TENNYSON AND HIS PUBLISHERS

Frontispiece Alfred Tennyson. From a photograph (circa 1860) by James Mudd of Manchester

TENNYSON AND HIS PUBLISHERS

June Steffensen Hagen

THE PENNSYLVANIA STATE UNIVERSITY PRESS
UNIVERSITY PARK AND LONDON

First published 1979 in the U.K. by
THE MACMILLAN PRESS LTD
London and Basingstoke

First published in the U.S.A. 1979 by
THE PENNSYLVANIA STATE UNIVERSITY PRESS
UNIVERSITY PARK AND LONDON

British Library Cataloguing in Publication Data

Hagen, June Steffensen
  Tennyson and his publishers.
  1. Tennyson, Alfred, *Baron Tennyson* – Friends
  and associates
  2. Authors and publishers – Great Britain
  I. Title
  821'.8   PR5583
  MACMILLAN ISBN 0-333-25931-9

THE PENNSYLVANIA STATE UNIVERSITY PRESS
ISBN 0-271-00249-2

Printed in Great Britain

In memory of my mother, Emma J. Steffensen,
and
for Jim

Contents

List of Plates

viii

by Gustav Doré for the folio edition of *Idylls of the King* (Moxon & Co., 1867). Reproduced by permission of the Mansell Collection

The frontispiece and plates 1, 2, 3, 4, 7, 8, 9 and 11 are from the Tennyson Research Centre Collection and are reproduced by courtesy of Lord Tennyson, the Tennyson Society and Lincolnshire Library Service.

Preface

Always the artist before the merchant, Alfred Tennyson was often reluctant to put his poems into print. In fact, early in his career only the efforts of persuasive friends such as Arthur Hallam and Edward FitzGerald and the dedication of such a committed poetry publisher as Edward Moxon enabled the poems ever to see publication. It was only after the appearance in 1850 of *In Memoriam*, for which Moxon particularly pressed, that the forty-one-year-old Tennyson felt sure enough of his own work to make such decisions by himself. After this success, he seldom allowed the convictions of others to undermine his own good judgment in the practical details of publication.

On the major occasion when Tennyson failed to heed his own instincts about format and yielded to his publisher's wishes, both poet and publisher soon regretted it. Later repercussions from this single miscalculation contributed heavily to Tennyson's breach with the Moxon firm. I speak here of the celebrated *Illustrated Edition of Tennyson's Poems* published by Edward Moxon in 1857. A decade of difficulty, centering first on this edition and then on others, followed Edward Moxon's death in 1858.

With Moxon himself Tennyson had a close friendship, which began when both men were just starting their respective careers and which continued into their respective heydays. They dined and smoked and laughed together; they went on holiday together in Switzerland; they knew and cared about each other's wives and children. Only at the end of his life, this time with Alexander Macmillan, who had been a family friend for a full thirty years before finally becoming the aging laureate's publisher, did Tennyson again go beyond the bounds of a cordial, business relationship. With various other publishers – J. and J. Jackson, Effingham Wilson, Alexander Strahan, Henry S. King, Charles Kegan Paul – his dealings were never primarily personal.

Tennyson expected his own tastes to be honored in the printing, binding and advertising of his poems, with the publishers being given a free hand in matters of distribution, sales, and demands for new editions. A natural business acumen made Tennyson decide early in his career to pay all costs of publication himself, dividing profits in varying proportions with his publishers through the years. Such a system allowed him greater control and ultimately greater income than he might have had from the outright sale of manuscript, leaving it to the publisher to bear the costs of production. Later he switched to a combination of publishers' commissions on old books and authors' royalties on new books. All in all Tennyson approached the commercial side of his art with the shrewd good sense and fiscal diligence of a person fully intending to live from it. And if there is any doubt that his livelihood was a good one, consider the following. At his death Tennyson left two fine country houses, Farringford on the Isle of Wight and Aldworth in Sussex, and a personal estate of £57,206 (at that time roughly the equivalent of $278,600, with a buying power today of $2,090,000).[1] Tennyson's estate may be seen in clearer perspective when we realize that a fellow poet, Robert Browning, left only £16,774. Two publishers of the day, however, managed to leave considerably more: George Routledge, £94,000, and George Bentley, £85,846.[2]

Although the records have demonstrated to me that Tennyson's income was substantial and his judgment sound, I have learned from them that in publishing activities Tennyson behaved ambivalently — that is, he both did and did not wish to be involved with the day-to-day minutiae of getting poetry into print and printed books to the public. He was notoriously careless with his own manuscripts and with what, ironically, no doubt, he termed his "fair copies," yet he tolerated no errors on the part of printers. He claimed to enjoy his isolation and privacy, yet at certain periods of his life he entered enthusiastically into what J. A. Sutherland calls the "conviviality [which] seems to have been the rule" of social contact between authors and publishers.[3] He gave all indication of not caring for money, yet he gained a reputation for driving a hard — albeit fair — bargain. He impressed many as being unimpressed by the whim of public taste and refused to write the kinds of poems for which his critics clamored, yet he nevertheless wrote much poetry which met with enormous popularity and he took delight in the appellation "Poet of the People."

In pointing to such contraries I do not mean to perpetuate the "modern myth of 'The Two Tennysons'" so favored by twentieth-century critics, for I agree with John D. Rosenberg's sensible observation that Tennyson "was remarkably of a piece from birth to death."[4] But by that I take Rosenberg to mean that Tennyson was consistent in his attitude towards himself and towards his art, and not that the poet was free from all conflicts between his aesthetic stance and his desire for the rewards of fame. And, just as Tennyson was both creator and purveyor of literary art, so, too, were most of his publishers themselves men of letters as well as businessmen. When these roles came into conflict, either between poet and publisher or within the poet himself, Tennyson almost without exception made his choices on artistic rather than mercantile grounds. His publishers, on the other hand, preferred to go with the trade. Tennyson even needed to be reminded often that the concerns of his publishers were legitimate ones. In what could be a keynote to this book, Charles Kegan Paul chided Tennyson in 1874 about the poet's resistance to advertising: "While we endeavor as far as possible to put ourselves in your position, and look on these matters as you do, in which we have not always succeeded, I am sure you will forgive our asking you to remember that the success of literature has two sides, and that the trade element is an important one, nor if rightly considered is it, I think, a wholly prosaic one."[5]

Acknowledgments

The publishers and I are grateful to the following for their assistance and for their permission to quote from published and unpublished material: Chadwyck-Healey Ltd for the extract from Brian Maidment's introduction to the microfilm "Archives of Kegan Paul, Trench, Trübner and Henry S. King, 1853–1912;" Columbia University Press for the extracts from "Edward Moxon: Publisher of Poets" (1939) by H. G. Merriam; the Macmillan Publishing Co. Inc. for the extracts from *Tennyson* by Christopher Ricks, © 1972 by the publishers; George Moore for a short quotation from his thesis "A Critical and Bibliographical Study of the Somersby Library of Dr. George Clayton Tennyson;" The Pierpont Morgan Library for permission to consult letters from Alfred Tennyson and Edward Moxon; and Catherine B. Stevenson for the quotation from her dissertation "Narrative Form and Point of View in *The Princess, Maud* and *Idylls of the King.*"

Most of the primary material for this study is in the Tennyson Research Centre, Lincoln, England. (Where there is no other source listed for a letter or account in my text or notes, it may be assumed to be from that collection.) I commend the Tennyson heirs for having this collection administered by the Lincolnshire County Library Service and housed where it is readily accessible to the public, at the Lincoln City Library; there the tradition of service to the public continues, making the work of visiting scholars most pleasant. In particular I thank Laurence Elvin, former Keeper of the Tennyson Collection, for his gracious help and friendship.

Susan Gates, Senior Reference Librarian of Lincolnshire County Library, has confirmed by her energy and insight my suspicion that reference librarians are the kingpins of scholarship. While I worked in Lincoln hospitality was extended to my family and to myself by Hope Dyson and Rose McIntosh. The late Sir Charles Tennyson, as he also did for so many others, encouraged me in my work and directed me specifically to his Notebooks. Sir Charles's unpublished typescript "Tennyson's Dealings with His Publishers" was called to my attention by James O. Hoge, who also sent me his own transcripts of relevant letters. William E. Buckler at New York University first sparked my interest in Tennyson. The Alumni Association of The King's College, Briarcliff Manor, New York, provided a grant from their Faculty Research Fund for the completion of this book, the manuscript of which was typed – at lightning speed – by my Brooklyn neighbor, Laurel A. Dietz. My aunt, Helen Adams Johnson, provided a most welcome quiet work area in her basement. I was buoyed up through the years of this project by the enthusiasm of my husband, James B. Hagen. To the above and to T. M. Farmiloe, editor at Macmillan Press, to Julia Brittain, editorial services controller and to Nancy Tuczek-Williams, picture researcher there, I extend my thanks.

Finally, I have been blessed with generous colleagues, Lynne Sacher and Catherine Barnes Stevenson, who read through the entire manuscript and offered invaluable suggestions, and with a copy-editor *par excellence*, Nerissa vom Baur. What felicities the book has I owe to these three – Lynne, Cathy and Nerissa. What it lacks I can blame only on myself.

1 Introduction: Tennyson's Early Publishing (1827–31)

The year 1830 marks two events in the history of poetry publishing which greatly, though unobtrusively, affected the literary world: Alfred Tennyson published his first independent volume, *Poems, Chiefly Lyrical*, and Edward Moxon set himself up in New Bond Street as a publisher. By 1832 they were working together. The story of this relationship and of Tennyson's dealings with his other publishers provides an intimate look at the nineteenth-century business of publishing poetry; it also reveals that anomaly, the poet who becomes wealthy solely from his pen.

The first third of the nineteenth century presented challenges for both writers and publishers of poetry which made the two groups uneasy. The most pervasive problem was the perpetual one of audience, for who writes – indeed, who publishes – without the hope of an audience? Certainly no one who wants to live by his trade. Once booksellers moved firmly into the higher-risk realm of publishing, and once rich patrons were no longer available to authors, publishers and poets alike had to take a new look at their major possibility of success – pleasing a book-buying public.

The public already available in 1830, one used to buying and reading books of poetry, had been raised on Scott and Byron. Two bits of publishing history illustrate Byron's popular success: he sold the first two cantos of *Childe Harold* to John Murray II for £600 and the third for £2000. "The first edition . . . was exhausted within three days, and every copy of the first printing of the *Corsair* – variously stated as 10,000 and 13,000 copies – was sold on the day of publication." Of Scott's success, only this need be said: in 1810, its first year, *The Lady of the Lake* sold 20,300 copies.[1] Keats and Shelley were by 1830 still barely noticed. Wordsworth, though still remembered for the more than thirty years old *Lyrical Ballads*, was unpopular. The other major Romantic poets, Landor, Southey, Campbell, Moore, had either switched to prose or written no significant poetry after 1815.

As a result, the field was wide open for new poets, but the popular demand was for new Scotts or new Byrons, and not for pioneers of new poetic idioms and forms. No wonder, then, that the successful poets of the day, the ones published in magazines such as Jerdan's *Literary Gazette*, produced the imitations of Scott and Byron their readers clamored for. Robert Montgomery, Letitia E. Landon, Felicia Hemans, Bernard Barton, Barry Cornwall and other poets of sentimentality and vapidity enjoyed a poetic renaissance in the early 1820s, in which English readers gave to poetry the attention modern English and American readers devote to the latest bestselling novel.[2] By the early 1830s, however, the quick poetry boom was over and the new "artistic" poets, Tennyson and Browning, faced the task of revitalizing jaded tastes and dwindling sales. Not unexpectedly, given what they knew about the market, they too began publication with imitations of the Romantics; but the works of relative newcomers, Keats and Shelley, rather than Byron and Scott, were their models. After Tennyson's and Browning's early publishing, however, both men developed from being facile imitators to being poets who found their objectivity and their own distinctive voices. Unfortunately, in 1840, by which time their themes, forms, and techniques were clearly their own, the audience that used to read poetry had discovered the novel — "easier to read than poetry, as well as being more topical in its application to ordinary experience."[3] Trade figures on sales show that no nineteenth-century volume of poetry in England ever matched the first-year sale of Harriet Beecher Stowe's novel *Uncle Tom's Cabin* in England — 1,500,000 sold between April 1852 and April 1853.[4] Even those volumes of poetry with outstanding sales records after the middle classes had begun reading novels voraciously, works such as Tennyson's *Idylls of the King* and *Enoch Arden*, never came near Stowe's record. In addition, these poems probably benefited in public opinion more from those same narrative qualities which were reminiscent of fiction than from their excellence as poetry.

Yet the audience's delight in Scott and Byron, its satiation with poetry and its growing taste for fiction were only three of the numerous challenges facing poets and their publishers in 1830. The Evangelical temper and the Utilitarian temper of the age told against them, too, for such an atmosphere stimulated a basic distrust of poetry. On both sides — from the religious one of Evangelicalism's capturing hearts to the secular one of Utilitarianism's capturing minds – powerful weapons were aimed at the nature of poetry itself.

But it was the economic reality of two trade depressions, a general one in 1826 and a specifically literary one in 1830, which made most publishers shy away from the high-risk business of publishing new poets. There always hung vividly before them the specter of major houses such as Ballantyne's and Constable's collapsing in the panic of 1826 and of others remaindering their stock. "The bankruptcies of 1826 revealed more than the financial instability of many firms. They augured a slump in literature, particularly in poetry. As a writer in Blackwood's *Maga* [*zine*] accurately remarked: 'Few write poetry . . . and nobody at all reads it. Our poets have over-dosed us.' "5 Even John Keats's publisher John Taylor felt the crunch, writing in 1827:

> The season has been a very bad one for new books, and I am afraid the time has passed away in which poetry will answer. All the old poetry buyers seem to be dead, and the new race have no taste for it. The fact is, Men's circumstances are not so good as they formerly were, and fancy book buying is a luxury which they can't afford to indulge in as they once could.

By 1830 most publishers had withdrawn new poetry from their lists, Taylor lamenting, "I am no publisher of poetry now."6 William Blackwood, who remained, complained in 1831, "There never has been so slack a year in our trade ever since I have been in business."7 As Mercurius Rusticus, the principal character in *Bibliophobia*, put it, "*FEAR* is the order of the day. To those very natural and long-established fears of bailiffs and tax-gatherers, must now be added the fear of *Reform*, of *Cholera*, and of BOOKS."8

With the audience diminishing and the publishers faltering, it is not surprising to find the poets themselves doubting their abilities, just as the successful poets of the generation before had done also. Byron and Scott "had their doubts about authorship as a profession."9 Southey, Wordsworth, and Moore considered law as an alternative profession for themselves; Coleridge and Crabbe tried the ministry.10 No doubt this fidgeting in the literary chair was partially caused by economic difficulty. Rosen argues forcefully that, "without exception, there is no writer one can think of between 1750 and 1830 (including Scott) who was able to live on what he earned creatively by his pen." Most chose not a new profession, but rather the backwaters of their own.

"Typically, the answer for the writer was to put his pen to less than creative tasks. It was newspapers, quarterlies, lectures, translations, collections of the poets, Vauxhall entertainments, hack novels, introductions to literary, philosophical, or historical works that added the necessary income."[11] The young Tennyson, writing in a remote, hilly section of Lincolnshire, itself a remote county, also struggled on the slopes of Parnassus. But, as far as we know, he never seriously considered being other than a poet.

Thus, taking everything into consideration, the prognosis for poetry in 1830 was dismal indeed. The audience was restless and increasing the pace towards fiction; the nature of poetry itself — and its worthiness as a serious pursuit in an enlightened age — was under attack both by secular Utilitarians and religious Evangelicals; once-prestigious publishing firms were going bankrupt; and the idea of a poet's being able to secure a livelihood from poetry alone was becoming more remote. Yet in the midst of this slough of despond Edward Moxon "opened his establishment in New Bond Street, in June, 1830, with the ambition of being a publisher of poetry," and Alfred Tennyson issued *Poems, Chiefly Lyrical*, with the hope that he would be the next great poet of the age.[12]

Both Edward Moxon and Alfred Tennyson were still going mainly on faith and not on sight when, two years later, in 1832, they joined together to publish poetry, speculating that a heretofore small audience could be nurtured into a much larger one.

Tennyson needed to break the bonds of isolation and severely limited income which had fettered his whole family. The isolation from the local community, not to mention wealth and fashionable society, stemmed from both the village of Somersby's physical apartness and Dr George Clayton Tennyson's emotional instability, which caused most of the Tennyson children to withdraw into a private world of their own making. For young Alfred, as well as for Frederick and Charles, his elder brothers, that world was poetry. They were thoroughly familiar with Horace (though he was not a favorite) and other Roman and Greek poets. They read Spenser, Shakespeare, Milton, Pope, Thomson, Collins, Gray, Campbell, Macpherson, Byron, Scott, and possibly Dante. Of contemporary poets other than Byron, Scott and Burns, Dr Tennyson owned a number of volumes now mainly forgotten but at the time probably read by his precocious children. Among these were Bloomfield's *Rural Tales* and *The Farmer's Boy*, West's *Mother*, and the poems of Samuel Rogers.[13] Missing from Dr Tennyson's library were works by Crabbe, Southey, Moore, Clare, Coleridge and Wordsworth. But the last omission, so egregious in our eyes, was not unusual at the time, for "the 1798 *Lyrical Ballads* was in fact a failure. Five hundred copies were printed, but the publisher was forced to sell the largest proportion of these at a loss. . . . It was not, in fact, till the 1820's when the peak of Dr Tennyson's book-buying was probably past, that Wordsworth began to achieve any sort of wide popularity."[14]

At age eight Alfred Tennyson imitated Thomson; at ten or eleven, Pope; at twelve, Scott; at fifteen, Milton, Shakespeare, Beaumont and Fletcher. In his early teens he also essayed odes in the style of Gray and Collins.[15] But the dominant early influence was Byron. Tennyson's reaction to Byron's death indicates the depth of the adolescent poet's feelings for his mentor: "I was fourteen when I heard of his death. It seemed an awful calamity; I remember I rushed out of doors, sat down by myself, shouted aloud, and wrote on the sandstone: 'Byron is dead.'"[16] He further described it as "a day when the whole world seemed to be darkened for me,"[17] a day when he "thought everything was over and finished for every one – that nothing else mattered."[18] Tennyson may have heard a line or two of Shelley from his older brother Frederick, "but it seems that he never saw a copy of any poem by Shelley until he went up to Cambridge two or three years later, and the same is probably true about Wordsworth and Keats."[19]

Tennyson's practice in the performance of poetry began even before he had learned to appreciate Byron or any of the other poets available to him. Hallam Tennyson records his father's saying, "'The first poetry that moved me was my own at five years old. When I was eight, I remember making a line I thought grander than Campbell, or Byron, or Scott.'" At eight, too, he said, "'I covered two sides of a slate with Thomsonian blank verse. . . .'"[20] Alfred's later fascination with mysticism and the reverberation of the past appeared quite early. "Before I could read," he recalled, "I was in the habit on a stormy day of spreading my arms to the wind, and crying out, 'I hear a voice that's speaking in the wind,' and the words 'far, far away' had always a strange charm for me."[21] Though cursed indeed by his father's ill temperament, alcoholism, and antisocial behavior, Tennyson nevertheless was fortunate in Dr Tennyson's ardent encouragement of his talent: "My father who was a sort of Poet himself thought so highly of my first essay [into poetry] that he prophesied I should be the greatest Poet of the Time."[22] Dr Tennyson's encouragement took a pragmatic turn at times: he helped Alfred master his meters, for

example. "Don't write so rhythmically," the father advised. "Break
your lines occasionally for the sake of variety."[23] His uncle Charles
Tennyson assisted the young poet also by showing some of his poems
to Thomas Moore. And, of course, Frederick and Charles added their
spurs of praise, joining Alfred in a publication, the 1827 *Poems by Two*
[really three] *Brothers*. All in all, the support for Tennyson's early
efforts was there -- and that, in combination with his own sense of
destiny, conspired to mold his resolve. "To his brother Arthur,
Alfred said as a child, 'I'm going to be famous,'" and the labels he
applied to his works at the age of ten -- "The Poetry of Tennyson,"
"The Lyrical Poetry of Tennyson," and "The Prose Writings of
Tennyson," -- evidence his decision to be among the literary
famous.[24] In doing this, as Sir Charles Tennyson, the poet's grandson
and chief biographer, observes, "Alfred was already thinking of
himself as 'Tennyson,' an established poet with a row of publications
to his credit."[25]

When Tennyson reached manhood his childhood dream had a
greater chance of becoming reality, for the time was propitious for a
new talent. The unusual circumstance of the second generation of
Romantic poets dying young, and the poetic powers of the first
generation fading during their later years (except for Wordsworth,
who, though not fading, was not currently popular) made the time
ripe for new poetry.

> Had Keats achieved full artistic maturity [writes Lionel Steven-
> son], he might have been the greatest author of the Victorian age,
> with Shelley, Byron, and other poets in their prime helping to
> dominate the scene. But the violent creative energy of the
> Romantic years seemed to have burned out the poets, either to
> actual death or to quiescence; and so the young generation which
> began writing about 1830 had an exceptionally clear field in which
> to seek distinction.[26]

Tennyson took to this clear field in spite of the extremely limited
popularity of his first publications, a condition that was not to be
removed for at least twenty years more. In 1850, however, *In
Memoriam* was widely read, not only by poetry's entrenched
disciples, but also by the general populace, and as a result Alfred
Tennyson became "the greatest Poet of the Time," as his father had
predicted.

But in 1827 the eighteen-year-old Alfred was so unsure of his audience that he included in *Poems by Two Brothers* only conventional verse in the style of Gray, Byron, Moore and Scott. He explained later "that he had at the time far better things by him than any contained in the volume, and that these were deliberately omitted as 'being too much out of the common for the public taste.'"[27] J. and J. Jackson, booksellers of Louth, Lincolnshire, and publishers of the young Tennyson brothers, no doubt felt they were risking enough with the book as it was and were relieved that Alfred excluded his more experimental, idiosyncratic efforts. They wanted to offend public taste not at all.

As it was, the Jacksons may have issued the volume more out of friendship than out of any business sense. Mrs Elizabeth Tennyson, the poet's mother, was the daughter of a former rector of Louth, and at Louth School, which he attended with great reluctance between the age of seven and ten, Alfred once wrote an English poem "for one of the Jacksons."[28] The firm offered the Tennyson brothers £20 for the privilege of publishing their book, of which £5 was to be taken out in books.[29] This monetary arrangement has been recorded differently through the years by various biographers, but a signed receipt at Trinity College supports the figures given here, which are also corroborated by James Knowles's quotation of notes dictated by Tennyson himself.[30]

One wonders how many copies were printed, and, more importantly, sold, but that information has not survived. We do know, however, that Jacksons printed too many, for "in 1870 a considerable stock of remainders, both bound and unbound, was found in the printer's warehouse."[31] There may even have been printed as many as 800. Sir Charles calculates thus: "The volume was offered at 5/-, large paper copies at 7/-, and on a ten per cent royalty basis, a sale of 800 copies of the 5/- edition would have been required to clear the £20 advance."[32] This estimate seems high, however; it is far more likely that the Jacksons bought the manuscript copyright outright — the common practice for first books by unknown authors — than that they paid a royalty. Ironically, "in 1892 the original manuscript was sold for £480," which must be at least £460 more than either publisher or poets made from the book.[33] The little volume in its plain gray boards was published on 20 April 1827 and distributed by Simpkin, Marshall & Co., a major London wholesale distributing agent with some Lincolnshire ties. Its founder, Benjamin Crosby, had been struck with paralysis in 1813 and had "retired to Louth,

Lincolnshire, where he died in the following year at the age of forty-six."[34]

The legend that the family coachman suggested publishing poetry as a way for the Tennyson brothers to make some extra money has been successfully challenged by Edgar F. Shannon, Jr, in *Modern Language Notes*, 64 (1949), 107–10. But no one who knows human nature need challenge Sir Charles's description of the singular delight the boys took in their achievement:

> Great was their pride when they sallied out with their mother to intercept the carrier who was to bring the first set of proofs from Louth over Tetford Hill. Even greater was the day of publication, when Charles and Alfred spent part of their cash advance in the hire of a carriage in which they drove fourteen miles over wold and marsh to Mablethorpe to share their triumph with the winds and waves.[35]

The only other detail we have of this publication event concerns its anonymity. Sir Charles reports,

> A letter sent by the brothers to Jackson while the arrangements for publication were in progress, is characteristic of Alfred's hatred of personal publicity and of his sound business instinct and common sense:

> "Dear Sir,
> The signature of Charles and Alfred Tennyson at the conclusion of the Preface was not in the contract and we have therefore erased it, nor do we think it would assist the sale of the book, since you are at liberty to say who are the authors of the book and 'Charles and Alfred Tennyson' in London would not be taken any more notice of than no signature at all."

> When the book was published, it contained no reference to the name of the authors, either on title page or elsewhere.[36]

But wishing to remain anonymous does not mean wishing to have one's book go unnoticed, and we can assume that the brothers were pleased to receive two brief reviews.

On May 19, 1827, the *Literary Chronicle and Weekly Review* quoted two of the poems, introducing them with the remark, "This little volume exhibits a pleasing union of kindred tastes, and contains several little pieces of considerable merit." In June the *Gentleman's Magazine* benignly commented, "These poems are full of amiable feelings, expressed for the most part with elegance and correctness. . . . The volume is a graceful addition to our domestic poetry, and does credit to the juvenile Adelphi."[37]

Tennyson's own sense of the insignificance of the volume, however, led him to call it in later years "early rot," and to keep its poems out of any collected edition. Christopher Ricks in our own day observes in the verses "many of the preoccupations that endured for Tennyson, such as the aged speaker; memory and time; prophetic denunciations; the assured simplicities of battle; and 'The Grave of a Suicide.'" But he rightly complains about the exclamatory or questioning endings, and a manner "too smoothly rapid." He concludes, as most critics would, "Though the knowledgeable admirer of Tennyson will find the stiff book stiff with anticipations, seeds, and nuances, its actual achievement was nugatory."[38] The book's insignificance notwithstanding, when Alfred and Charles entered Trinity College, Cambridge, the next fall they did have this to their credit: they had published a volume of poetry.[39]

At the university Alfred soon became part of the Apostles, which had been founded in 1820 under the title "The Cambridge Conversazione Society" and was now under the heady leadership of John Sterling and F. D. Maurice. Charles Merivale, who was one of the Apostles and whom the shy Tennyson asked to read his prize poem "Timbuctoo" at Commencement in 1829, described the activities of these young men with "common intellectual taste, common studies, common literary aspirations" − and, he might have added, a common palate for anchovies on toast, which they called "whales":

> We lived . . . in constant intercourse with one another, day by day, meeting over our wine or our tobacco; but every Saturday evening we held a more solemn sitting, when each member of the society, about twelve in number, delivered an essay on any subject, chosen by himself, to be discussed and submitted to the vote of the whole number. Alas! alas! what reckless, joyous evenings those were. What solemn things were said, pipe in hand; how much serious emotion was mingled with alternate bursts of laughter;

how every one hit his neighbour, intellectually, right and left, and
was hit again, and no mark left on either side; how much sentiment
was mingled with how much humour![40]

The essay subjects were wide-ranging – in reporting an 1832 meeting
Merivale mentions Heath's essay on Niebuhr, Alford's on Chris-
tianity, and his own on Mrs Trollope's *America*.[41] Tennyson once had
to speak on "Ghosts"; failing to do so, he forfeited official
membership but retained his place in the comradely discussion circle.
F. D. Maurice's influence made itself felt in the attention the young
men paid to poetry, particularly to poetry not yet appreciated by
what they called the world of "Philistines, or Stumpfs."[42] They
prided themselves on having "discovered" Shelley, for example, and
once debated against Oxford (December 1829) on "The Superiority
of Shelley to Byron," with Hallam, Milnes and Sutherland taking the
affirmative for Cambridge.[43] But it was not long before they devoted
their fervor to advancing the career of their own poet, Alfred
Tennyson.

A living poet as their spokesman was a greater prize; their Samson,
he would "do the Lord's work against the Philistines of this
viperous generation." They urged Tennyson to live up to his
responsibility as one of the elect and anticipated important results
in combatting, as Blakesley wrote to him, "the monstrous opinions
and feelings which pervade the age." They hailed him as a "first-
rate poetical genius," as "one of the mighty of the earth," and even,
in the words of Fanny Kemble, sister of an Apostle, as "our hero,
the great hero of our day."[44]

Furthermore, by developing as their major critical tenet Wordsworth's idea (filtered through Maurice) that a true poet has hearers
only "few and scattered," the Apostles were able to ease Tennyson's
anxiety about his limited number of readers. As the poet of the future,
they assured him, he need not worry about the present – particularly
when he already played to a stimulating, intelligent and appreciative
audience.

Finding a coterie which would thus admire and recite his poetry,
copy his compositions into commonplace books, engage him in
exciting conversation and expand his social and intellectual horizons
proved just the thing for the self-conscious poet from the country.
Years later, Tennyson still regularly sent new poems to his brother

Apostles or asked for their response to his trial editions before being willing to publish. The Apostles in turn, even several years after Tennyson had left Cambridge to head his by-then fatherless family in Somersby, kept up the "Tennyson cult" by reading favorite poems, particularly "The Palace of Art" and "The Lotos-Eaters," "as canonical scripture to every new member."[45]

The reciprocal admiration thus expressed was doubly appreciated by Alfred because the admirers themselves were talented and promising men in their own fields. Among those active in the Apostles in 1830, 1831 and 1832, along with Arthur Hallam and Alfred Tennyson, were Richard Chenevix Trench, who became Dean of Westminster and then Archbishop of Dublin; John Kemble, later an authority on Anglo-Saxon history and literature; Charles Merivale, who would become Dean of Ely; William Hepworth, a future Master of Trinity College; Henry Alford, later Dean of Canterbury; Joseph W. Blakesley, who advanced to be Dean of Lincoln; Richard Monckton Milnes, who became an editor of Keats and his first biographer; Edmund Lushington, a classical scholar and later Tennyson's brother-in-law; James Spedding, the great biographer and editor of Sir Francis Bacon; and others of similar accomplishment.[46] Of these, however, "it was Hallam who proved himself the most urgently and enduringly perceptive admirer of Tennyson's poetry."[47] Moreover, Hallam took action when action was needed.

Arthur Henry Hallam, eighteen months Alfred Tennyson's junior, entered Trinity College in October 1828 and was elected to the Apostles in May 1829 along with the Lincolnshire poet. In one letter explaining the closeness they developed as one of mutuality of feeling, Arthur wrote to Alfred,

> I, whose imagination is to yours as Pisgah to Canaan, the point of distant prospect to the place of actual possession, am not without some knowledge and experience of your passion for the past. To this community of feeling between us, I probably owe your inestimable friendship, and those blessed hopes which you have been the indirect occasion of awakening.[48]

(The "hopes" are those Hallam entertained of marrying Alfred's sister, Emily, with whom he had fallen in love immediately upon meeting her at Somersby in December 1829.) To others, Arthur extolled Alfred's praises in a similar way, once predicting to his Eton friend W. E. Gladstone, "I consider Tennyson as promising fair to be the greatest poet of our generation, perhaps of our century."[49] Alfred, in turn, responded to Hallam as all his Cambridge friends did: he considered him the most promising mind among them, the best-natured, the most congenial, the most stable. Hallam possessed, too, literary talent admired by many. His father said that the boy at about age nine "felt a keen relish for dramatic poetry, and wrote several tragedies, if we may so call them, either in prose or verse, with a more precocious display of talents than the Editor remembers to have met with in any other individual."[50] A later critic tellingly compares the language in poems by Hallam and Tennyson to "strengthen . . . our sense of the close community of spirit and thought which bound the two."[51] Further strengthening these ties was a shared political spirit, which encouraged the two idealists in an expedition to Spain in summer 1830 to aid the revolution of General Torrijos against King Ferdinand. "No harm came to Hallam and Tennyson, who met some of the rebels and gave them money and stirring words," but a cousin of John Sterling was executed in the fall for his part in the conspiracy.[52]

Although Arthur Hallam was thought of after his death as a man of unshakable faith and unfailingly bright spirits, he actually shared the doubts and depressions which were an acknowledged part of his friend's life. At one point "he confided in Milnes his fears of going mad and of turning atheist: 'In my fits of gloom I so often look death and insanity in the face, that the impulse to leave some trace of my existence on this bulk of atoms gathers strength with the warning that I must be brief.'"[53] Tennyson and Arthur Hallam, then, shared their gloom as well as their "passion for the past," their literary bent, their intellectual abilities, and their political spirit.

When it came to the publication of Tennyson's poetry, however, the two men differed — Alfred procrastinating, worrying, and Arthur acting.

Hallam "good-naturedly claimed some credit for Tennyson's victory [in the prize poem competition in 1829], as is clear from a letter by J. M. Gaskell, dated 25 June 1829:

Have you heard that Alfred Tennyson, a great friend of Hallam's, was successful at Cambridge in the Timbuctoo business? I received a letter this morning from Hallam. He is delighted that Tennyson is successful. He says that Tennyson deserved it, but that he borrowed the pervading idea from him, so that "he is entitled to the honours

of a Sancho Panza in the memorable victory gained in the year
1829 over prosaicism and jingle jangle. . . ."⁵⁴

Exactly what Hallam means by "the pervading idea" is not clear,
since Tennyson had simply taken an old poem, "Armageddon,"
altered the beginning and the ending, entering it in the competition
only because his father had insisted he must do so: "You're doing
nothing at the university," Dr Tennyson had told his recalcitrant son.
"You might at least get the English poem-prize."⁵⁵ Perhaps Hallam
meant that he had inspired Tennyson's production by the excellence
of his own submission, for he too had submitted a poem to the
competition, a poem which Tennyson later called "everyway so
much better than that wild and unmethodized performance of my
own."⁵⁶ Although Tennyson never reprinted it himself, his "Timbuctoo" was published in several Cambridge collections.⁵⁷

The first major publication in which we can discern Hallam's
influence came in June 1830. He and Tennyson had planned to issue
together a volume of poetry, following the example of Coleridge and
Wordsworth a generation before with the *Lyrical Ballads*, but Arthur
reluctantly withdrew his contributions at the request of his father,
who perhaps disliked their revelation of Arthur's religious doubts and
irreligious love affairs. From May 1830 on, however, Arthur's
printed *Poems* were circulated, sometimes by himself, as when he
wrote to Mrs Tennyson,

> As I have at last the pleasure of sending to Alfred his long-expected
> book, I take this opportunity of begging that you will accept from
> me a copy of some poems, which I originally intended to have
> published in the same volume. To this joint publication, as a sort of
> seal of our friendship, I had long looked forward with a delight
> which, I believe, was no-way selfish. But there are reasons which
> have obliged me to change my intention, and withdraw my own
> share of the work from the press. One of these was the growing
> conviction of the exceeding crudeness of style, and in parts
> morbidness of feeling, which characterised all my earlier at-
> tempts.⁵⁸

Arthur probably saw the Tennyson poems as well as his own through
the press that spring — his own were in print when his father stopped
their publication — and may have proof-read them as he was to do for

the 1832 *Poems*. (Some extant proofs indicate that Tennyson did at least some proof correction himself.) From the letter above we are sure of Hallam's role in picking up a copy from Effingham Wilson to send out to Alfred at Somersby. *Poems, Chiefly Lyrical*, then, though officially Alfred Tennyson's first independent volume, proceeded almost to its publication date as a joint effort with Hallam. One stage of its history, however, belongs only to Alfred: "as he was coming home one night from Spilsby, the manuscript, which he had just got ready for the printers, fell out of his overcoat pocket and was never recovered. He was, however, able to re-write all the lost poems immediately from memory."[59]

The most notable of the poems — "Recollections of the Arabian Nights," "The Kraken," "The Sleeping Beauty," "The Ode to Memory," "A Spirit Haunts the Year's Last Hours," "Mariana," "The Dying Swan," "The Mystic," "The Poet," "The Poet's Mind," and the anguished "Supposed Confessions of a Second-rate Sensitive Mind Not in Unity with Itself" — fulfilled the Apostles' expectations of their Samson poet. The least notable — "Lilian," "Isabel", etc., "Lost Hope," "The Tears of Heaven," "Love and Sorrow" — were rightly condemned. But certainly anyone who knew the tradition of English poetry and had ears to hear must have heard in "Claribel," which opened the volume, a new voice singing. That voice not only sounded an experimental idiom independent of Tennyson's major predecessors Keats and Shelley, but also spoke with a lyric force beyond that of anyone else publishing in 1830.

Tennyson's publisher for this volume, Effingham Wilson, a noted London bookseller who had just added publishing to his activities, must have had a gift for recognizing young talent, for in addition to this volume he published Browning's *Paracelsus* (1835) after Edward Moxon had refused it. Wilson issued 600 copies of the Tennyson book, some bound in drab paper boards, some in pink, in June 1830, at a retail price of five shillings per copy.

In his first year of publishing, Wilson, who advertised himself as "Bookseller to the Emperor of all the Russias," listed these works: *The Real Devil's Walk*, with designs by R. Cruikshank; Coventry's *On the Revenues of the Church of England*; "Raphael, the Astrologer's New Work," *The Royal Book of Dreams*; *The History of Christ's Hospital*; two books of French grammar; his own *New Stranger's Guide through London*; and what sounds like an indispensable book by "an Old Physician," called, believe it or not, *Health without Physic; or, Cordials for Youth, Manhood, and Old Age; Including Maxims, Medical,*

Moral, and Facetious, for the Prevention of Disease, and the Attainment of a Long and Vigorous Life!
Wilson himself wrote a description of the new Royal Exchange, published in 1844, and, a year after his Tennyson venture, a thirty-two-page argument for repeal of the newspaper and advertisement taxes. This appeared in the *Westminster Review*, 1 July 1831, under the title, "On the Taxes on Knowledge," and may have contributed to the lowering of the stamp duty on newspapers in 1836 from fourpence to a penny. Wilson died in 1868, but his firm flourished as late as 1895, with continued interest in trade matters, publishing, for example, Charmier's *Law Relating to Literary Copyright and the Authorship and Publication of Books.*
The publisher prospered more on his other publications than he did on Tennyson's; exactly how many copies of *Poems, Chiefly Lyrical* were sold we do not know, but in 1833 Tennyson apparently owed Wilson £11. Their agreement probably called for half shares on both risks and profits, with the £11 thus being Tennyson's share of the production costs not covered by sales. Hallam reported to Tennyson in a letter,

I went again to Effingham Wilson's shop today, I saw the old codger himself; he was bland & submissive, promising to send me the account as soon as he should have time to make it out. I am confident the £11 will be found a mistake – perhaps a bravado of that saucy cub his son. Come what may you need not pay it. Take no step yourself. Leave it to Moxon, Tennant, Heath & myself.[60]

This action on Hallam's part represents a most significant strand in their tightly woven friendship. Hallam had an eye for business tactics and for the practical matters of promotion which counterbalanced the poet's own diffidence. As Ricks notes,

It is important . . . to realize that what Tennyson gratefully loved in Hallam was not limited to the grandly platonic marriage of true minds, but included the shrewd and generous practicalities with which Hallam furthered the publication and promotion of Tennyson's poems. And, moreover, what Hallam loved in Tennyson was partly the opportunity which all this provided for some energetically disinterested and honorable activity such as Hallam's life would otherwise have lacked.[61]

Later in his career, though he took a more active part in his business affairs, Tennyson always had some friend or relative handling the nitty-gritty correspondence, the proofs, the copying, the back-and-forth negotiations which publishing involved. At first it was Arthur Hallam; next Edward Moxon and Edward FitzGerald; then his wife Emily, her brother-in-law Charles Weld, and their friend John Forster. Later, his own son Hallam Tennyson gave up Cambridge and a career to become his father's secretary, after Emily's health had broken down. At the height of his success Tennyson added the services of Arnold White, solicitor, of White, Broughton and White. A good part of the story of Tennyson's dealings with his publishers, then, depends on the correspondence of these intermediaries. No helper, however, even tireless Emily and Hallam Tennyson, ever took matters completely into his own hands as did Arthur Hallam.

Hallam's "honorable activity" on behalf of his friend took four forms in the year following publication of *Poems, Chiefly Lyrical*: first, he asked Leigh Hunt to review Alfred's book along with Charles Tennyson's *Sonnets and Fugitive Pieces*, published in March 1830; secondly, he wrote his own review for Moxon's *Englishman's Magazine*; thirdly, he sent one of Tennyson's sonnets to Moxon for publication in the same periodical; and, finally, he tried to arrange payment to Tennyson from Moxon for regular submissions to the magazine. Of these endeavors, all were successful except the last.

Tennyson's little volume required such diligent support because it had appeared at what Frederick Shannon calls

> an inauspicious moment. George IV died on June 26, and parliamentary elections with agitation for reform occurred in England during the summer. On the Continent revolution swept triumphantly through France and Belgium, and war between these countries and the Holy Alliance seemed imminent. It was a time when the periodicals, supplied with a plethora of news, were unlikely to evince much interest in a little book of poems by an almost unknown author.[62]

Yet by the end of the year generally favorable reviews had appeared in the *Atlas*, the *Spectator*, and *Felix Farley's Bristol Journal*, but not in the two strictly literary weeklies, the *Athenaeum* and the *Literary Gazette*. Hallam therefore worried aloud to Tennyson in October, "I cannot make out that you have been reviewed anywhere."[63] But in January the *Westminster Review* ran fourteen pages of praise, allaying his fears somewhat. Nevertheless he wrote to Leigh Hunt, editor of *The Tatler*, hoping to encourage that noted man of letters to review the poems favorably. In this letter Hallam shows both the tactful force which characterized all his efforts on Alfred's behalf, and, in the last paragraph, his assimilation of Maurice's poetic theory:

> Will you excuse the liberty that a perfect stranger to you takes in sending you two little volumes of Poetry [Alfred's and Charles's] with which I cannot but think you will be pleased? They are the compositions of two brothers both very young men, and both intimate friends of mine. The larger volume was reviewed in the last number of *The Westminster Review* . . . and the high praise bestowed upon it by the reviewer is not higher in my opinion, and I hope in yours, than its merits demand. I flatter myself you will, if you peruse this book, be surprised and delighted to find a new prophet of those true principals of Art which, in this country, you were among the first to recommend both by precept and example. Since the death of John Keats, the last lineal descendant of Apollo, our English region of Parnassus has been domineered over by kings of shreds and patches. But, if I mistake not, the true heir is found. . . .
>
> The other, and smaller, volume, written by his brother, contains poetry of a very different character, but sterling, I think, and showing a mind capable of noble thoughts, although inferior in depth and range of powers to that which I first described. Should you agree with me to any extent in my judgment of these volumes, you will not perhaps object to mentioning them favourably in *The Tatler*, which I believe you at present conduct.
>
> I do not suppose that either of these poets is likely to become extensively or immediately popular: They write not to the world at large, which "lieth in wickedness" and bad taste, but to the elect Church of Urania, which we know to be small and in tribulation. Now in this church you have preferment, and what you preach will be considered by the faithful as a sound form of words. Should you after all, Sir, not like these books, I can only hope you will pardon the liberty that has been taken by one who has derived pleasure and benefit from your writings, and therefore subscribes himself as
>
> Yours in gratitude and respect,
> Arthur Henry Hallam.[64]

The editor did take up the cause, reviewing both volumes extensively in four numbers of *The Tatler* at the end of February and the beginning of March. But Hallam intended even better coverage. He began preparing his own review for Edward Moxon's new *Englishman's Magazine*. "On Some of the Characteristics of Modern Poetry and on the Lyrical Poems of Alfred Tennyson" appeared in due course in August 1831 and proved to be a fine piece of literary criticism, justly pointing out Tennyson's poetic virtues and extravagantly estimating *Poems, Chiefly Lyrical*.[65] The "five distinctive excellencies of [Tennyson's] own manner" which Hallam elucidates are

First, his luxuriance of imagination, and at the same time his control over it. Secondly, his power of embodying himself in ideal characters, or rather moods of character, with such extreme accuracy of adjustment, that the circumstances of the narration seem to have a natural correspondence with the predominant feeling, and, as it were, to be evolved from it by assimilative force. Thirdly, his vivid, picturesque delineation of objects, and the peculiar skill with which he holds all of them *fused*, to borrow a metaphor from science, in a medium of strong emotion. Fourthly, the variety of his lyrical measures, and exquisite modulation of harmonious words and cadences to the swell and fall of the feelings expressed. Fifthly, the elevated habits of thought, *implied* in these compositions, and imparting a mellow soberness of tone, more impressive, to our minds, than if the author had drawn up a set of opinions in verse, and sought to instruct the understanding, rather than to communicate the love of beauty to the heart.[66]

Knowing that Moxon, the young poet–publisher, had been favorably impressed with *Poems, Chiefly Lyrical*, Arthur Hallam was further encouraged in his efforts to advance Tennyson's fame. On 15 July 1831 he wrote to Alfred,

I write in some haste. Moxon who has some sparks of poetry in his composition has got into his possession the *Englishman's Magazine* a periodical of last year's growth. He wants to start with a flash number if possible; and has already pressed Wordsworth, Southey and Charles Lamb into his service, but he is especially anxious to have something of yours. I very much wish you to comply with this request. Send the "Two Maidens" or "Rosalind" or something of that calibre or if you will commission me to get the Southern Mariana from Spedding which will save you all trouble. If you choose I have no doubt that you can become a permanent contributor on terms; and why should you disdain a mode of publication which Schiller and Goethe chose for their best compositions. It will not interfere with your collecting the pieces hereafter into a volume. You have no reason to be ashamed of your company and if a friendly name pleases you more than a famous one, I shall be along with you, at least if Moxon thinks me worthy of admission. Suggest the state of things to Charles and Frederick; one or both of them may be tempted to proffer their assistance. Only we want the answer directly because July is passing rapidly to the tomb of all the Julys.

When Tennyson failed to reply quickly, Hallam took matters completely into his own hands, only bothering to inform Alfred, "You perhaps will be angry when I tell you that I sent your sonnet about the 'Sombre Valley' ['Check every outflash'] to Moxon, who is charmed with it, and has printed it off. I confess this is a breach of trust on my part, but I hope for your forgiveness. . . ."⁶⁷ How could Alfred object when Hallam's "long, discriminating, and enthusiastic essay" on his *Poems, Chiefly Lyrical* appeared in the same number?⁶⁸
   For his final effort that year, Hallam had to request aid: would Merivale visit Moxon's office?

I may venture to ask you to take a little trouble for me in London, or rather for Alfred Tennyson, who according to custom has devolved his business on me. . . . Alfred, not intending to go into the Church, as the grandfather who has *patria potestas* over him wishes, and not having yet brought himself to cobble shoes for his livelihood, is desirous of putting his wits to profit, and begins to think himself a fool for kindly complying with the daily request of Annuals without getting anything in return. Now the aforesaid Moxon is a very good sort of fellow, and knows what's what in poetry, which, you know, "is as high as metaphysic wit can fly," and wishes Alfred to send him poems for his Mag. The matter I entrust to you is to call upon Mr. Moxon, 64 New Bond Street, introducing yourself under shelter of my name, and Alfred's, and to pop the question to him, "What do you pay your regular contributors? What will you pay Alfred Tennyson for monthly contributions?" Also, while your hand is in, to ask whether, if

Alfred was to get a new volume ready to be published next season, Moxon would give him anything for the copyright, and if anything, *what*. You might dextrously throw in, that I have a promise that any article I might write should be admitted either in the *Edinburgh* or *Quarterly*, and that I could therefore vouch for the books being reviewed in one or both. Nevertheless, I know the trade is at present in a most ticklish situation, and I suspect Moxon will fight shy; but I should be obliged to you if you will make the attempt, and write me word of the result in the course of next week. . . .

Moxon never did receive more contributions from Tennyson for the *Magazine* — which died in early 1832 — but it certainly was not for want of trying on Hallam's part. By these efforts, Hallam was setting up the acquaintanceship which would move Tennyson towards choosing Moxon as publisher for his next volume. That choice began a twenty-eight-year publishing relationship during which publisher and poet were able to meet the aesthetic and economic challenges confronting them in the early 1830s. Even by 1832 Tennyson had begun staking out his share of the current poetry audience and had begun to change its tastes. By so doing, his share of that audience increased dramatically and both he and Moxon eventually prospered.

2 Persuasive Friends: Moxon, Hallam, FitzGerald (1832–41)

Edward Moxon, the young publisher whom Arthur Hallam in 1832 decided was just right for Tennyson's next publication, had the background and meteoric business success which even Samuel Smiles of *Self-Help* fame would have applauded. Born on 12 December 1801 in Wakefield, Yorkshire, the eldest son of Michael Moxon, a textile worker, Edward received at most three or four years of formal schooling before being apprenticed at age nine to Edward Smith, a local bookseller. Yet this youngster, whom Leigh Hunt was later to describe as "a bookseller among poets, and a poet among booksellers," somehow picked up enough love of poetry to devote his life to publishing it.[1] That he also wrote poetry himself no doubt set him apart from the more mundane purveyors of books and helped to insure his success.[2]

At age sixteen, Moxon left Wakefield for London, effectively disappearing but surfacing again four years later as a clerk at Longmans, where he gained a reputation as one of the firm's "best hands."[3] During these years, in addition to learning the country trade, he read steadily and wrote verse so extensively that in 1824 he could submit "his poems to Charles Lamb for criticism."[4] This single act brought Moxon more fruitful relationships than usually accrue from such a request. First, Charles Lamb and his sister Mary became his life-long friends; secondly, he fell in love with and later married the Lamb household's "sort of adopted daughter," Emma Isola;[5] and, thirdly, through Lamb he met Samuel Rogers, William Wordsworth and Leigh Hunt, who became not only his friends but also prime authors on his list once he had set out as a publisher. Lamb's and Rogers's encouragement moved Moxon to submit his poems for publication. Longmans thus issued in January 1826 *The Prospect, and Other Poems*, dedicated to Samuel Rogers.

These highly derivative verses, full of Wakefield countryside and mildly Romantic diction, were prefaced by a very humble and apologetic statement in which Moxon self-pityingly revealed both his struggle to educate himself and, probably inadvertently, his lack of confidence in his own abilities. Wordsworth, when presented a copy by Moxon after the two men met for the first time in the fall of 1826, graciously offered this sage advice:

> Your poem I have read with no inconsiderable pleasure; it is full of natural sentiment and pleasing pictures. . . . This little volume, with what I saw of yourself during a short interview, interests me in your welfare; and the more so, as I always feel some apprehension for the destiny of those who in youth addict themselves to the composition of verse. It is a very seducing employment, and, though begun in disinterested love of the Muses, is too apt to connect itself with self-love, and the disquieting passions which follow in the train of that, our natural infirmity. Fix your eye upon acquiring independence by honourable business, and let the Muses come after, rather than go before. . . .[6]

Moxon, although not deterred from writing poetry, did indeed head for "independence by honourable business" by leaving Longmans to join with Hurst, Chance and Co., with whom he may have been a literary advisor.[7] A few years later, in May 1830, he set up his own shop. His partner in these early years was one Frederick M. Evans, later of Bradbury and Evans, who printed most of what Moxon published, and, at his death, were to become managers of the firm and his trustees. Hurst, Chance and Co. published in 1829 Moxon's second volume of poetry, *Christmas*, which was dedicated to Charles Lamb. Merriam points out that, "with all its worthy intention and often cheery spirit, the poem is not exhilarating," because of its overshadowing gloom.[8]

Moxon's next effort, *Sonnets*, he published himself as the second volume to issue from his new shop at 64, New Bond Street:

> [The *Sonnets*] were inscribed "most affectionately" to his brother William, then a young man preparing for the bar. There were thirty-two sonnets, one on a page, beautifully spaced, with clear, well-cut type, followed by a poem in twenty-three quatrains "To the Muse." The book was finely bound. It, too [like Lamb's *Album Verses*, Moxon's first publication], was issued for publicity rather

than for profit and was distributed as a gift to influential persons. Unfortunately, it drew no immediate comment from the press. The sonnets, which were quite the equal of much of the contemporary versifying, brought notice, however, to the new house in this way — a young publisher was himself a writer of verse: was a second Dodsley among them? Surely, also, Moxon was bidding for the manuscripts of poets.[9]

Three years later, on 25 May 1833, Arthur Hallam wrote to his fiancée, Emily Tennyson, about a book he had sent to Alfred Tennyson: "It is a volume of sonnets by Moxon. . . . The verses are very respectable and the binding the most lovely I ever saw." Thus, Tennyson probably never saw the *Sonnets* until after he had entered into publishing with Moxon, but we can surmise that Moxon's writing of poetry contributed to the friendship between them.

During his first six months as a publisher, in addition to his own *Sonnets* and Lamb's *Album Verses* (which attracted customers to the shop because of the harsh reviews it received!), Moxon also issued a cheap reprint, *Songs of Shakespeare and Milton.* "Throughout his publishing career," the biographer Merriam remarks, "Moxon's cheap reprints of accepted writings at a half-crown apiece or at four or five shillings played no small part in support of his other, more venturesome, enterprises."[10] A final edition that first year, Rogers's *Italy*, jointly issued with T. Cadell and "superbly illustrated" by twenty-four Turners among the fifty-six plates, "gave the new house its first solid contemporary importance."[11] Rogers, who had loaned Moxon £500 to start his business, paid all costs himself. Moxon printed 10,000 copies, selling them at £1 8s. each, which meant that he needed to sell 7448 before costs could be met on this very expensive undertaking.[12] He probably did not make any money on it, but this volume (which, incidentally, introduced the young John Ruskin to Turner's painting), also introduced Moxon's quality publishing to the world:

> It is hardly possible to exaggerate the importance of the book to the new publishing house. Rogers was influential among literary people; he enjoyed a long-established reputation for taste in art and literature; he was the friend of men and women in high society. The *Italy* gave prestige to the firms that put it out and attracted customers to their premises. Leigh Hunt caught the significance when he commented in the *Tatler*, in June, 1831: "Mr. Moxon has

begun his career as a bookseller in singularly high taste. He has no connection but with the select of the earth." Further, the volume of trade which came from its sale enlivened the shop and bestowed a pleasant feeling of success on the bookseller. It is to be noted, also, that no severer test could be placed on a publisher than the production of so fine a book for so fastidious a man as Samuel Rogers.[13]

During 1831 Moxon added to his expanding list Lamb's two poems *The Wife's Tale* and *Satan in Search of a Wife*; James Kenney's opera *Masaniello*; Landor's *Begir*; Tieck's tales from the German, translated by Julius Hare; James Kennedy's *History of the Contagious Cholera*; and two volumes of *Selections* from Southey and Wordsworth.

This same year a second publishing opportunity became available and Moxon made the most of it: he took ownership of the monthly *Englishman's Magazine*, which had "started well and steadily improved. From the first Moxon may have edited it himself. If so, he showed a surprising grasp of public affairs, a good feeling for relative values in materials, and a courageous and vigorous spirit."[14] A recent historian of periodicals, Walter Graham, claims that

by reason of its contributors [the *Englishman's Magazine*] has a clear title to a place among the better literary magazines of the century, in spite of its short career of little more than a year [seven numbers]. Tennyson, at that time almost unknown, Thomas Hood, Charles Lamb (signing himself "Elia"), Leigh Hunt, James Sheridan Knowles, Thomas Pringle, Mrs. Norton, William Motherwell, John Clare, and the precocious Arthur Hallam were represented in its columns.[15]

Its articles included ones supporting the Reform Bill, exposing the mishandling of the Indian cholera, opposing slavery, and evaluating the management of the British Museum. Regular space was given to dramatic reviews, music, painting, sculpture, drama and science. Commentary on current events, usually with a liberal bent, appeared in special columns. Though the magazine failed for lack of support, Moxon's publishing business reaped good publicity from it, enabling Moxon a year later to take ownership of yet another magazine, this time "a weekly series of essays called the *Reflector*, edited by John Forster, a new friend."[16] The three issues of the *Reflector*, however, "brought [the] firm no prestige and gave the publisher no fresh contact with literary men."[17] Not surprisingly, therefore, Moxon's brief excursion into publishing periodicals ended with the short-lived *Reflector*.

In 1832 Moxon acquired four important associations by publishing these new books on his list: the plays of Sheridan Knowles, works of Leigh Hunt, Shelley s *Masque of Anarchy*, and Tennyson's *Poems*. The Knowles plays influenced Moxon to undertake printing a whole series of dramas. Leigh Hunt was a noted reviewer and literary figure whom it was advantageous to know. The Shelley poem brought Moxon other Shelley compositions (some, such as the forged letters and *Queen Mab*, attended by court cases), and the Tennyson *Poems* netted him what proved to be his biggest publishing catch. However, before attending to the behind-the-scenes details of this first Moxon–Tennyson enterprise, it would be well to delineate the business policies which Moxon was developing and would continue to employ over his twenty-eight years as a publisher.

That Moxon's prime interest was poetry is clear from his list, which included almost every important poet of the period: Coleridge, Wordsworth, Keats, Shelley, Southey, Rogers, Lamb, Hunt, Campbell, Taylor, Knowles, Browning, Barrett, Patmore, Baillie and Longfellow, in addition to Tennyson. Although he was not as committed to fiction, he did publish Dana's *Two Years Before the Mast* and Harriet Martineau's novels, in addition to six other fiction titles. Of the few religious works, those of R. C. Trench predominated. Plays, books on public affairs, such as Kennedy's *History of the Contagious Cholera*, and especially travel narratives, such as Thomas Pringle's *Residence in South Africa*, reflected Moxon's personal enthusiasms. Like all successful publishers, Moxon needed a potboiling staple. For him it was not the usual cookbook, textbook or Sunday School tract, but a universal, compact reference work in use to this day, Haydn's *Dictionary of Dates*. The steady income from the many editions of this book helped to underwrite the firm's more speculative ventures into poetry. "With few histories on his list of publications, few religious books, no textbooks, few biographies, little fiction, practically none of the classics, no foreign books, and with the sale of poetry exceedingly slow, Moxon, one would think, must have had a difficult task to finance his business. Yet he prospered."[18]

Part of that prosperity can be attributed to his extremely good taste in getting up a book. "The type in Moxon's books was clear-cut and well spaced, even in cheap editions with double-columned pages. The title pages were simple and dignified, usually without rulings or ornaments. The binding was simple but elegant for his more expensive books, and simple and substantial for his cheaper ones."[19] Moxon's Tennyson editions, for instance, were usually done up in plain green cloth boards with simple gilt lettering on the spine. The exceptions to this practice were equally elegant: the 1857 *Illustrated Edition* appeared in bright blue, silk-like cloth with a gilt urn on the cover, and the 1850 *In Memoriam* came out in suitable dark purple cloth boards. Always the print and spacing attracted the eye and facilitated reading.

For publicity Moxon relied little on paid advertisements, but those he did run were brief and understated. Often the same copy, consisting of a simple announcement that a certain book had been published by Edward Moxon, appeared week after week. For an average spate of ads in the *Athenaeum*, Hunt's *London Journal*, and, of course, *The Times*, Moxon expended only about £20–40 per book. What he valued for publicity more than advertising were "social talk, business reputation, and reviews. 'A review,' he wrote to Wordsworth in 1842, 'even with a sprinkling of abuse in it, is, in my opinion, worth a hundred advertisements.'"[20] The abuse in reviews of his books was sometimes more a deluge than a sprinkling. His own sonnets, Lamb's *Album Verses*, the forged Shelley letters (which Moxon published unwittingly) and a few other volumes were attacked ferociously. Most of his books, however, received good notices, in large measure because Moxon understood the reviewing system and cultivated influential friends, such as noted reviewer John Forster. In addition to these methods of attracting attention, Moxon used each book to publicize others by running four- or eight-page listings of his publications on the flyleaves. For example, a first edition of Tennyson's 1832 *Poems*, now in the Tennyson Research Centre, advertises in this way: Richman's *Population Returns of 1831*; Cunningham's *The Maid of Elvar*; Rogers's *Italy*; Barry Cornwall's *Songs*; Southey's *Selections from the Poems* and *Selections from the Prose Works*; Wordsworth's *Selections*; Knowles's *The Hunchback*; Kennedy's *The History of the Contagious Cholera*; Madame d'Arblay's *Memories of Doctor Burney*; and Shelley's *The Masque of Anarchy*.

Such conservative advertising techniques appealed to publicity-shy authors such as Tennyson, but dismayed more flamboyant ones. "Browning," for example, "complained of [Moxon's] slowness, his lack of advertising, his lack of enterprise: 'If one of his books can only contrive to pay its expenses, you may be sure that a more enterprising brother of the craft would have sent it into a second or third edition.'"[21] And Leigh Hunt once called Moxon "a secreter rather than a publisher of books."[22]

Moxon's business dealings, of course, centered on his contracts with authors. Here, too, he usually took the financially conservative tack of encouraging the "half profits" agreement whereby the publisher paid all costs of production and advertising, and then, after reimbursing himself for these costs, shared whatever profits remained with the author. The agreement quoted below between Moxon and Leigh Hunt is typical, and probably represents in large part the terms held by Moxon and Tennyson for the 1832 *Poems*. Apparently they were able to function agreeably without a formal statement. All we have, actually, is Tennyson's statement in a letter of 13 October 1832, "Some time ago Mr. Hallam (to whom I gave full powers to treat with you) informed me that you are willing to publish my book, going shares with me in the risks and profits, neither of which, I should fancy, would be very considerable."[23]

The Moxon–Hunt "Memorandum of Agreement" reads,

> Mr. Moxon agrees to publish a new edition of Mr. Hunt's Poetical Works to consist of 2000 copies and to be comprised in one pocket volume and the selling price to be two shillings and sixpence, the same to be printed, stereotyped, published, and advertised by and at the sole risk of Mr. Moxon.
>
> That the profits to arise from the publication of such new edition of the said book as aforesaid, after deducting and paying thereout the costs and expenses to be incurred by Mr. Moxon in printing, stereotyping, publishing, and advertising the same and all other expenses incidental thereto, shall be equally divided between Mr. Hunt and Mr. Moxon.
>
> That Mr. Moxon shall from time to time be at liberty to print and publish any further such edition or editions of the said Poetical Works (to consist of 1000 copies) as by him shall be deemed advantageous, the profits of such future edition or editions being divided as aforesaid.
>
> That Mr. Moxon shall at the end of every six months (at midsummer and Christmas) render an account to Mr. Hunt of the sale of each edition and shall thereupon pay him his share of the profits arising from the sales of such edition or editions.[24]

The conservative business tactics which Moxon adopted do not reflect an accurate overall picture, however, for two noteworthy episodes attest to rather more liberal attitudes, which may.explain the sense of the "kindred spirit" which Tennyson felt towards him. One event occurred in 1840, when Moxon went against the trade's advice and published the full text of Shelley's *Queen Mab.* Moxon's consequent trial for "blasphemous libel," which resulted in conviction but no punishment, endeared him to civil libertarians. Furthermore, Moxon went against the Booksellers' Association in 1852 on the matter of free trade in bookselling — that is, he wished to allow booksellers to set whatever retail price they wished once they had bought books from a publisher, while the Association wanted to control retail prices and prevent special bargains or sales. When quizzed about this controversy, most authors, including Carlyle, Dickens, Kingsley, Lewes, Tennyson, Trench, Spencer and Mill, agreed with Moxon. Tennyson wrote, "I am for free trade in the bookselling question, as in other things."[25]

During the spring of 1832, when Edward Moxon was beginning to be known as a "publisher of poets," Alfred Tennyson was home in Somersby polishing his stanzas for a new volume. Upon the death of his father the year before he had had to leave Cambridge without his degree in order virtually to head his family of mother and eight younger brothers and sisters. His Cambridge friends, as usual, had become quite familiar with the poems in manuscript and had pronounced them good. "Tennyson's career," we are reminded by Charles and Frances Brookfield, "was followed closely from the start by sanguine friends who never failed to extend to him their enthusiastic admiration and encouragement; and who, whenever a poem appeared, wrote comments upon it to each other, discussing it line by line, sympathetically criticising, and invariably finding beauty throughout."[26] The correspondence that spring was filled with urgings towards publication. Hallam on 10 February wrote to Tennyson from Tunbridge Wells, "Your M. S. S. are exceedingly popular at Cambridge especially I think the 'Maidens' which perhaps would if published establish you at once in general reputation. . . ."[27] After visiting Alfred in March, Hallam reported to Trench,

Alfred I was most glad to find better than I had apprehended. I see no ground for thinking he has anything really serious to ail him. His mind is what it always was, or rather brighter, and more vigorous. . . . I have persuaded him, I think, to publish without further delay. There is written the amount of a volume rather larger than the former, and certainly, unless the usual illusion of manuscript deceives me, more free from blemishes and more masterly in power.[28]

Yet Hallam was to reverse himself a few weeks later, voicing to Alfred a reservation founded partly on a justified concern about care of the manuscripts:

> I don't know that you ought to publish this Spring but I shall never be easy or secure about your M. S. S. until I see them fairly out of your control. The Ballad of the Sisters was very popular at Cambridge. Indeed it is very perfect. . . . All were anxious for the 'Palace of Art,' etc., and fierce with me for not bringing more.[29]

Merivale wrote to Frederick Tennyson from Cambridge in late May, "As Cato took to Greek at eighty, so have I begun writing out Alfred's MSS. in a very neat book. — Poets who won't publish put their friends to great trouble. . . ."[30]

These supportive Cambridge friends shored up Alfred's shaky confidence almost to the point of publication — that is, until Professor John Wilson's ("Christopher North's") devastating article in the May *Blackwood's Edinburgh Magazine*. His February article had only stung a little, but this one burned. As Sir Charles puts it, Wilson "dealt with the young poet and his critics in the rowdy, blackguardly, patronizing and at the same time discriminating way which was peculiarly his own."[31] Hallam's essay in the *Englishman's Magazine* the previous year received a lethal blow, Wilson writing:

> The *Englishman's Magazine* ought not to have died; for it threatened to be a very pleasant periodical. An Essay "on the Genius of Alfred Tennyson" sent it to the grave. The super-human — nay, supernatural — pomposity of that one paper, incapacitated the whole work for living one day longer in this unceremonious world. The solemnity with which the critic approached the object of his adoration, and the sanctity with which he laid his offerings on the shrine, were too much for our irreligious age. The Essay "on the genius of Alfred Tennyson" awoke a general guffaw, and it expired in convulsions.[32]

Tennyson seemed more hurt by this attack on Hallam's essay than he did by Wilson's vigorous abuse of his own work, but Hallam took the pragmatic position that "all things considered the review will do good rather than harm," something that, by this time, Moxon already knew too.[33]

In spite of injured feelings after the Wilson article, Hallam multiplied his own efforts for getting Alfred published again, discussing the possibility with Moxon and even reporting to Emily, Tennyson's sister, whom he was now courting,

> I was speaking the other day to Moxon about books and the polite publisher touched upon Alfred's, talked of the favourable light with which it was received and asked if Alfred had any views of further publication. I don't doubt that Moxon would publish any volume Alfred might make up for him free of expense. It is worth his considering; a 2nd book just now would set Alfred high in public notice, and afford him the means of putting money in his pocket.[34]

Alfred's own worries at this time over his finances and career (of which more will be said later) did not lead him into gloom, however. For example, when news of the passage of the Reform Bill reached Somersby in June,

> My father [writes Hallam Tennyson] and some of his brothers and sisters at once sallied out into the darkness, and began to ring the church bells madly. The new parson, horrified at hearing his bells rung and not merely rung but furiously clashed without his leave, came rushing into his church, and in the pitch blackness laid hold of the first thing which he could clap hand to, and this happened to be my aunt Cecilia's little dog — which forthwith tried to bite. The Tennysons then disclosed themselves amid much laughter; and the parson, who I suppose was a Tory of the old school, was with difficulty pacified.[35]

The Tennyson children were not the only ones cheered by the Reform Bill. Edward Moxon had published articles in support of it in the *Englishman's Magazine* the year before. This affinity of spirit in political matters, tempered by Moxon's conservative tastes in getting up his books and in advertising them, may have disposed Tennyson to choose Moxon as publisher once the poet had finally decided to let his poems loose upon the world. Then, too, Alfred tended to take

Hallam's advice, and Hallam, as we have seen as far back as his 1831 letter to Merivale, advocated Moxon.

Little was done that summer on the book, though news of its publication, considered to be imminent, had reached the Cambridge circle. Tennyson went to London for a few days in late June and early July, where he basked in his friends' admiration. Two letters addressed to W. B. Donne on 2 July 1832 relate to this visit. J. W. Blakesley writes, "Kemble is in town; he is reading law five hours a day (or at least was doing so before Alfred Tennyson came up to town, for now those five hours are consumed (together with much shag tobacco) in sweet discourse on Poesy). . . ." And Kemble writes to Donne,

> Alfred Tennyson is about to give the world a volume of stupendous poems, the lowest toned of which is strung higher than the highest of his former volumes. He has been in London for some time, and a happy time it was; a happy time and a holy time, for it is the mighty privilege of such men to spread their own glory round them, upon all who come within the circuit of their light, and to exalt and purify them also.[36]

Later in July Alfred and Arthur toured the Rhine country together, enduring a miserable week in cholera quarantine while doing so, but otherwise delighting in new sights. In September Hallam manned a full-scale assault on Tennyson's reluctance to make important decisions about his volume. On 4 September, "I called on Moxon the other day but he was out of town. . . . When you write to me which I trust you will do without delay, tell me if you wish anything to be done about your M. S. S." And on 13 September he exhorts once more: "Moxon is impatient to begin the volume, unless I hear before Wednesday concerning the order I shall take that upon myself."[37] Hallam's efforts were rewarded at last: Tennyson pushed himself quite hard that very week in order to send off to London more manuscripts and a proposed order. On 24 September Hallam wrote a long letter to him, a letter which, along with the others following, indicates the minute attention Hallam was devoting to this project:

> I felt a thrill of pleasure on opening the packet this morning, for, to say the truth, I had begun to despair of your volume getting on, as you seemed so indignant at our endeavours to hasten it. They are good sonnets especially the 2nd. Your stanzas "All good things,"

most beautiful & to me especially should be most precious, since whether you choose or not, to descend from your convenient station in the Ideal, the world will consider them addressed to me. "Mariana in the South" seems the right title, I perceive you mean to refer only to the former one, not to republish it. Is "looming" rightly used? Its precise meaning I know not, but rather think it applies to ships at sea seen thro' mist or fog. I read some of Oenone to my Father today. He seemed to like Juno's speech and the next but was called away in the middle of Venus. I have the "Sisters". I like extremely the new stanzas in the "Palace." . . . I would hint a change of Livy into some other body. What think you of "Goethe & Raffael." I have not a perfect copy of the Hesperides. I wish you would send me one entire. Are we to have Amy or Margaret? Send the Old Year. I shall go into town Wednesday, & give the M. S. S. to Moxon; but will direct him to wait till Monday, before he begins printing, in case you should think to alter your proposed order. Should you wish to correspond with him directly the address is New Bond Street. I have not time to write more now for I am very busy. If neither Moxon nor I hear from you to the contrary, the printing shall commence next week in the order you specify. . . .[38]

A week or so later Hallam again thanked Tennyson for more MSS and expressed continued anxiety about the delays in getting the book out:

Moxon is in ecstasies with the "May Queen"; he says the volume must make a great sensation. He and your friends are anxious that it should be out before the storm of politics is abroad. The French Fleet has got the start of you, and I fear Antwerp may be taken before your last revise is ready; but still you may be beforehand with the elections, which is more important. There has been some delay this week, owing to want of types, but the [printer's] devils are full of promise to set up immediate. Moxon has sent me the revises of "The Palace," with the notes; they are, I believe, correct. . . .[39]

Consider, if you will, Hallam's influence thus far on this volume: he pushed Tennyson into publishing; he virtually chose the publisher; he carried the manuscripts to the printer; he helped decide the contents; he suggested changes in wording. Furthermore, it was he who read both first proofs and revises, though these often required help. On 10 October he gave Tennyson this progress report:

> I must snatch a few minutes from the overwhelming mass of law business which is now on my hands, just to talk with you about the first-proof. I had it sent down to me while I was staying at Heath's. The weather was miserably rainy, so, after breakfast, we adjourned to an arbour in the garden, and while Thompson, who was also staying there, furnished cheroots, I furnished proof-sheets. After mature examination, we came, in full conclave, to some decisions, of which you shall have the benefit. We think the type very pretty, but are rather sorry the book will not bind up with its predecessor. We admire the Buonaparte sonnet but we strongly urge the substitution of "dreamer" for "madman." The stanzas "All good things" seem to us perfect. The "Lady [of Shalott]" reads charmingly in print: the more I read it, the more I like it. You were, indeed, happily inspired when the idea of that poem first rose in your imagination. We had a long battle with Mr. Heath, a famous lawyer, but no man of letters, about the last stanza in the proof. We flatter ourselves we floored him; to be sure we were three to one, but he fought well. . . . In one place a whole line was omitted. Douglas Heath read, "sudden laughters of the Tay" [Jay]; without ever suspecting the misprint. I hear Tennant has written to dissuade you from publishing "Kriemhild," "Tarpeia" [in the "Fair Women"]. Don't be humbugged, they are very good; you may put a note or two if you will, yet Milton did not to "Paradise Lost." Rogers the poet has been staying here, and speaks of you with admiration. Have you written to Moxon? He is anxious to have the rest of the MSS.[40]

In all this, surprising as it may be, it seems that Tennyson had not yet written to Moxon on his own or spoken to him in person; Hallam was the intermediary. But, owing to Hallam's continued urging, Tennyson finally was forced to address Moxon directly. He did so in a letter dated 13 October:

> Some time ago Mr. Hallam (to whom I gave full powers to treat with you) informed me that you were willing to publish my book, going shares with me in the risks and profits, neither of which, I should fancy, would be very considerable.
> You will have received by this time the first proof-sheet

corrected. I think it would be better to send me every proof twice over. I should like the text to be as correct as possible. To be sure this proceeding would somewhat delay the publication, but I am in no hurry. My MSS (*i.e.*, those I have by me) are far from being in proper order, and such a measure would both give me leisure to arrange and correct them, and ensure a correct type.

I scarcely know at present what the size of the volume will be, for I have many Poems lying by me with respect to which I cannot make up my mind as to whether they are fit for publication. Most probably it would be nearly the size of that published by Effingham Wilson, about 150 pages. If such be the case, and you send me every proof twice, how long would your printer be in getting the book ready? I will send you the remaining MSS as soon as possible.

P. S. May I act upon the principle contained in that pithy apothegm "Better late than never," and thank you for your very polite present of Charles Lamb's Album Verses, made to me two or three years ago?[41]

From this we know that, after Moxon had started printing the book, Tennyson was still not sure of either the order or the contents of the volume. Since we have none of Moxon's letters from this period, we can only imagine the consternation which such dawdling and mind-changing, such revisions in proof, must have caused. Even receiving the MSS in installments — with the order yet undecided — would have led a lesser publisher to protest. But Moxon was no ordinary publisher. He had the patience to keep pressing on because he sensed that Tennyson's poems were in themselves extraordinary and therefore worth struggling for.

No doubt the biggest struggle over the *Poems* of 1832 centered on Tennyson's urge to withdraw "The Lover's Tale," a blank verse poem of about sixty pages which was slated to end the volume and was already set up in print.[42] In this, Tennyson adamantly went against the protestations of Hallam, Heath and even Moxon himself.

Early in November Tennyson presumably wrote to Hallam informing him that he intended to withdraw "The Lover's Tale" after having thought the whole matter over carefully.[43] Hallam wrote back to him, most vehemently,

By all that is dear to thee — by our friendship — by sun, moon and stars — by narwhals and sea-horses — don't give up "The Lover's Tale." Heath is mad to hear of your intention. I am madder. You must be point-blank mad. It will please a vast number of people. It pleases the wise. You are free from all responsibility as to its faults, by the few lines of preface. Pray – pray – pray – change your mind again. I have ordered Moxon to stop proceeding till I hear from you again – therefore write instanter.[44]

In a second letter, before Tennyson's reply reached him, Hallam expostulated further,

> I hope to have a line from you today stating your ultimatum as to the Lover's Tale. I fear it will not be favorable [sic] as you say you made up your mind after deliberation. If so I shall be very sorry. There are magnificent passages in that poem. The present casket, faulty as it is, is yet the only one in which the precious gems contained therein can be preserved. I have begun a sort of article upon you, which I think I shall send to the "Edinburgh." For several reasons the "Edinburgh" is preferable if I can manage it. If however Macaulay would review you favourably it would be much better. Do you intend printing any sort of preface to the volume? "Poems" is not a sufficient title. People will think it is the old book & not buy. Moxon's advertisements have been "A second series of Poems by etc" but I don't much like the word "series". Let me or him have a line about this. . . .

While Hallam was writing this, a letter arrived from Tennyson, apparently requesting the return of all printed copies of "The Lover's Tale," for Hallam continues, "I have just got your note. It can't be helped. *Nescit vox missa reverti.* In a selfish point of view I shall gain; for mine is the only printed copy of the 'Tale' and I shall lend it at 5 /- a head."

After these vigorous protestations from Hallam, Tennyson felt that he must at least give the withdrawal message to Moxon in his own hand, although usually nothing except extreme necessity could induce him to write letters. And so, on 20 November 1832, he sent off these instructions to his publisher:

> After mature consideration I have come to a resolution of not publishing the last poem in my little volume entitled "Lover's Tale" – it is too full of faults and tho' I think it might conduce towards making me popular, yet to my eye it spoils the completeness of the book and is better away – of course whatever

expenses may have been incurred in printing the above must devolve on me solely.

The volume can end with that piece entitled "To J. S." Half of this last I have received in Revise: there are 9 stanzas more which it will not be necessary to send me – if I remember right they only contained one material blunder viz. "Bleeding" for "Bleedeth." Should this last revise be already on its way to me it will be better for me to retain it, and if there be any other mistake, which is scarcely probable I will give you notice by letter. We who live in this corner of the world only get our letters twice or thrice a week: this has caused considerable delay but on the receipt of this you may begin to dress the Volume for its introduction into the world as soon as you choose.

> P. S. The title page may be simply – Poems
> by Alfred Tennyson
> (don't let the printers squire me)
> Be so good as to send me five copies.[45]

One must conclude from Tennyson's withdrawal of "The Lover's Tale" and from a few other small points, such as his retaining the title "Poems," that Hallam's influence, strong as it was, could not prevail against Tennyson's stubborn insistence on judging the worth of his own art. When it came to the test, Tennyson had the last word on what went in and what stayed out.

The contents finally decided upon reveal Tennyson as a poet who grappled with finding his own voice, forms, and themes, while retaining some of the imitative impulses from his earlier days, impulses seen in the 1830 *Poems, Chiefly Lyrical* and in the juvenilia. A few sonnets, some insipid "women portraits" ("Eleanore," "Rosalind," "Margaret," "Kate"), a few brief lyrics in adolescent style, a sentimental trifle ("O Darling Room") and an inane retort ("To Christopher North") were among the backward-looking pieces, and these the critics properly denounced. But the strength of the volume lay in other directions: in poems of English life ("The May Queen," "The Miller's Daughter"); poems on the Arthurian theme ("The Lady of Shalott"); poems based on the classics ("Oenone," "The Hesperides," "The Lotos-Eaters"); on traditional learning ("Mariana in the South," "The Palace of Art," "A Dream of Fair Women"); or in mature lyrics such as the lovely "To J. S." and "The Death of the Old Year." These poems, some in revised form, are now among the mainstays of the Tennyson canon, and are certainly an amazing output for a twenty-three-year old.

When the book was finally on its way, Arthur Hallam stepped up his campaign for obtaining good reviews. He wrote to Leigh Hunt, who had so enthusiastically greeted the earlier volume,

> I hope soon to have the pleasure of presenting you a second collection of poems by my friend Alfred Tennyson, much superior in my judgment to the first, although I thought, as you know, highly of those. His brother, the author of *The Sonnets*, has entered the Church, and is, I fear, lost to the Muses. Alfred has resisted all attempts to force him into a profession, preferring poetry and an honourable poverty. [46]

One way to guarantee a good review, as Hallam well knew, was to write it oneself. This he had already begun to do, but, since it was unsolicited, he was unsure of its acceptance. It never appeared. [47]

Moxon placed an announcement on the flyleaf of Hunt's *Poetical Works*, published late that year, to this effect: "Just Published: "In Foolscap Octavo / A Second Series of Poems / By Alfred Tennyson." The December printing of 450 copies, which sold at six shillings, proved more than a sufficient supply, for "two years later only 300 of the edition of 450 copies had been disposed of." [48] Moxon bound the volume in drab paper boards with a white paper label on the spine. Hallam reported on sales and attitudes towards the book when he wrote to Emily on 12 December 1832:

> Alfred's book is very prettily got up; there are, I believe, no errors except here & there in the stopping, [which] the reader's eye easily connects. The heaviest [?] errors alas! consists [sic] of Alfred's own alterations. I hear the most awful complaints from Cambridge of what he has done to the Lotus [sic] eaters, Palace etc. [49] However the men of Cambridge have bought *seventy-five* copies; a fact infinitely to their credit. There is a savage & stupid attack on poor Nol [nickname for Alfred] in the Literary Gazette — with such a parody on the Lady of Shalott! Poor Nol will die of it. But nobody minds the Lit. Gazette.

But it was not the review in the *Literary Gazette* which troubled Alfred's spirit. Rather it was an anonymous one in the April *Quarterly Review*. We now know this was written by John Wilson Croker [no relation to Professor John Wilson, "Christopher North"], whose attack on Keats in *Blackwood's* fifteen years before is justly famous as the epitome of vitriolic, small-minded criticism. Sir Charles's summary of the Croker attack captures its essence:

> As if to emphasize the malice and folly of his onslaught, Croker prefaced it with sarcastic reference to Keats and a mock apology for his own review of *Endymion*. Of course, this was done in order to lead up to a classification of Tennyson as a member of the "Cockney school." Croker then proceeded to employ every device known to the dishonest critic, in order to discredit and ridicule the book before him. He made no effort to find any beauty or merit in it. In his comments he alternated between savage sarcasm and ponderous jocosity. When he quoted, he either picked out the worst lines and poems or separated passages from their context with the sole object of making them seem ridiculous.[50]

The choice of Croker for this review of a new young poet probably came from editor John Lockhart's personal fondness for Professor John Wilson ("Christopher North"). Wilson disdained to say anything publicly about Tennyson's epigram on him, but no doubt he resented it enough to seek some kind of devastating revenge. Since Croker devoted two of his fifteen pages to the insignificant mistake, "To Christopher North," we can guess that Wilson had asked him to give Tennyson tit for tat, or worse. Moxon's biographer ponders the publisher's willingness to include the North epigram: "One marvels what could have been in Moxon's mind when he left in the book such an obvious bid as those childish lines for at least one unfavorable review in a powerful journal. The only answer is that he was inexperienced, that Tennyson was young and stubborn, and that both were overconfident."[51] But Moxon, as usual, claimed not to mind the bad review, maintaining that bad notice was still preferable to no notice at all. We gather this from Hallam's letter to Tennyson in late spring, 1833:

> Your book continues to sell tolerably and Moxon says the *Quarterly* has done good. Rogers defends you publicly as the most promising genius of the time. Sir Robert Inglis told my father he had heard from unquestionable authority that Alfred Tennyson was an assumed name like Barry Cornwall. I endeavoured to shake

his scepticism, I fear without effect. I hear to-day that a question is put up at the Cambridge Union, "Tennyson or Milton, which the greater poet?" . . . Rogers thinks the first volume decidedly superior to the second. . . . I don't quite understand this.[52]

But Tennyson, always sensitive to even the mildest censure of his poetry, was disturbed by Croker's violence. The review hurt his pride, hurt sales, and therefore hurt Moxon indirectly, too, for it prevented him from achieving the success with the volume which it probably would have had without the *Quarterly*'s influence. The few favorable reviews were in minor periodicals such as *The Monthly Repository* and *The True Sun*. Later, in July 1835, John Stuart Mill wrote a sympathetic review of both the 1830 and 1832 volumes for the *London Review*, but it came too late to stop the damage done by the powerful *Quarterly*. That Tennyson fully repented including the North epigram there can be no doubt.[53]

Yet he kept working. Tennyson's so-called "Ten Years' Silence" which followed was not really silence at all, but rather a hum of artistic energy devoted to revision of his old poems and creation of many new ones which were to fully establish him later as the leading poet of his generation. More on these revisions later, however. The point here is that, in spite of the *Quarterly*, Alfred passed a quietly contented summer at Somersby, "with writing, revision and study, which was his normal routine of existence."[54] He did not mope about. In fact, these months brought him great contentment, owing to his deepening friendship with Arthur Hallam, who could once again spend vacations at the Somersby Rectory now that his engagement to Tennyson's sister Emily was acknowledged by both families. Sir Charles attributes some of the eroticism of "The Gardener's Daughter" (mild, indeed, by today's standards), composed at this time, to an expansion of spirit experienced by Alfred because of this double tie to Hallam, who was both friend and soon to be brother. In this poem Tennyson may also have been drawing on his awakening interest in the lovely Rosa Baring of Harrington Hall, two miles from the Somersby Rectory. After all, he writes of "Rose, the Gardener's daughter" and "Eden where she dwelt" – possibly a veiled reference to her stepfather, Arthur Eden, who had leased the Hall around 1825 and had entered his family into the community's social life.[55] Yet the sorrow in human experience soon came unbidden into Tennyson's own Edenic life.

At the beginning of August Arthur was to go with his father on a Continental tour. Alfred came down to London from Scotland [where he had been on brief holiday] to see him off, and gave a supper in his lodgings at which Moxon and Leigh Hunt were present. Afterwards he recited glorious fragments of *The Gardener's Daughter*, and the party did not separate till half past four in the morning.[56]

That farewell party is the first recorded evidence of Tennyson's meeting socially with a new friend – his publisher, Edward Moxon. Chances are, however, that the two had actually met before, as Moxon's bookshop also served as one of the literary meeting places of its day.

On 15 September 1833 Arthur Hallam died suddenly in Vienna. The news reached the Tennyson family on 1 October, and it is no exaggeration to say that that date was the most significant in Alfred's life up to that time. At one blow he lost his closest friend, his intellectual focal point, his best advisor, his literary agent, his editor, his proof-reader. Moreover, Alfred had to witness the devastating grief of his sister at the loss of the man she was to marry. As for Tennyson himself, he sought comfort in the only path open to the creative intellect: he turned to his art, and in doing so acquired a new potency and attained a new level of excellence.

Later that fall, Edward FitzGerald, another new friend, who, in tandem with Moxon, was to fill the oppressive void left by Hallam's death, emphasized Tennyson's art when commenting to W. B. Donne on 25 October,

> Tennyson has been in town for some time: he has been making fresh poems, which are finer, they say, than any he has done. But I believe he is chiefly meditating on the purging and subliming of what he has already done; and repents that he has published at all yet. It is fine to see how in each succeeding poem the smaller ornaments and fancies drop away, and leave the grand ideas single. . . .[57]

During this melancholy period, elder brother Frederick also made the mistake of assuming that so much activity would result in Alfred's publishing again that next spring.[58] One can easily understand why Frederick should have received this impression, for, by the end of the year, when the family had received word that the ship bearing the body of Arthur Hallam had finally arrived in England, Alfred had already worked out some of the best stanzas of *In Memoriam*; he had probably also begun "Morte d'Arthur," and had worked on versions of "The Two Voices" (first called "Thoughts of a Suicide"), "Ulysses," "St. Simeon Stylites," "St. Agnes," "Sir Launcelot and Queen Guinevere," "Sir Galahad" and "The Beggar Maid." These poems, which were to be included in the next published volume, mark the threshold of mature poetic achievement, with none of the occasional flaccidity of his earlier work. He continued this creation of important new poems, including "Tithonus," "O! that 'twere possible" (the germ of *Maud*), and many more *In Memoriam* stanzas, throughout the decade 1833—42.

A second important accomplishment in this period was Tennyson's extensive revision of those poems he felt worth saving from the earlier volumes.

The effect of the critics' words on these revisions is open to question. It has been the received opinion that Tennyson revised out of obsequiousness as a way of circumventing the same kind of criticism he had suffered earlier. This view, however, ignores the actual changes he made. Although he did excise or rewrite some passages objected to by reviewers, he also changed some about which there had been no complaint. In a number of cases he left highly criticized lines just as they were. In short, he was exercising his own critical judgment throughout.

Tennyson's attitude towards revision is evident from a number of comments in the *Memoir*. Hallam Tennyson writes about the period from 1833 to 1835:

> From the letters of that time I gather that there was a strong current of depreciation of my father in certain literary quarters. However he kept up his courage, profited by friendly and unfriendly criticism, and in silence, obscurity, and solitude, perfected his art. "First the workman is known for his work, afterwards the work for the workman": but it is "only the concise and perfect work," he thought, "which will last."[59]

Again, "My father pondered all that had been said, and — after a period of utter prostration from grief, and many dark fits of blank despondency — his passionate love of truth, of nature, and of humanity, drove him to work again."[60] Through all of this there runs the refrain of poetry as work, apparently because Tennyson considered it so. Of his own development as a worker with words, a poet, he said, "I suppose I was nearer thirty than twenty before I was anything of an artist."[61] Tennyson was thirty in 1839, right in the midst of these creative years. According to the *Memoir*, one of Tennyson's favorite adages was, "The artist is known by his self-limitation," a quotation Hallam Tennyson puts in the same paragraph with the famous one about Tennyson's dislike of having anyone see his "chips in the workshop."[62] Ignoring this dislike, however, has enabled modern scholars to contribute to our understanding of Tennyson's methods by studying these "chips," these revisions, at length.[63] One scholar writes that Tennyson often "sought to curb his own excesses by removing needlessly replete descriptions, reducing the number of fulsome epithets, and regularizing his metres and stanza patterns."[64] One might say that, in sum, Tennyson in his revisions simplified diction, dignified movement, dramatized action and theme, and clarified structure. Although occasional critics prefer a few lines of an original version here and there to the revised lines, in most cases Tennyson's revisions are admitted improvements. It was the *revisions* of the earlier poems, plus a few important new poems, which finally established Tennyson as a poet of the first rank.

Of Tennyson's personal life during the 1830s more information can be gleaned from the occasional references made in letters from friends and in some of Tennyson's own recently published ones than from the traditional source, Hallam Tennyson's *Memoir* of his father. Apparently Tennyson's personality, even after the shock of Arthur Hallam's death and his sister's great sorrow, had a much lighter and even roguish side to it than his reticent son admitted. Here is what Mary Joan (Donahue) Ellmann says of the correspondence she discovered:

In these letters the private and young man, sometimes grumpy, sometimes gay with a labored raillery, almost always direct and blunt, shows less self-consciousness [than in his Laureate years]. The serious, almost exalted temper which Hallam Tennyson constructs as dominant in these years [1833–6] is not reflected here. And the poetic temper of "The Lady of Shalott" and "St. Agnes" and "Tithonus" seems to have been independent, separate from the temper of his daily life.[65]

Ralph Rader, in his *Maud* book, argues at length that, although

Hallam's death was indeed "a very great blow to Tennyson . . . without doubt the most severe shock of his life," the poet's mood was not one of despair. "The facts seem to indicate that during 1834 Tennyson largely recovered from that shock and was addressing himself once more to life."[66] One of his projects was the stretching of his intellectual muscles by a program of daily studies to make up for his truncated Cambridge education. His subjects included history, chemistry, botany, electricity, animal physiology and mechanics, for mornings; German, Italian and Greek, for afternoons; poetry, for evenings; and theology, quite properly, for Sundays.[67] Social and family life, too, filled his time. He kept up with his friends by means of letters and visits; he danced, dined, smoked, flirted. Moreover, he began to concern himself to a greater extent with the health of his brothers — Charles's opium addiction; Edward's complete mental breakdown; Septimus's deteriorating mind — and his own financial straits, and the wave of stunned sadness over Hallam's death began to ebb.

Tennyson's financial troubles went back to the death of his father, Dr George Clayton Tennyson, Rector of Somersby and Bag Enderby, in March 1831. His death left Mrs Tennyson and her eleven children dependent upon the grandfather, George Clayton Tennyson the elder, of Bayons Manor, who was called, none too affectionately, "The Old Man of the Wolds." Since he had disinherited his eldest son, driving him into the Church, had displayed constant favoritism towards the younger son, Charles Tennyson d'Eyncourt, had harbored a dislike for the Somersby Tennysons which was exacerbated by their eccentricities and apparent indolence, it comes as no surprise to find that the provisions he made for the Rectory family centered on a severe plan. In order to pay Dr Tennyson's debts of almost £900 without having to sell his books and furniture, and to cover £800 of Cambridge debts accrued by Frederick, Charles and Alfred, the Old Man "drew up two bonds totaling over £1,400 (formalized in September 1832) which bore upon the three eldest sons and their mother; the bonds were to be realized for the younger children after his death. Mrs Tennyson was allowed £800 a year, less interest on the bonds and less any expenses which the Old Man incurred on her younger children's behalf." Ricks explains further that the grandfather "disliked the idea that the three eldest sons, already fortunate in their education compared with their siblings, should in effect have more than their fair share of their eventual bequest from him."[68]

What this meant in practical terms was that, unless Alfred took to making some money for himself, he would have to live on funds which Mrs Tennyson could ill afford to provide for him. A family friend, the Rev. T. H. Rawnsley, Vicar of Halton Holgate, less than ten miles from Somersby, urged Frederick and Alfred "by all the affection and regard I bear, and they ought to bear, to their Father's memory, and their own situation, to put their great talents into exercise, and to exert themselves for their own maintenance and respectability."[69] But this prudent advice was countermanded by the Old Man. According to him, both Frederick and Alfred should head for the Church, to which Charles, who seems to have had an actual vocation, was already firmly committed and ready to be ordained. One would think that the tragic life of his son George, rife with violent fits of temper and bouts with alcholism which caused frequent upheavals in the Rectory household would have cured the Old Man of his proclivity for driving people into Holy Orders, but it did not. George's sad misplacement he now wanted to visit upon the children. The coercion towards the Church reveals itself in a letter from Uncle Charles, chief negotiator, to his father in May 1831:

> We discussed what was to be done with the children. Alfred is at home – but wishes to return to Cambridge to take a degree. I told him it was a useless expense unless he meant to go into the Church. He said he would. I did not think he seemed much to like it – then suggested Physic or some other profession. He seemed to think the Church the best and has I think finally made up his mind to it. The Tealby living was mentioned and understood to be intended for him. [In fact, the Tealby curacy went to Charles until the livings at Grasby and Caistor should be available to him.] . . . Alfred seems quite ready to go into the Church although I think his mind is fixed on the idea of deriving his great distinction and greatest means from the exercise of his poetic talents.[70]

Alfred managed to resist these proddings, however. After Frederick took himself out of the country and Charles took up the curacy at Tealby, Alfred was left at home, far from the Cambridge circle of friends who so supported him, in order to head what remained of the family. He stayed in that position, dependent on his mother (who in turn was dependent on her father-in-law), until he gained some slight measure of financial independence by the Old Man's death in 1835. Alfred received property at Grasby worth about £3000. The income from the rents on that land, occasional pocket money from his aunt, Elizabeth Russell, and a later bequest of £500 from Arthur Hallam's aunt formed his only income until the moderate success of the two-volume *Poems* published in 1842. Taking room and board from his mother and money from his aunt during these years must have been irksome to him, but not irksome enough, apparently, to make him forgo his plan of becoming a great national poet who could sustain himself on the earnings from his pen. Thus far all he had received for his poems was the Cambridge gold medal — and that he sold for £15 in 1835! Yet he would not take a job or prepare for any of the usual professions; indeed, few of the Tennyson children other than Charles ever did. Rawnsley wrote of them, with much understanding and some ruefulness, in a letter to their Uncle Charles during the mid-1830s, "I wish they would earn more either of fame or profit, but then they are leading a harmless and quiet life and this is what the ancient poets and philosophers say is after all the highest state of permanent enjoyment."[71] Fame and profit were to come to Alfred eventually, and they would come by the very means he espoused — poetry.

During the decade beginning in 1832, however, this virtually penniless, "sometimes grumpy, sometimes gay" young poet published only a few poems — and these few *gratis* in the elaborately illustrated "annuals" which graced Victorian parlor tables. Arthur Hallam referred to the first few of these efforts in these words: "Alfred, not intending to go into the Church, as the grandfather who has *patria potestas* over him wishes, and not having yet brought himself to cobble shoes for his livelihood, is desirous of putting his wits to profit, and begins to think himself a fool for kindly complying with the daily requests of Annuals without getting anything in return."[72] Although Tennyson despised this method of publication, the insistence of his friends overruled his own wishes. For example, on 3 August 1832 he had written to Brookfield,

How have you the conscience to ask me to annualize for Yorkshire. Have I not forsworn all annuals provincial and metropolitan — I have been so be-Gemmed and be-Amuletted and be-forget-me-not-ted that I have given all those things up. . . . Would you have me break my vow because you sing pleasantly over a winecup? Shall I forswear myself because you can make punch? . . . No — by St. Anne — No. I wouldn't do it for Tennant — no — not for Hallam yet peradventure for thee, William Henry, I might be brought to it. . . . But seriously, Brookfield, I have a very strong objection to appearing in annuals and it is only because *you* ask me that I have written for you the following sonnet.[73]

In July 1836 Alfred wrote to Brookfield again on the subject of publication in annuals; this time he sent "St. Agnes" for *The Keepsake*, edited by Lady Emmeline Stuart Wortley, but he complained all the while,

> I have sent you a little poem written some three years back; had there been any prospect of filthy lucre, or perhaps had the lady herself wooed me with her fair eyes, I might have sent something which would have filled a larger space in her annual, but
>
> > If she be not fair to me,
> > What care I how fair she be.
>
> I think it will be easily decipherable even to the dull eyes [and] blunt wits of printer's devils and, as you see, I have written it on a blank leaf, so that you may tear it off and transmit it as soon as you choose to Lady E.S.W. I trust that she will not take it in earnest of anything to be sent her next year, for I have a sort of instinctive hatred towards annuals each and all —
>
> I am much better in health than when I saw you and altogether more cheerful. Plans for the summer I have none, for my walking tour seems to be quashed for want of a companion, nor do I think it probable that I shall be in town at all till Autumn and perhaps not then.
>
> I am in a great hurry just going to dine out.[74]

The next year a very important little poem, "O! that 'twere possible," which was the germ of *Maud*, published eighteen years later, was sent to *The Tribute*.[75] This, though not an annual in the technical sense, but rather "an isolated volume, published by Murray for the benefit of Edward Smedley," had as its contributors "an illustrious band: Wordsworth, Landor, Aubrey de Vere, Henry Taylor, Southey, Milnes, and others."[76] Tennyson's friend Richard Monckton Milnes was responsible for gathering contributions for the volume and of course asked his Apostle friend. Two letters went from Tennyson to Milnes about this request, the first refusing in a bantering way, leading Milnes to misinterpret it. Tennyson said, among other things, "To write for people with prefixes to their names is to milk he-goats;

there is neither honour nor profit." Milnes replied with an angry note which required that Alfred send a second, this time conciliatory, letter — in which he ended up promising contributions not only from himself but also from Charles and Frederick![77]

These *gratis* publications notwithstanding, Tennyson made it quite clear to his friends and publisher alike that he was not ready to publish again on his own because he was working hard at both new compositions and revisions of the old ones. To James Spedding he wrote, probably in 1835,

> John Heath writes me word that Mill is going to review me in a new Magazine, to be called the *London Review*, and favourably; but it is the last thing I wish for, and I would that you or some other who may be friends of Mill would hint as much to him. *I do not wish to be dragged forward again in any shape before the reading public at present*, particularly on the score of my old poems, most of which I have corrected (particularly "Oenone") as to make them much less imperfect. . . .[78]

We have already noted FitzGerald's observation that Tennyson "repents that he has published at all yet," which may have been a reaction to the severe reviews of the 1832 *Poems*, but this hesitancy about publishing was more the rule than the exception.

The close members of Tennyson's coterie realized that his unusual methods of composition often precluded his producing even a manuscript, much less a published book. Milnes expressed this tersely to Aubrey de Vere: "Tennyson composes every day but nothing will persuade him to print, or even write it down."[79] Throughout his life Tennyson was given to composing long stretches of poetry in his mind as he walked about the hills and lanes or sat over his pipe during the morning and evening hours in his study. Some of these passages he revised mentally and eventually, with suitable grumblings, no doubt, wrote down.[80] But not all of them. William Michael Rossetti commented in 1850: "Patmore says that Tennyson has in his memory, and on occasion recites, an immense quantity of poetry which he never intends to commit to paper."[81] This habit of mental composition accounts for some of the faults of the early volumes, which really needed pruning more than anything else. Sir Charles speculates on this, after mentioning the "great quantity of material lying by him from which to select [the contents of the 1832 volume]":

One may be sure that many other ideas for poems were simmering in his mind. The reduction into final form of the material selected from this mass, involved an intense effort of concentration from a mind seething with ideas and creative activity, which made the exercise of the critical faculty difficult and irksome. Sometimes, especially in the longer poems, it could not stand the strain. There were lapses, and his friends' enthusiasm and their respect for his own sensitiveness tended to obscure these from him. [82]

Even after Tennyson's poems managed to get written out in longhand, the long siege to preserve them was far from won. Remember Hallam's writing to him in 1832, "I shall never be easy or secure about your M. S. S. until I see them fairly out of your control." We can well appreciate Hallam's worries on this score when we read some of the comments made about Tennyson's notorious carelessness about his papers. (I say "notorious" advisedly, because the account of his having lost the manuscript of *Poems, Chiefly Lyrical* in a Lincolnshire lane became well known.)

Rawnsley's nephew reports, "My Uncle Edward . . . was sitting in Tennyson's room once, when he was burning letters and papers, and he rescued literally out of the fire a lyrical gem, possibly the poem 'Break, Break,' saying 'You must not burn that, that is one of the best things you have written.'" [83]

Hallam Tennyson writes, "'The Brook' in later years was actually rescued from the waste-paper heap." [84] But the most horrendous loss of a manuscript, from a modern critical perspective or, indeed, from the point of view of Tennyson's personal life, fame or financial security, occurred when he left the *In Memoriam* butcher's book in his Mornington Place lodgings early in 1850. [85] After noticing his loss, Tennyson wrote calmly to Coventry Patmore,

> I went up to my room yesterday to get my book of Elegies: you know what I mean, a long Butcher ledger-like book. I was going to read one or two to an artist here: I could not find it. I have some obscure remembrance of having lent it to you. If so, all is well. If not, will you go to my old chambers and institute a vigorous inquiry? I was coming up today on purpose to look after it, but as the weather is so furious I have yielded to the wishes of my friend here to stop till tomorrow.

But Patmore did not have the volume. And the second of those possibilities Tennyson voiced in his letter created some consternation in one London landlady:

> Patmore had considerable difficulty in gaining access to the room which Alfred had occupied, as it was now let to someone else. Indeed, the landlady stoutly refused him admittance, but he pushed past her, ran upstairs and, after some search, found the "butcher's book" at the back of the cupboard in which the poet had been used to keep his tea and bread and butter.[86]

Tennyson seemed more amused by his friends' concern than anxious to mend his ways; in fact, even when he finally wrote his manuscripts out for the printers, he teased his friends by tearing off the ample margins of the butchers' books for pipelights.

This recklessness about his manuscripts — the losses, not the pipelight foolery, that is — Sir Charles attributes "in part to his feeling that [the poems] were living things, part of his own being, with a life quite independent of any visible existence." Undoubtedly, too, a man known as slovenly in his dress was probably simply slovenly in his papers. Yet somehow more seems to be involved when a larger view is taken. Consider this if you will: Tennyson lost manuscripts; entered publishing reluctantly, almost dragged in by his friends; published two of his first four books anonymously (*Poems by Two Brothers* and *In Memoriam*) — yet insisted that he wanted fame and profit only from poetry. Such a double message usually indicates some lack of confidence, some holding back, some doubting of one's powers. But the revisions Tennyson made on his old poems were sure and forceful. In them he indicated no doubting of his own abilities *as a poet*. No, what he questioned, I believe, was his ability to please a wide audience, a questioning only reasonable after his small sales. After *In Memoriam*'s popular success, however, Tennyson's customary reluctance to publish gave way so much so that he even took the (for him) unprecedented routes of publication in pamphlet form ("The Ode on the Death of the Duke of Wellington") and in periodicals ("The Charge of the Light Brigade," "Britons, Guard Your Own," "The Third of February, 1852," "Hands All Round!" and others, for example, in *The Examiner*).[87] The persuasiveness of Tennyson's friends was not needed after 1850, by which time Tennyson had easily adjusted to having as support only the secretarial and critical help of his wife, Emily, who had no need to persuade Alfred to publish, for he had by now persuaded himself. What was once a coterie of rarified admirers was now supplanted by mass popularity, and concomitantly his fear about "being dragged forward . . . before the reading public" was replaced by a new confidence. He did make one small change in his working habits later in life. Allingham visited Aldworth in 1884 and noted the change:

> He writes his poetry now in trim small quarto books, in limp covers, the writing as neat as ever, tho' sometimes a little shaky. He keeps these books handy and takes them up very often, both at set times and odd moments, considering them and correcting, and frequently reading new poems aloud from them, first to his family and afterwards to visitors. After the compositions are put into type he usually keeps them by him in proof for a long time, months or even years, reconsidering and perfecting every part.[88]

No change was ever made in these proof habits. In his first letter to Moxon about the 1832 *Poems*, more than fifty years before Allingham's visit, Tennyson had asked for more than one set of proofs. It was his life-long practice to have double sets of proofs sent to him twice; he, Edward Moxon, and Arthur Hallam referred to these sets as "first-proofs" and "revises." Each time, Tennyson would copy his revisions from the working proofs to the clean proofs, which he would then send back to his printer. Tennyson's custom in reading proof was not only to correct the printer's errors but also to adjust punctuation, to which he never paid much attention when writing out the poems in manuscript. John Pfordresher explains,

> Many times he would write on for lines without a single punctuation mark, frequently even neglecting to capitalize the first word of a sentence. . . . He sent [his publishers] manuscript copies of his poems and they would send him back proof sheets on which he would make innumerable additions and alterations, most of them in punctuation. Evidently he preferred to create his punctuation when he could see how a poem looked in print.[89]

On his proof pages, moreover, Tennyson completely revised lines and even whole passages. "Such fastidiousness was not appreciated by the poet's publisher, Mr. Moxon," observes Cuthbertson, "who looked upon him as 'a great torment, keeping proofs a fortnight to alter, and then sending for revises.'"[90] This habit of page-proof revision created problems for Tennyson's publishers no doubt, but, more importantly, helped eliminate aesthetic problems in the published poetry.[91]

Like most authors, Tennyson felt that printers were inordinately careless in the mistakes they made in setting his material. Numerous references throughout his life reflect this feeling, only two of which I need give here. One occurs in an 1847 letter to Moxon about proofs of *The Princess*, in which Tennyson wrote, "I have written one or two passages twice over for greater clearness: don't let them print these twice over in their stupidity."[92] A second example is recorded in a sympathetic letter from Frederick Locker-Lampson, in which he says,

> In the first issue of "The Princess," edition 1875, King & Co., vol. IV, p. 120, line 8 runs thus:
>
> And followed by a hundred hairy does.
> [This should have read: "airy does."]
>
> Was not this unkind of the printer? I was with the unlucky author when the proof reached him. He gazed at it with horror and gave a very prolonged and remarkable groan, which not having been set to music, I cannot do justice to here.[93]

Careless printers, however, were no bother to Tennyson during his publishing quiescence following the 1832 *Poems*, though his friends Milnes, FitzGerald and Moxon continued to press him to publish or at least reprint. FitzGerald wrote to Bernard Barton in November 1839, "Moxon . . . has been calling on [Tennyson] for the last two years for a new edition of his old volume."[94] Yet, for the few years immediately after the 1832 *Poems* appeared, Moxon was far from anxious for *more* Tennyson books; he had in stock more than would sell. He was hardly receptive to new poems when Browning tried to show him *Paracelsus* in April 1835:

> Browning presented himself with a letter of introduction. No sooner was the letter read, Browning tells us, "Than the Moxonian visage lowered exceedingly thereat – the Moxonian accent grew dolorous thereupon." "Artevelde," he assured him, had not paid expenses by thirty-odd pounds. "Tennyson's poetry is *popular at Cambridge*," he continued. His further remark, however, gave the impression that Cambridge was the only place where it was

popular. "Of 800," he said, "which were printed of his last, some 300 only have gone off." Under the influence of these and other depressing facts, Moxon assured his visitor that it was doubtful if he would ever again venture into a transaction so unprofitable as the publication of poetry. There was no money in it at all. Accordingly he begged to decline even the inspection of Browning's manuscript.[95]

No doubt Moxon was piqued that Henry Taylor's *Philip Van Artevelde*, a poetic tragedy which had been refused by John Murray's advisors, should have been what Browning called "the literary event of the day," and yet a debit in the Moxon firm's ledger.[96] On other fronts Moxon's publishing house was doing well. The companion to Rogers's *Italy*, called simply *Poems*, sold steadily in its handsome illustrated edition. Moxon's undertaking to publish *Memorials of a Tour in Greece* and several volumes of poetry for Richard Monckton Milnes was not in vain, though the verses were meritorious more for their expression of sympathy for working people than for any intrinsic value. Other successes, with dramas by Sheridan Knowles and T. N. Talfourd, followed. Thus, although Moxon was not always financially successful with poetry — he said much later that "Tennyson was the only poet he did not lose by" — other books kept him in business as a "publisher of poets." He began regularly to issue well-printed, tastefully bound books by both new and established poets. Moxon's expansion into wider literary and social circles followed. In the 1830s he added Rogers's famous breakfast parties and Milnes's breakfasts and luncheons to his steady diet of more homely dinners at the Lamb cottage.

At this same time Alfred Tennyson's social life was also expanding. For one thing, he fell in love with lovely Rosa Baring and enjoyed a year or two of pleasant infatuation before becoming frustrated, owing to an understandable preference on her part for more promising, gentlemanly suitors. He also developed at least one new friendship which was to be life-long — that of Edward FitzGerald. Fitz, as he was called by his friends, had been at Cambridge with Alfred, but there is no suggestion of the two having become acquainted before about 1833 in London. The shy, anti-intellectual FitzGerald had long been impressed by Alfred's poetry. In May 1831 he wrote this postscript to his friend John Allen, "How good Mariana is!" Furthermore, while at Cambridge in the spring of 1832, FitzGerald read a manuscript copy of "The Lady of Shalott." He wrote to Allen on his return to London: "I forgot to tell you that when I came up on the mail, and fell a-dozing in the morning, the sights of the pages in crimson and the funerals which the lady of Shalott saw and wove, floated before me: really, the poem has taken lodging in my poor head."[97]

For three rainy weeks in the spring of 1835, Tennyson and FitzGerald visited James Spedding at his home, Mirehouse, by Bassenthwaite in the Lake District. They did what hiking they could, but the weather forced them indoors most of the time, where they sketched or talked. In the evenings, while Fitz played chess with Mrs Spedding, James and Alfred discussed poetry, or Alfred read aloud the works of Wordsworth, Keats and Milton. Also,

> from a little red book into which he had copied them, he read some of his own poems, "mouthing out his hollow oes and aes," FitzGerald said, "his voice very deep and deep-chested, but rather murmuring than mouthing, like the sound of a far sea or of a pine wood." At Mirehouse FitzGerald heard for the first time the "Morte d'Arthur" and other poems not published until 1842.[98]

After the Mirehouse visit, Tennyson and Fitz spent a week together at Ambleside. They stopped their rowing one day on Windermere long enough to give attention to composing "the weakest line of poetry in the language," which FitzGerald's chance remark about his brother-in-law, "A Mr Wilkinson, a clergyman," had precipitated. Fitz's original won the prize.

The friendship between FitzGerald and Tennyson had so deepened by the summer that Fitz could try to ease Alfred's financial worries by offering a loan:

> I have heard you sometimes say that you are bound by the want of such and such a sum, and I vow to the Lord that I could not have a greater pleasure than transferring it to you on such occasions; I should not dare to say such a thing to a small man: but you are not a small man assuredly: and even if you do not make use of my offer, you will not be offended but put it to the right account. It is very difficult to persuade people in this world that one can part with a banknote without a pang. It is one of the most simple things I have

ever done to talk thus to you, I believe: but here is an end; and be charitable to me.[99]

This has led to the idea that Alfred took £300 a year from FitzGerald as a sort of pension; all evidence suggests, though, that for only one year, 1843, was this the case.

About a year after the Lakes visit, Alfred's life took a new turn when he escorted Emily Sellwood into the church for her sister Louisa's marriage to Charles Tennyson. Emily and Alfred had first met in 1830, when the Sellwoods had driven over from Horncastle to visit at the Somersby Rectory, but during the interim the two had seldom seen each other – and Tennyson had been occupied, among other things, with Rosa Baring. But, as they stood at the altar as bridesmaid and best man, Alfred found Emily's quiet beauty of person as appealing as her beauty of spirit. Emily had warmth, a capacity for deep thought, and a gentle sensitivity to the needs of others, which made her a fine match for Alfred: she tempered his gruffness, and he added zest to her life.

Unfortunately, however, although Alfred courted her assiduously at first, her family was hardly enthusiastic about the prospect of her marrying a penniless poet who refused to work at anything which might make a steady income. Then, in 1837, the Burton family of Lincoln, which had control of the contiguous church livings of Somersby and Bag Enderby and had given them to the late Dr Tennyson upon the request of his father, wanted to allow the current Rector to live in the Somersby Rectory. The Tennyson family therefore had to make their long delayed move from their old home, set in the wolds Alfred had roamed over so exuberantly all his life. But at least their new home, High Beech in Epping, Essex, though far from Lincolnshire – and Emily Sellwood – brought Alfred within closer range of the literary ferment he had lost upon leaving Cambridge. In London Alfred stayed with various friends, particularly Spedding, FitzGerald and John Allen. "As time went on the family took rooms in Mornington Place, Hampstead, which could be used by any of the brothers or sisters who had reason to stay overnight in London."[100] Fitz wrote to a friend about these London visits: "We have had Alfred Tennyson here. Very droll and very wayward: and much sitting up of nights till two and three in the morning with pipes in our mouths; at which good hour we would get Alfred to give us some of his magic music, which he does between growling and smoking. . . . "[101] When the friends dined out, it was usually at a tavern, where Tennyson rarely "varied from his favourite dinner of a chop or steak and cut of cheese with a pint of port, followed by a pipe of shag Tobacco."[102]

When not in London, Alfred worked at his poetry in the High Beech study: "not the top attic, according to his usual preference, but a large room over the dining-room, with a bay window, red curtains, and a Clytie on a pedestal in the corner."[103] Though the suburban life of Epping was a far remove from the country remoteness of Somersby, Alfred enjoyed the house and park. "There was a pond in the park," reports Hallam Tennyson, "on which my father might be seen skating, sailing about on the ice in his long blue cloak."[104]

Gradually Alfred expanded his London circle, adding the young Gladstone, Arthur Hallam's Eton friend, and some of the aspiring politicians who gathered for Richard Monckton Milnes's "Young England" evenings. Furthermore, he joined the Sterling Club and there hobnobbed with many former Apostles. His literary set included Samuel Rogers, Carlyle, Forster, Macready and Landor.[105]

Edward Moxon was a part of London's literary life and apparently went about a bit with Tennyson himself. A glimpse of them together is given in Jane Carlyle's description of their visit one evening in 1839 or early 1840:

Carlyle went to dine at Mr. Chadwick's the other day, and I, not being yet equal to a dinner altho' I was asked to "come in a blanket and stay all night!" had made up my mind for a nice long quiet evening of looking into the fire, when I heard a carriage drive up, and men's voices asking questions, and then the carriage was sent away! and the men proved to be Alfred Tennyson of all people and his friend Mr. Moxon — Alfred lives in the country and only comes to London rarely and for a few days so that I was overwhelmed with the sense of Carlyle's misfortune in having missed the man he likes best, for stupid Chadwicks, especially as he had gone against his will at my earnest persuasion. Alfred is dreadfully embarrassed with women alone — for he entertains at one and the same moment a feeling of almost adoration for them and an ineffable contempt! adoration I suppose for what they might be — contempt for what they are! The only chance of my getting any right good of him was to make him forget my womanness — so I did just as Carlyle would have done, had he been there: got out pipes and tobacco — and brandy and water — with a deluge of tea over and above. — The effect of these accessories was miraculous — he professed to be

ashamed of polluting my room, "felt," he said, "as if he were
stealing cups and sacred vessels in the Temple" — but he smoked on
all the same — for three mortal hours! — talking like an angel — only
exactly as if he were talking with a clever man — which — being a
thing I am not used to — men always adapting their conversation to
what they take to be a woman's taste — strained me to a terrible
pitch of intellectuality.[106]

Thomas Carlyle wrote down his impression of Alfred Tennyson in
1840: "A fine, large-featured, dim-eyed, bronze-coloured, shaggy-
headed man is Alfred; dusty, smoky, free and easy; who swims
outwardly and inwardly, with great composure in an articulate
element as of tranquil chaos and tobacco smoke: great now and then
when he does emerge: a most restful, brotherly, solid-hearted man."
But Carlyle, who had little affection for what seemed to him the
more useless arts, also thought of Tennyson as "a life-guardsman
spoilt by making poetry."[107]

Even the London literary scene and poetry writing at High Beech
did not keep Alfred from pursuing Emily Sellwood, however, who,
if the truth be told, was not exactly running away. In 1838 her family
recognized their engagement, only to become disturbed over
monetary settlements; in consequence, Mr Sellwood forbade all
correspondence between the two, and the engagement was broken
off in 1840. The break was influenced, too, by Alfred's own financial
and emotional insecurity about his future as a poet who could support
a family from his pen.

Alfred's mother offered to share her annuity with him, to enable
him to make a definite arrangement with the Sellwoods, but this he
would not accept. Nor would he attempt to meet the situation by
bringing out a new volume of poems. No doubt he felt that this
would be doomed to failure and would, therefore, serve no useful
purpose. Nor would he, as some of his friends suggested, write
short popular poems for the magazines and newspapers. "I only
write what I feel," he said, "and will never write anything else."[108]

In retrospect we can applaud Tennyson's decision, knowing as we do
that he would eventually become self-sufficient from writing alone,
but at the time his stubbornness was seen as some sort of wilful
caprice, and understandably so. As though fulfilling the Sellwoods'
fears, 1840 began a period of catastrophic years for Alfred. The family

moved again; Alfred invested his whole fortune of about £3000 in a mechanical wood-carving scheme fostered by a Dr Matthew Allen — and lost it. With that failure went Alfred's seemingly last-ditch attempt to finance a married life for himself and Emily.

These years, then, from 1832 to 1842, during which time his friends played such a large part in his life, were on the one hand tumultuous but on the other tremendously creative for him. He was distressed by the bad reviews of his 1830 and 1832 volumes, shattered by Arthur Hallam's death, forced to move with his family from the boyhood home he deeply loved, burdened by his brothers' weaknesses, engaged to and disengaged from Emily Sellwood, and finally, rendered penniless. These Job-like early years (and later in life came the sorrows of a still-born child, the untimely death of his son Lionel, and further deaths of friends) serve to refute those critics who mistakenly insist that Tennyson was removed from "real" experience, by which they invariably mean tragic or painful experience.

In these years, despite the personal turmoil, Tennyson did some of his most enduring work. He began the series of stanzas which was later to form *In Memoriam*. He wrote and published "O! that 'twere possible," the germ of *Maud*. He composed other new poems, most notably "The Two Voices," "Ulysses," "St. Simeon Stylites," "Tithonus," "Morte d'Arthur," the English idyls, "Sir Launcelot and Queen Guinevere," "The Vision of Sin," and "Break, break, break." He also revised his old poems extensively. This continued activity resulted, naturally enough, in more pressure for publication, from both friends and strangers.

3 Heyday for Publisher and Poet Laureate: Edward Moxon (1842–58)

Towards the end of Tennyson's active period of composition and revision in the 1830s, Edward Moxon redoubled his efforts to get the poet to publish again. Edward FitzGerald, the friend who was beginning to perform some of the duties which Arthur Hallam had fulfilled before, added his exhortations to Moxon's. In 1839, Fitz reported to Bernard Barton, the Quaker poet, "I want A. T. to publish another volume: as all his friends do . . . but he is too lazy and wayward to put his hand to the business. He has got fine things in the large Butcher's Account that now lies in my room."[1] It took a new and different kind of pressure, however, finally to move the hesitant Alfred.

Copies of Tennyson's early poems were scarce in America, but the leading literary figures were so vociferous in his praise that people began demanding copies. In 1838

Emerson . . . urged C. C. Little & Co., of Boston, to reprint the early volumes in America, and this they agreed to do, borrowing Emerson's and Longfellow's copies for the purpose. In May, 1838, Tennyson had a letter from Messrs. Little announcing their intention. No reply from him survives, but no doubt he protested strongly, for nothing more was heard of the project.[2]

Two years later, however, continuing American pressure showed no surcease, and Tennyson was forced to start the laborious task of readying his poems for publication. Three letters from this period sum up the situation and indicate clearly Tennyson's restrained politeness but definite feeling against republication of old, unrevised poems. On 25 December 1840, Charles Stearns Wheeler, Harvard Greek scholar and friend of Emerson and Lowell, wrote to Tennyson suggesting "that he would cheerfully see [the poems] through the press" if Tennyson would agree to have Little & Brown (C. C. Little's successor) publish an American edition. "He spoke of his work with the editions of Carlyle, of their great success in America, and of his eagerness to perform a similar service for Tennyson."[3] Tennyson's initial reaction is given in a personal letter to FitzGerald, written from Mablethorpe on the Lincolnshire coast at the beginning of 1841: "You bore me about my book; so does a letter just received from America, threatening, tho' in the civilest terms, that, if I will not publish in England, they will do it for me in that land of freemen. I *may* curse, knowing what they will bring forth. But I don't care."[4] The fact that he did care very much, however, is suggested by the reply he gave to Wheeler in a letter dated 22 February 1841:

I thank you for your polite & kindly communication, as also for the offer of your services in the correction of the press, supposing that my book were publisht in America. I am rejoiced that I have made myself friends on the other side of the Atlantic & feel what a high privilege it is for a writer to be born into a language common to two great peoples; & so believe me not insensible – or if that seem to savour too much of the coldness of mere courtesy – believe me deeply sensible of the honour my American friends have done me even in making a request to which I feel it impossible to accede as they, perhaps, might wish. I am conscious of many things exceedingly crude in those volumes that it would certainly be productive of no slight annoyance to me, to see them republisht as they stand at present, either here or in America. But I will tell you what I will do, for when I was wavering before, your letter has decided me. I have corrected copies of most that was worth correcting in those two volumes & I will in the course of a few months republish these in England with several new poems & transmit copies to Little & Brown & also to yourself (if you will accept one) & you can then of course do as you choose with them.[5]

Many years later Tennyson referred back to this decision with these words: "I hate publishing! The Americans forced me into it again. I had my things nice and right, but when I found they were going to publish the old forms I said, By Jove, that won't do!"[6]

The rest of 1841 "was spent by Alfred in giving a final polish to the poems which he had by him. In March Fitz met him in town 'with a little bit of dirty pipe in his mouth and a particularly dirty vellum

book of M.S.S. on the sofa.'"[7] And by October Fitz could write to
Frederick Tennyson, in Italy, "Just heard from Edgeworth that
Alfred is in London 'busy preparing for the press'!!!"[8] But Alfred's
"busy preparing for the press" was not as energetic a state as his
friends supposed. Early in 1842 Tennyson wrote to his brother-in-
law and fellow Apostle, Edmund Lushington,

> I have not yet taken my book to Moxon. Spedding's going to
> America has a little disheartened me, for some fop will get the start
> of him in the *Ed. Review* where he promised to put an article and I
> have had abuse enough. . . . However I intend to get it out
> shortly, but I cannot say I have been what you professors call
> "working" at it, that indeed is not my way.[9]

Edward FitzGerald caught on to Tennyson's "way" and switched
from encouragement to direct coercion.

In March 1842 Tennyson appeared in London. "He had still not
sent his poems to the printer, but, fortunately, his first act was to call
on Fitz, who 'carried him off with violence to Moxon' to complete
arrangements for publication. Fitz then made him settle to the task of
writing out his manuscript neatly for the printer." The description of
this manuscript which follows in Sir Charles's account of these days
indicates some of the problems Moxon must have faced with his
recalcitrant author.

> The poems were mostly written in a long ledger-like volume (a
> "butcher-book" Fitz called it) in a fine small hand leaving a good
> margin, which Alfred had often stripped off for pipelights "taking
> care" as he observed to Fitz' amusement, "not to damage the
> manuscript." The pages were now carefully torn from the book
> and despatched to Moxon.[10]

After they came back with proofs and were checked, these manuscript pages were consigned to the fire, except for a few which Fitz
saved and later gave to Trinity College library. Almost twenty years
later, in a letter dated 9 December 1861, Fitz said to W. H. Thompson,

> I wish I had secured more leaves from that old "Butcher's Book"
> torn up in old Spedding's Room in 1842 when the Press went to
> work with, I think, the Last of old Alfred's Best. But that, I am
> told, is only a "Crochet." However, had I taken some more of the

Pages that went into the Fire, after serving in part for pipelights, I might have enriched others with that which A. himself would scarce have grudged, jealous as he is of such sort of Curiosity.[11]

Even though Tennyson despaired of ever publishing again once he saw some of the proof sheets, it was too late; he was in FitzGerald's hands, and FitzGerald persevered with a mixture of needling and encouraging in an effort to convince Alfred of the probable success of the poems. That Fitz's judgment was astute and his praise genuine cannot be doubted. He wrote to Barton on 17 March 1842,

Poor Tennyson has got home some of his proof sheets: and, now that his verses are in hard print, thinks them detestable — there is much I had always told him of — his great fault of being too full and complicated — which he now sees, or fancies he sees, and wishes he had never been persuaded to print. But with all his faults, he will publish such a volume as has not been published since the time of Keats: and which, once published, will never be suffered to die. This is my prophecy: for I live before Posterity.

I don't know that you will care for most of his poems, which are in the heroic way: but there are some on quieter themes which you cannot fail to like. "Lady Exeter" is among them: and an English Eclogue called "Dora," which comes near the book of Ruth. . . .[12]

The beginning of another letter from Fitz to Barton, a week or so later, suggests the strain Tennyson put upon his personal relationships when it came time to prepare poems for the press: "I am going this morning with Tennyson to Dulwich," Fitz writes; "when we get there of course the Gallery will be shut because of Easter. Well, then we shall go in a bad humour to dine at a tavern: get heartily sick of each other: and so back to town."[13] But Fitz was not to be easily deflected from his task and pursued the volumes through to publication, inquiring after them even when he was away from London. In early May he asked Pollock by letter, "How does Tennyson get on with his book? I wish you would tell me that."[14] And he kept up his honest appraisal of his friend's work. To Pollock he wrote after getting news that Moxon had finally published the two-volume *Poems* on 14 May 1842,

So Alfred is come out. I agree with you quite about the skipping-rope, etc. [brief, inconsequential poems in the volumes]. ... Alfred, whatever he may think, cannot trifle – many are the disputes we have had about his powers of badinage, compliment, waltzing, etc. His smile is rather a grim one. I am glad the book is come out, though I grieve for the insertion of these little things, on which reviewers and dull readers will fix: so that the right appreciation of the book will be retarded a dozen years.[15]

After receiving his own copies of the books, Fitz wrote once more to Pollock, again with strong criticism:

It is a pity he did not publish the new volume separately. The other will drag it down. And why reprint the Merman, the Mermaid, and those everlasting Eleanores, Isabels, – which always were, and are, and must be, a nuisance, though Mrs. Butler (who recognized herself in the portrait of course) said that Eleanore (what a bore) was the finest thing he ever wrote. She has sat for it ever since, I believe. Every woman thinks herself the original of one of that stupid Gallery of Beauties.[16]

Here then, ten years after Hallam's influence on the 1832 *Poems*, we see another friend's influence; but the differences between Arthur Hallam and Edward FitzGerald say something important about Tennyson's development during the interval. In his youth Alfred needed not only the expediting force of Hallam, but also his almost unswerving praise. Now, as a maturer artist, Tennyson could have as his expediter a friend who criticized his poetry forcefully.

When the volumes appeared in print on 14 May 1842, Tennyson, as he had promised he would, rushed off copies to America, where they were quickly published by W. D. Ticknor of Boston. Wheeler had decided to use this house in preference to Little & Brown because they had offered him better terms. Tennyson ended up with a $150 payment for copyright, "possibly the earliest copyright payment by an American publisher to a foreign author."[17] Such honesty on the firm's part at a time when many publishers were pirating left and right so impressed Tennyson that to the end of his life he always considered William D. Ticknor & Co. and their successors (now Houghton Mifflin) his official American publishers. In 1889 he referred to the firm's founder, William D. Ticknor, as "one who gave so honourable an example to his countrymen of justice in the highest sense."[18] Ticknor put out 1500–2000 copies in his first edition, which attempted to be as close a facsimile as possible of the English first edition.

The English publisher was more cautious about expected success than his American counterpart, perhaps because of his greater experience with Tennyson sales. 800 copies of the 1842 *Poems* were printed by Moxon, bound in drab paper boards with a white spine label and priced at twelve shillings the two volumes. Whereas the 1830 *Poems, Chiefly Lyrical* had appeared in a 600-copy edition, the 1832 *Poems* had a run of only 450. Apparently the 1830 edition had not sold well and Moxon was careful not to commit himself too much in 1832. Thus he appears to have undertaken something of a risk by running 800 in 1842, since Tennyson's few publications in annuals during the interim had not done much to increase his reputation. But Moxon really need not have feared: "Five hundred of the 800 copies printed had been sold . . . four months after publication," notes Marshall.[19] Sir Charles calls it "evidence of the modesty of Moxon's expectations that he should have interpreted this as a 'sensation,'"[20] but, in terms of Moxon's previous Tennyson sales, 500 copies probably *was* a sensation.[21] FitzGerald must have been gratified, after his persistent efforts to see the book materialize, to report to Frederick Tennyson on 16 August 1842, "As to Alfred's book, I believe it has sold well. . . . Thompson . . . told me that very many copies had been sold at Cambridge, which indeed will be the chief market for them."[22]

A general slump in the book trade, starting in 1836, probably added to Moxon's "modest expectations." In 1840 he had said, "Books of a much more popular cast [than Trench's latest] sell badly now," and by 1842 he felt the market getting worse.[23] Browning wrote to his friend A. Domett on 13 July 1842, "I shall print nothing till October – the book season has been, says Moxon, no season at all, the trade flourishing (same authority) more in one month, January, last year, than in the whole of these present six months. (Same cry in Town and Country.)"[24] Although we do not have intimate details of Moxon's personal and family life at this time – or at any other, for that matter – we know from two events in June 1841 that Moxon had his share of other troubles: for example, his trial for printing Shelley's *Queen Mab* took place while the Moxons were mourning the death of their first-born son, Edward.[25] Nonetheless, Tennyson's publisher had enough equanimity to take less drastic steps against the slump in trade than did some of his competitors: John Murray, for instance, "withdrew every work he had in the press and returned many manuscripts to their authors."[26] The wonder, then, is not that 500 copies of Tennyson's *Poems* sold in a few months, but that Moxon would push to publish him at all given the sad state of the book business. Moxon, in short, was willing to take some risk in order to publish a poet whose work he admired. His business had now prospered to the point where in 1842 his author's list could be divided into categories. The flyleaf advertisements to Tennyson's *Poems* announced "Poetical Works" (Wordsworth, Rogers, Campbell, Shelley), "Dramatic Library" (Beaumont and Fletcher, Ben Jonson, Shakespeare, Massinger and Ford, Wycherley, Congreve, Vanbrugh and Farquhar) and "Cheap Editions of Popular Works" (fiction, essays, travel narratives and some more poetry).

Most of Tennyson's fellow authors, particularly Rogers, Dickens and Carlyle, praised the *Poems* highly. Samuel Rogers, for example, who had been of such help to Moxon when he started business on his own and who had encouraged the young Tennyson, wrote to Alfred on 17 August 1842, "Every day have I resolved to write & tell you with what delight I have read & read again your two beautiful volumes: but it was my wish to tell you so, face to face. That wish however remains unfulfilled & write I must, for very, very few things, if any, have ever thrilled me so much." Robert Browning's response, on the other hand, was his characteristic concoction of wild praise and wild blame. In a letter to Alfred Domett on 13 July he laments,

I send with this Tennyson's new vol. and, alas, the old with it — that is, what he calls old. You will see, and groan! The alterations are insane. *Whatever* is touched is spoiled. There is some woeful mental infirmity in the man — he was months buried in correcting the press of the last volume, and in that time began spoiling the new poems (in proof) as hard as he could. "Locksley Hall" is shorn of two or three couplets. I will copy out from the book of somebody who luckily transcribed from the proof-sheet — meantime one line, you will see, *I have* restored — see and wonder! I have been with Moxon this morning, who tells me that [Tennyson] is miserably thin-skinned, sensitive to criticism (foolish criticism), wishes to see no notices that contain the least possible depreciatory expressions — poor fellow! But how good when good he is — that noble "Locksley Hall," for instance — and the "St. Simeon

Stylites" — which I think perfect. Do you (*yes*) remember our day on the water last year? To think that he has omitted the musical "Forget-me-not song," and "The Hespirides" — and the "Deserted House" — and "everything that is his," as distinguished from what is everybody's![27]

Yet Browning understood enough about the dramatic in Tennyson's poetry to make this astute observation about Leigh Hunt's review of the 1842 *Poems* which appeared in the *Church of England Quarterly Review* that October: "Hunt's criticism is neither kind nor just, I take it — he don't [*sic*] understand that most of Tennyson's poems are *dramatic* — utterances coloured by an imaginary speaker's moods."[28]

Critics took to the *Poems* slowly, but with increasing enthusiasm. By the appearance of James Spedding's review in the April 1843 *Edinburgh*, most critics were ranking Tennyson "among the foremost of our young poets" even when voicing some reservations about him.[29] Spedding "emphasized the lighter and freer handling; the increase of humanity; the deeper and purer interest; the closer adherence to truth and greater reliance for effect upon the simplicity of Nature."[30] He also paid due attention to the improvements made in the previously published poems. By 1844 Tennyson's achievement was being recognized throughout the world of those who read poetry. "R. H. Horne in his *New Spirit of the Age* [London: Smith, Elder, 1844] . . . referred to his position as thoroughly established, and it was significant that the Decade Society at Oxford held a meeting about this time to discuss the relative merits of Tennyson and Wordsworth."[31] Moxon issued four successive editions of the *Poems*, each one larger than the previous one, in order to bring to an expanding audience the polished poetry of one they began to acknowledge as England's leading poet.

Not all the poems in the volumes were new. Volume I consisted mainly of poems previously published in 1830 and 1832, but the best of them, works such as "Mariana," "The Lady of Shalott," "Oenone," "The Palace of Art" and "The Lotos-Eaters," had been so extensively revised in the interim as to be strikingly different. Volume II contained, with the exception of "St Agnes" and three stanzas, "The Sleeping Beauty," poems never before published. Of these, "Morte d'Arthur," "Ulysses," "Locksley Hall" and "The Two Voices" are still widely judged to be among Tennyson's most distinctive achievements. Of this second volume of the 1842 *Poems* the poet's grandson and chief biographer observes, "Never before or

since has an English poet produced a volume treating so wide a range
of subjects with such a high level of accomplishment."[32]

Tennyson received regular payments from Moxon as the publisher
issued successive "editions" of the *Poems*.[33] For example, the extant
Moxon–Tennyson accounts, which start with 1843, show that
Tennyson's share of the profits for that year's second edition of 1000
copies was £156 2s. 6d., which was paid into his bank accounts in
£40–50 installments until 1846. In 1845 Moxon listed another
printing of 1500 of the *Poems* as giving him £129 16s. 9d., being
one-third of profits, the publisher's share, with Tennyson receiving
£259 18s. 1d. In 1846 Moxon printed an additional 2000 copies,
providing Tennyson with £330 7s. 6d. Aside from indicating
Tennyson's gradually increasing income, these accounts are important because they show that the agreement relating to publication of
the 1842 *Poems* gave the poet the larger share of the profits: two-
thirds, to the publisher's third. No written agreement exists for this
period, so the accounts must be taken as evidence of the terms they
worked under. There is, however, a written agreement for the "Fifth
Edition" of *Poems*, 1848, probably because the terms were changed
for this special volume "illustrated by 30 vignettes engraved on
steel." Tennyson therein agreed to pay for all expenses, he and
Moxon to divide profits in equal shares. These terms duplicate those
for the 1832 *Poems*.

However gratifying the modest profits from these volumes, they
only slightly lessened the financial worries and physical and
emotional ailments which weighed upon Tennyson during the
early 1840s. He lamented to Edmund Lushington in September 1842,
"What with ruin in the distance and hypochondriacs in the
foreground, God help all."[34] Ruin came closer in 1843 when the
wood-carving scheme in which Tennyson had invested his entire
£3000 inheritance failed. In the foreground, at home, all the brothers
except Frederick, who was abroad, were suffering in some way or
another. Edward was in Lincoln Asylum, where he would remain for
the rest of his life; Charles's health was bad, though he had overcome
his opium habit; Arthur was drinking; Septimus had some undefined
"nervous ailment"; and Horatio was depressed over his failure in
Tasmania.[35] These troubles took their toll on Alfred's health, driving
him in the next years to a number of water-cures at hydropathic
hospitals near the Tennyson family's new home, in Cheltenham.
Little new composing was done before 1845, and only the burgeon-
ing critical respect for the 1842 *Poems* and the steadying friendship of

FitzGerald, Aubrey de Vere, Carlyle and Moxon, among others, kept Tennyson reminded that he was, beyond a doubt, an important poet.

"Honest, bustling, capable Edward Moxon," as Sir Charles describes him, offered Tennyson a reliable, comfortable friendship which not only included hospitality but also an unshakable belief in his genius.

He acted as Alfred's banker, advancing him money as he needed it and sending small sums on his behalf to the needy authors who, as his reputation grew, approached him in ever increasing numbers and were always met with uninquiring generosity. Moxon understood exactly the informal hospitality which Tennyson enjoyed and introduced him unobstrusively to men and women likely to interest and stimulate him.

Mrs Moxon, "whom Lamb described as the best female talker he had known," even allowed the poet to smoke in her drawing-room, on condition, no doubt, that she be a part of the conversation. Moxon "was in an excellent position to [entertain] for he was now firmly established and publishing for Rogers, Wordsworth, Leigh Hunt, Talfourd, Monckton Milnes, Elizabeth Barrett and Robert Browning."[36]

As would be expected, Moxon supplied Tennyson with reading matter. In January 1843, for example, Tennyson wrote from dreary Mablethorpe, "There is nothing here but myself and two starfish, therefore, if you have any stray papers which you do not know what to do with, as you once told me, they would be manna in the wilderness to me."[37]

Moxon acted as a tonic for Tennyson's spirits almost as much as did the water-cures. Dr Gully, the most famous of the practitioners under whose care Tennyson came, forbade alcohol, tobacco, rich foods and late hours for his patients and encouraged long walks in the bracing Malvern air. Exactly what this regimen was supposed to correct in Tennyson's case is not clear from the nineteenth-century vocabulary in which his condition is discussed, for "nerves" and the notorious "black blood of the Tennysons" and "ruining [oneself] by mismanagement and neglect of all kinds" are hardly medical diagnoses by today's standards. I suspect, however, that Tennyson's neurasthenia was aggravated by a vitamin B_1 (thiamine) deficiency, which would have produced all his symptoms: sleeplessness, fatigue, loss of memory, constipation. His suppers of mutton, cheese and port would have aggravated this condition; after his marriage his "nerves" mysteriously cleared up, probably because of a more balanced diet. Be that as it may, the only life-long physical disorders we can document are hay fever, extreme short-sightedness, eczema, and occasional bouts of influenza. Tennyson, it should be remembered, lived eighty-three years, and, as far as we can tell, spent most of them in vigorous health. The stories which attest to this are almost as numerous as the ones which refer to his bad "nerves." In his twenties, for instance, he reportedly carried a small pony about the Rectory lawn; in his sixties he took twenty-mile walks and mountain climbs in the Pyrenees; and in his eighties he "did exercises for his arms and legs, and delighted to challenge visitors to get up quickly, twenty times running, from a low chair without use of the hands, a feat which he himself would perform with ease."[38] But in his thirties this strong man suffered enough to submit himself to the rigors of hydropathy and to allow his composition of new poems to lag. His friends lamented such lapses, of course. "In 1848 FitzGerald said prophetically, albeit inelegantly, 'Tennyson is emerged half-cured, or half-destroyed, from a water establishment; has gone to a new Doctor who gives him iron pills; and altogether this really great man thinks more about his bowels and nerves than about the Laureate wreath he was born to inherit.'"[39]

Tennyson's financial situation improved dramatically in 1845: he recouped £2000 of his loss in the wood-carving fiasco by means of an insurance policy on Dr Allen's life which Franklin Lushington had taken out (Allen conveniently dying shortly thereafter). Furthermore, his friends, particularly Henry Hallam, the historian and father of Arthur, and Samuel Rogers prevailed upon Sir Robert Peel to grant Tennyson a Civil List pension of £200. Of this Carlyle remarked in his dour fashion, "Alfred looks haggard, dire, and languid: they *have* got him however to go and *draw* his Pension; that is reckoned a great achievement on the part of his friends! Surely no man has a right to be so lazy in this world; – and none that is so lazy will ever make much way in it, I think!"[40]

There was marked improvement, too, in Tennyson's treatment by the reviewers. For example, in 1846, when Bulwer Lytton, a close friend of his Uncle Charles, attacked Alfred ferociously in *The New Timon*, Alfred's reply, "The New Timon and the Poets" in *Punch*, and his retraction, "After-thoughts," found the critics on his side rather than on Bulwer's.

No paper of standing, except the Literary Gazette, ventured to show any approval [of Bulwer], and the Gazette's sympathy was rather implied than expressed. In the edition of *The New Timon* issued just before the end of the year, the passage was withdrawn. There could hardly have been stronger evidence of the growth of Tennyson's hold upon the public.[41]

During a remission of his neurasthenia in 1845, Tennyson's literary and social activity increased dramatically. Fitz related to Frederick Tennyson, "Alfred was in London the first week of my stay there. He was looking well, and in good spirits; and had got two hundred lines of a new poem [*The Princess*] in a butcher's book."[42] That spring must have been a lively time for all the literati in London. Mrs Brookfield, Robert Browning, FitzGerald, Caroline Norton – all report on the dining and drinking parties. Aubrey de Vere, however, provides the most detailed references to Tennyson and Moxon in social gatherings. The extracts below speak for themselves:

April 17. I called on Alfred Tennyson, and found him at first much out of spirits. He cheered up soon, and read me some beautiful Elegies, complaining much of some writer in "Fraser's Magazine" who had spoken of the "foolish facility" of Tennysonian poetry. I went to the House of Commons and heard a good speech from Sir G. Grey – went back to Tennyson, who "crooned" out his magnificent Elegies till one in the morning.

April 18. Sat with Alfred Tennyson, who read MS. poetry to Tom Taylor and me. Walked with him to his lawyer's: came back and listened to the "University of Women." Had talk with him on various subjects, and walked with him to Moxon's.

April 25. Moxon sent me Tennyson's portrait.

April 29. Went to Spedding's rooms, and found Stephen Spring Rice, Tennyson, Brookfield and Moxon – all very jolly.

May 4. Brought Alfred Tennyson, murmuring sore, to Hampstead, to see Mr. Wordsworth. Mr. W. improved upon him.

May 7. Asked Tennyson to dinner: we dined with Stephen and A. B. We all made speeches on our health being drunk, and were merry.

May 9. [De Vere goes with Rogers and Wordsworth to the Exhibition.] Returned to tea, and received a letter from my mother. Alfred Tennyson came in and smoked his pipe. He told us with pleasure of his dinner with Wordsworth – was pleased as well as amused by Wordsworth saying to him, "Come, brother bard, to dinner," and taking his arm; said that he was ashamed of paying Mr. Wordsworth compliments, but that he had at last, in the dark, said something about the pleasure he had had from Mr. Wordsworth's writings, and that the old poet had taken his hand, and replied with some expressions equally kind and complimentary. Tennyson was evidently much pleased with the old man, and glad of having learned to know him.

May 10. I went to Alfred Tennyson, who read me part of his "University of Women," and discussed poetry, denouncing exotics, and saying that a poem should reflect the time and place. May 11. Called on Tennyson. Spent three hours with him and Edward FitzGerald, trying to persuade him to come to Hither Green. At last he agreed. We passed through Greenwich Park, and he was delighted with the view and pointed out all the rich effects of colour in the landscape. We had a merry dinner and a pleasant talk till 12:30, when we drove away in a fly. I got home after two. . . .[43]

Not all was glee for Tennyson in 1845, though. A few months after their spirited spring parties, de Vere found him depressed once more:

July 16. On my way in, paid a visit to Tennyson, who seemed much out of spirits, and said he could no longer bear to be knocked about the world, and he must marry and find love and peace or die. He was very angry about a very favourable review of him. Said he could not stand the chattering and conceit of clever men, or the worry of society, or the meanness of tuft-hunters, or the trouble of poverty, or the labour of place, or the preying of the heart on itself. . . . He complained much about growing old, and said he cared nothing for fame, and that his life was all thrown away for want of a competence and retirement. Said that no one had been so much harassed by anxiety and trouble as himself.

De Vere's sensible reply to this jeremiad — "I told him he wanted occupation, a wife, and orthodox principles, which he took well" — proved to be prophetic, for, once Tennyson became Poet Laureate, worked on his poetry with daily regularity, and married Emily Sellwood, his depression lightened.[44]

Tennyson continued work on "The University of Women" (*The Princess*) and "The Elegies" (*In Memoriam*) throughout 1846, except

for a month-long holiday in Switzerland with Edward Moxon.
Planning the trip proved no easy matter for Tennyson's cohorts. For
example:

> Dickens, like all Tennyson's friends, wanted to organize his life for
> him, to extricate him from his gloomy indecision, and tried to
> get him to join the Dickens family party when they left for
> Switzerland [in] June. Tennyson would not go. He told Elizabeth
> Barrett's brother George, whom he met one day in the Inns of
> Court, that if he went with Dickens they would be bound to
> quarrel over Dickens' sentimentality, and break up their friend-
> ship; it was safer to decline the invitation. So he stayed behind in
> London, and mooned about in a haze of short sight, depression and
> tobacco smoke.[45]

FitzGerald, too, expressed his concern: "Alfred Tennyson was in
London," he wrote, "for two months striving to spread his wings to
Italy or Switzerland. It has ended in his flying to the Isle of Wight till
Autumn, when Moxon promises to convey him over. . . ."[46]
Alfred's vacillations about foreign travel ended when Moxon was as
good as his word, taking him off on 2 August, a month before Fitz
had expected. The solid, imperturable Edward Moxon, of whom
Mrs Brookfield once said, "Mr. Moxon has just cheerily bounced into
the room with hearty shakes of the hand, 'Sir' . . ."[47] was a fit
traveling companion for the often morose poet. Sir Charles, too,
alludes to the balance of their friendship when he describes Alfred in
May 1846 as "sometimes going into general society, shepherded by
the faithful Moxon. Browning saw them at a public dinner on 13
May and found the publisher's care of the poet "the charmingest
thing imaginable.'"[48] But even "the faithful Moxon's" patience may
have been tried by the chronic complaining in which Tennyson
engaged as the tour began. Alfred's journal, kept in a manuscript
book of "The University of Women" which he had with him on the
journey, has entries for the first few days which invariably end with
some reference to insomnia:

2 August — "hot nervous night with me. Man 'hemmed' overhead
enough to shake the walls of Jericho"
3 August — "nervous night"
4 August — "not quite four hours' sleep"
5 August — "Woke at 5 or earlier, clash and clang of steamboat
departure under me. . . ."[49]

A retrospective letter from Tennyson to FitzGerald captures Tennyson's attitude towards his trip once his memory of those first days and nights of tourist brigades, noisy hotels, bad beer and fleas had vanished:[50]

> Well, Moxon went to Switzerland; saw Blanc, he was very sulky, kept his nightcap on, doff'd it one morning when I was knocked up out of bed to look at him at four o'clock, the glance I gave did not by any means repay me for the toil of traveling to see him. Two other things I *did* see in Switzerland, the stateliest bits of landskip I ever saw, one was a look down on the valley of Lauterbrunnen while we were descending from the Vengern Alp, the other a view of the Bernese Alps: don't think that I am going to describe them. Let it suffice that I was so satisfied with the size of crags that (Moxon being gone on before in vertigo and leaning on the arm of the guide) I *laughed* by myself. I was satisfied with the size of crags, but mountains, great mountains disappointed me.[51]

A chance comment from Moxon, though, added to Tennyson's chronic fears about his health that of going bald. In December 1846 Henry Hallam's remaining son received this letter from one of Alfred's friends,

> Mr. Moxon said Alfred one day while travelling said to him, "Moxon, you have made me very unhappy by something you said to me at Lucerne," the unfortunate speech having been "Why Tennyson you will be as bald as Spedding before long." Poor Alfred brooded over this till on his return to England he put himself under a Mrs. Parker (or some such name) who rubs his head and pulls out dead hairs an hour a visit, and ten shillings an hour, besides cosmetics *ad libitum*. Your father's hair would bristle up at the idea of the Queen's pension being spent in this manner, but really his hair is such an integral part of his appearance it would be a great pity he should lose it — and they say this woman does really restore hair, and she is patronised by Royalty itself! Can I say more in her favour or in extenuation for A. T.[52]

In spite of Alfred's frequent grousings, the trip to Switzerland nevertheless cemented the friendship between poet and publisher more than the dinner parties in London society had, for no disagreements regarding publishing practices or attitudes marred their ensuing years together. The trip also contributed the stanzas beginning "Come down, O maid, from yonder mountain height" to *The Princess*, which Tennyson was still working on.

Tennyson's choice of topic for *The Princess* (1847) provides some insight into the workings of his artistic judgment *vis-à-vis* critical responses to his previous poems. Tennyson told William Allingham that he had given up the idea of writing an Arthurian epic in twelve books after John Sterling had attacked "Morte d'Arthur" in his review of the 1842 *Poems*.[53] Tennyson felt that if his prelude to an epic could not work well, he certainly should not attempt the epic itself — at least not yet. "An artist should get his workmanship as good as he can," he said, " and make his work as perfect as possible. A small vessel, built on fine lines, is likely to float further down the stream of time than a big raft."[54] *The Princess* was Tennyson's attempt to see how well another of his "small vessels," though larger than the others, would sail. He needed no further experimentation with lyrics, or narrative poems, or dramatic monologues — those he felt confident would be welcomed by a receptive public, but a long poem, not epic, yet equally formidable, how would that be received?

Early in 1846 Elizabeth Barrett wrote Robert Browning her response to Tennyson's new composition, which she may not even yet have seen or heard:

> But the really bad news is of poor Tennyson. . . . He is seriously ill with an internal complaint and confined to his bed. . . . Which does not prevent his writing a new poem — he has finished the second book of it — and it is in blank verse and a fairy tale, and called the "University," the university-members being all females. . . . I don't know what to think — it makes me open my eyes. Now isn't the world too old and fond of steam, for blank verse poems, in ever so many books, to be written on the fairies?[55]

All Tennyson's friends were aware of his new poem, but few reacted as negatively as did Miss Barrett, perhaps because they realized that Tennyson was in effect carrying out the literary doctrines which most of the reviews of his 1842 *Poems* had expressed. In Shannon's summary, these doctrines were:

> (1) modern poetry must idealize and mirror contemporary life and thought; (2) the highest type of poetry must be concerned with human experience; (3) the poet's primary duty is to teach; (4)

Tennyson's poetry must display more human sympathy; and (5) Tennyson, if he is to establish his claim to greatness, must write a long poem — a sustained work on a single theme.[56]

Poets other than Tennyson, including Miss Barrett herself, wrote long poems between 1847 and 1862 dealing with the same essential subject as *The Princess* — namely, the nature of women, as positioned in love and marriage. Barrett's *Aurora Leigh* (1857), Clough's *The Bothie of Tober-na-Vuolich* (1848), and Patmore's *The Angel in the House* (1854) all came to be written not by some strange coincidence but by the same earnest desire to respond to a vigorously debated and vital question of the day. Tennyson's poem, as John Killham reminds us, "was really a serious attempt, artfully disguised, to change an outworn attitude to an important human problem."[57] As far back as 1831 one of Tennyson's reviewers had placed the problem squarely before him:

Upon what love is, depends what woman is, and upon what woman is, depends what the world is, both in the present and in the future. There is not a greater moral necessity in England than that of a reformation in female education. The boy is a son; the youth is a lover; and the man who thinks lightly of the elevation of character and the extension of happiness which woman's influence is capable of producing, and ought to be directed to the production of, in society, is neither the wisest of philosophers nor the best of patriots.[58]

These critical responses to his poems, though encouraging him towards this topic, were only part of a more pervasive influence. For one, socialists in both France and England kept the emancipation of women and the reform of the institution of marriage before the eyes of the Apostles during Alfred's Cambridge stay. Furthermore, the predicament of Tennyson's own mother, caught in a tumultuous marriage with a violent alcoholic, was always before his eyes. In addition to his mother's plight at home, Tennyson had a positive example of the intellectual capacities of women, in the persons of his sisters Mary, Emily and Cecilia, who had been given a substantial, though an "at home," education. At one point these three girls "became members of a romantic circle of friends and correspondents, known as the 'Husks,' the main function of which was the writing and study of poetry," especially that of Tennyson, Keats and Shelley.[59] These influences on Alfred in the 1830s were followed in the 1840s by his socializing with the leading female lights in London intellectual life. Caroline Norton, Mrs Brookfield, Emma Moxon, Elizabeth Barrett – he probably spoke to all of them with the same attitude Jane Carlyle noticed when he spoke to her: "talking like an angel – only exactly as if he were talking to a clever man."[60] Moreover, in Emily Sellwood Alfred had chosen for himself a woman who stimulated his own creation of poetry by suggesting topics and who could listen to all he wrote with discriminating ears.[61]

Tennyson espoused a clear-eyed view of the sexes, one which saw them as being complementary, in marriage, to the formation of a single whole. More exactly, he specified that "Men should be androgynous and women gynandrous, but men should not be gynandrous nor women androgynous."[62] In *In Memoriam*, for instance, he praises Hallam for being "manhood fused with female grace" (CIX, 17), and in "Locksley Hall Sixty Years After" (l. 48) he has the speaker lament the death of his wife Edith, "She with all the charm of woman, she with all the breadth of man, / Strong in will and rich in wisdom . . . ." In *The Princess* this particular attitude is expressed more vividly when the Prince's vision of the two sexes, "Self-reverent each and reverencing each / Distinct in individualities," rouses Ida's fear that such ideals will not be possible for them. He responds to her anxiety with a dream he has learned from his mother:

> Dear, but let us type them now
> In our own lives, and this proud watchword rest
> Of equal; seeing either sex alone
> Is half itself, and in true marriage lies
> Nor equal, nor unequal: each fulfils
> Defect in each, and always thought in thought,
> Purpose in purpose, will in will, they grow,
> The single pure and perfect animal,
> The two-celled heart beating, with one full stroke,
> Life.   (VII, 281–90)

Tennyson's unusual feminist perspective, based as it was on Apostolic discussion, his mother's situation, his sisters' abilities, his association with spirited literary women, and his love for Emily Sellwood, was not shared by extremists on either side of the "Woman Question."

The speaker in *The Princess* announces his role as mediator:

> Then rose a little feud betwixt the two,
> Betwixt the mockers and the realists:
> And I, betwixt them both, to please them both,
> And yet to give the story as it rose,
> I moved as in a strange diagonal,
> And maybe neither pleased myself nor them.
>
> (Conclusion, 23–8)

Tennyson himself struck a "strange diagonal" between the warring factions by choosing a form and context intentionally ambiguous and complex. The Prologue and Conclusion are set in a country house near an abbey. (Tennyson used the Lushingtons' Park House in Kent as his model, just as the Maidstone Mechanics Institute festival in that park which he attended on 6 July 1842 found its way into the Prologue.) The context of myth and romance, of time here and time there, of a country house in the Greek style near a ruined Gothic abbey, of industrial workers enjoying cricket and country dances, imitated the confused sense of time and place in the England of his day. The narrative form itself came from a Cambridge game in which different people improvised a story one after another. "It was Tennyson's search for a new form of expression, one capable of representing the singular diversity of his time, that led him to forgo conventional unity in preference for a 'Medley'"[63] Such ambiguities and complexities of both form and context have troubled many critics. Ricks, for example, considers the "strange diagonal" passage an uneasy statement indicating Tennyson's unwillingness – or inability – to deal with his "truthful fears"; Ricks's reading emphasizes, consequently, the evasions of the poem. Yet those evasions can themselves be part of the "medley" and thus expressive of artistic subleties. Catherine Barnes Stevenson interprets the medley form and theme as a valuable aid to our reading: "If the poem is to be fully understood, it must be read in terms of the tensions, contrasts, parallels and interfusings that comprise its poetic process. Furthermore, it must be read in terms of the creative role of the reader in discerning the various components of the whole poem's drift."[64] Reading form and theme together, apprehending its essence and its existence simultaneously, is no easy task; indeed, it is a far more difficult task than many readers are willing to take on, preferring as they do an easier reading based on the biography of the poet, yet, as

Stevenson points out, only a composite reading reveals Tennyson's view of the role of art:

> In *The Princess*, the multi-levelled, many-voiced form into which the particulars of human experience are cast is the essential component of the poem's meaning. For, in addition to being about the relationship between sexes; the mixture of qualities that makes up a complete human being; and the relationship between human memory, time, and art; *The Princess* is also about the *way* in which the "meaning" of a situation or a proposal can be approached and the role of art in suggesting this method of approach.[65]

Tennyson constructed *The Princess* carefully; extant manuscripts indicate at least three main stages of composition. The time he spent in its composition was unusually long for him at this stage of his career; "it had seemingly taken more than two and a half years in continuous composition, and perhaps as long as eight years in the gestation."[66] Sir Charles attributes the maturity of thought and polish of phrase in the poem to Tennyson's solitary existence alternating with an intense social life, which were to produce his great understanding of human behavior.[67]

As for the manuscript itself, Tennyson sent it to Moxon and worked on the proofs himself, all this during the spring of 1847, but his new independence in these preliminary stages of publication did not diminish his reluctance finally to publish. A letter to Moxon written that spring when Tennyson was at one of Dr Gully's water-cures epitomizes the usual Tennysonian concerns about a forthcoming volume: what people will say; when to publish; what fools printers are:

> I wish you would make up your mind to come down on Saturday. . . . I want to talk with you. I find it very difficult to correct proofs under the treatment, but you shall have them all back with you on Monday; don't show them to people. I have not at all settled whether I shall publish them now or in the Autumn, yet an Edinburgh paper mentions that I have a poem in the press. Confound the publicities and gabblements of the 19th century! Now, I hope you will come. If you do, bring two copies of my poems with you, two persons in this house want them; if you don't come (but I hope you will) send two. The printers are awful zanies,

they print erasures and corrections too, and other sins they commit of the utmost inhumanity. Come! Send a line first.[68]

Tennyson may have had his troubles with printers, but Moxon too had his troubles with Tennyson – at least when it came to proofs. Mary Russell Mitford wrote in August that year, "[Tennyson] is a great torment to Mr. Moxon, keeping proofs a fortnight to alter, and then sending for revises."[69] Such delays naturally slowed down the whole process of issuing the book. By autumn, Tennyson was still correcting proofs, informing Moxon, "I am putting the last touches to the 'Princess.' I trust there will still be time when I come up to get the book out by Christmas."[70] In spite of Moxon's best efforts, *The Princess* did not make it for pre-Christmas sale, only for the day itself, being published 25 December 1847. Sales, nonetheless, were immediately brisk and continued so for many years. "No less [*sic*] than seventeen editions appeared in England in the thirty years after publication," records Killham, and in both England and America, "for over sixty years, *The Princess* was a really popular poem."[71]

It took five editions (in the modern sense of the term this time) before the text reached its final form. A second edition in early 1848 included a dedication to Henry Lushington; the third edition in late January or early February 1850 was made up of an extensively revised text and six rhymed songs placed between the poem's seven sections; the fourth edition in late March or early April 1851 had added to it the "weird seizures" of the Prince; and the fifth edition, in February 1853, had an expanded Prologue.[72] Shannon notes "the remarkable extent" to which Tennyson was influenced by the reviewers in all these changes; but at least for the intercalary songs it was the public's response which made him resurrect an old idea. He said,

> The child is the link through the parts, as shown in the songs [inserted in 1850], which are the best interpreters of the poem. . . . Before the first edition came out, I deliberated with myself whether I should put songs between the separate divisions of the poem; again I thought that the poem would explain itself, but the public did not see the drift.[73]

Sales of these five editions brought in substantial profits to both Tennyson and Moxon. The book, published on a one-third/two-thirds division of profits system, as was *Poems* in 1842, differed from those volumes in that it was issued in green cloth boards, with gilt lettering; this became Tennyson's standard binding from this point on, from Moxon right through to Macmillan. The original 1500 copies at five shillings each brought in £103 13s. 7d. to Tennyson. The second edition had similar results: £118 4s. 7d. And the third, also of 1500 copies, brought in £106 19s. 4d. For the fourth edition, Moxon increased the run to 2000, for a £147 3s. 10d. profit for Tennyson. The fifth edition, also of 2000 copies, was the first one which took more than a year to sell out. During 1853, 1304 copies sold, yielding £82 3s. 2d. for the poet; by the end of 1854, the rest had been sold, with profits of £66 4s. 10d. for Tennyson. Thenceforward, sales held steady at about 1000 a year, bringing with them an annual revenue of roughly £75 for Tennyson.

What with this income from *The Princess*, an average of £100 a year from the *Poems*, £200 from the Civil List pension, the interest on the £2000 recouped from Dr Allen's folly, and continued small gifts from Aunt Elizabeth, Tennyson's financial pains were subsiding, though not yet completely cured. (It took *In Memoriam* to effect his full health.) We can gain perspective on Tennyson's income by knowing that a skilled artisan, a printer perhaps, earned on the average £400 a year at that time. Tennyson in 1848 was at least £100 beyond this in annual income.

His opinion of his own craft, though, did not depend on sales records and income from *The Princess*. In fact, the poem did not please him once it was out. He wrote to FitzGerald, "My book is out and I hate it and so will you," a judgment which proved correct, in that Fitz thought the poem "a wretched waste" of Tennyson's abilities.[74] Also, Frederick Locker-Lampson revealed that in 1869 Tennyson spoke to him about *The Princess* "with something of regret, of its fine blank verse, and the many good things in it: 'but,' said he, 'though truly original, it is, after all, only a medley.'"[75] That Tennyson did not like this creation as well as he did some others is evident from his failure to read it aloud in later life, though he often read *Maud*, the various Lincolnshire dialect poems, "The Charge of the Light Brigade," and "Guinevere." Current critical opinion certainly assigns a greater place to some of the songs in *The Princess*, particularly "Tears, idle tears," "Now sleeps the crimson petal, now the white," and "Come down, O maid, from yonder mountain height" than to the whole long poem, yet that might be endemic to our age's inability to deal critically with long poems and not truly reflective of the actual merits or demerits of *The Princess*.[76]

The early reviewers of the poem found it disappointing in its apparent lack of seriousness and confusing in its form, failing, as they did, to understand the implications of "medley." Nevertheless, reviewers overall in the first four years were more approving than disapproving, although they expressed a hope for a clearer, more fervent application of Tennyson's powers to a subject compelling public interest.[77]

With *In Memoriam*, they, the public and Emily Sellwood were to receive just that.

In late May 1850, after seventeen years of intermittent composition, *In Memoriam* was published anonymously; on 13 June, after fourteen years of intermittent courtship, Tennyson married Emily Sellwood; and on 19 November, after months of wavering, Queen Victoria officially appointed him Poet Laureate. These three events of that *annus mirabilis* formed a matrix, which makes it difficult to analyse cause-and-effect relationships between them, yet certain connections are clear: Emily Sellwood was so impressed with the religious affirmation – or what she thought was the religious affirmation – of *In Memoriam* after she had seen a copy of the trial edition that her fears about Tennyson's orthodoxy were calmed and her answer to his renewed marriage proposal changed from the "No" she had given him in 1848 to "Yes." It was she also who suggested the poem's title. Their marriage was expedited, moreover, by Edward Moxon's advancing Tennyson £300 against *In Memoriam*'s profits. Finally, the popular success of the poem and the evidence it offered of Tennyson's sustained poetic capacity in a serious, elevating vein convinced the Queen, her advisors, and even the critics, of Alfred's suitability for the Laureateship. Thus, in a few months, great personal happiness, financial security and popular and official recognition were showered on the same Tennyson who had before been living in a drought of intermittent distress and a flood of water-cures.

After publication of *The Princess* Tennyson had not immediately turned to the composition of *In Memoriam*; rather, he began quite consciously gathering material for the King Arthur poem always somewhere on his creative agenda. Fitz wrote to E. B. Cowell in November 1848, "he meditates new poems; and now The Princess is done, he turns to King Arthur – a worthy subject indeed – and has consulted some histories of him, and spent some time on visiting his traditionary haunts in Cornwall."[78] Fitz might have added "Devon and Ireland" as well, for Alfred's Arthurian search took him there also. By early 1849 de Vere could report that Tennyson "is more full than ever of King Arthur, and promises to *print* at least his exquisite

Elegies, and let his friends have a few copies."[79] Thus, although the material for the epic mounted, King Arthur was pushed aside once again as Tennyson began tinkering with the arrangement and final publishing of a lengthy lyric work, called variously "Elegies," "Fragments of an Elegy," and "The Way of the Soul" by Tennyson and his friends, but published as *In Memoriam*.

Since fall 1833, when the news of Arthur Hallam's death had reached the Tennyson family, Alfred had been making jottings, writing line fragments, composing short verses, and piecing together stanzas and sections of this quasi-autobiographical, reflective poem. Like Gray's "Elegy Written in a Country Churchyard," which Tennyson may have had in mind when he developed the distinctive "a-b-b-a" *In Memoriam* stanza, the poem turns on the "I," and is removed by both form and voice from the declamatory public mode of previous elegies. The pace is different, the rhyme is not insisted upon (even Tennyson's middle, "bb," lines do not chime) and the element of artificality is eliminated. Both Tennyson and Gray, for that matter, are far from the previously normative classic elegy, Milton's "Lycidas." But Tennyson, even more than Gray, changes the usual elegiac themes, too. Tennyson has themes of unity, identity, and the affirmation of faith, with a principle aesthetic theme operative throughout; at least thirty lyrics examine the function of art, some quite compellingly, as when the speaker announces,

> I sometimes hold it half a sin
>   To put in words the grief I feel;
>   For words, like Nature, half reveal
> And half conceal the Soul within.
>
> But, for the unquiet heart and brain,
>   A use in measured language lies;
>   The sad mechanic exercise,
> Like dull narcotics, numbing pain.
>
> In words, like weeds, I'll wrap me o'er,
>   Like coarsest clothes against the cold:
>   But that large grief which these enfold
> Is given in outline and no more.   (v)

Later he finds the narcotic effect of his art, his "measured language," modified into a playful, even "wholesome" exercise:

> If these brief lays, of Sorrow born,
>   Were taken to be such as closed
>   Grave doubts and answers here proposed,
> Then these were such as men might scorn:
>
> Her care is not to part and prove;
>   She takes, when harsher moods remit,
>   What slender shade of doubt may flit,
> And makes it vassal unto love:
>
> And hence, indeed, she sports with words,
>   But better serves a wholesome law,
>   And holds it sin and shame to draw
> The deepest measure from the chords:
>
> Nor dare she trust a larger lay,
>   But rather loosens from the lip
>   Short swallow-flights of song, that dip
> Their wings in tears, and skim away.   (XLVIII)

The "short swallow-flights of song" image captures *In Memoriam*'s form in one sense, but it underplays the unity which is created through the sustained, though changing, voice of its single speaker. Though Tennyson admitted, in the note below, to the haphazard development of the whole poem, he knew quite well that by the time seventeen years of composition were finished it had been worked into an artistic whole. Thus, in the same note, he likens it to the *Divine Comedy*:

> It must be remembered . . . that this is a poem, *not* an actual biography. It is founded on our friendship, on the engagement of Arthur Hallam to my sister, on his suden death at Vienna, just before the time fixed for their marriage, and on his burial at Clevedon Church. The poem concludes with the marriage of my youngest sister Cecilia. It was meant to be a kind of *Divina Commedia*, ending with happiness. The sections were written at many different places, and as the phases of our intercourse came to my memory and suggested them. I did not write them with any view of weaving them into a whole, or for publication, until I found that I had written so many. The different moods of sorrow as in a drama are dramatically given, and my conviction that fear,

doubts, and suffering will find answer and relief only through Faith in a God of Love.[80]

Despite Tennyson's warning against such readings, the poem has been read as straightforward biography, autobiography, spiritual diary, religious tract, philosophical treatise, and more. Yet it remains alive most notably as a re-creation of grief and doubt, and a tentative exploration of the artistic spirit's response to both.

Sir Charles points to at least three distinct stages of composition of *In Memoriam* before the final butcher's book got copied for the printer. In these various stages Tennyson brought to bear on the randomly composed lyrics his consummate skill as polisher of verse and refiner of sensibilities. Work now being done by Susan Shatto at the Tennyson Research Centre on the manuscripts should reveal in considerable detail how this particular poet labored over his words. (We already know how careless he was with the pages on which those words were written.)

The *In Memoriam* butcher's book had to be rescued once by Coventry Patmore, who said to William Allingham one cold night in August 1849,

> I have in this room perhaps the greatest literary treasure in England — the manuscript of Tennyson's *next poem*. It is written in a thing like a butcher's account-book. He left it behind him in his lodging when he was up in London and wrote to me to go and look for it. He had no other copy, and he never remembers his verses. I found it by chance, in a drawer; if I had been a little later it would probably have been sold to a butter-shop.

Allingham then wrote, "Before I went away Patmore took out this MS. book from a cabinet and turned over the leaves before my longing eyes, but Tennyson had told him not to show it to anybody. Mrs. Patmore had copied it out for the press, and T. gave her the original."[81]

Late that year Moxon was eager to publish *In Memoriam* and therefore advanced Tennyson £300. Their new, unwritten agreement called for the poem to be issued at Tennyson's risk, with Moxon taking one-third of the profits and 5 per cent on the gross sales and Tennyson getting the balance. We have noted that earlier accounts show that the *Poems* of 1842 and *The Princess* were published under an agreement whereby Moxon had borne production costs and profits had been strictly divided one-third to him and two-thirds to Tennyson. By this new agreement Tennyson seems to have been reaching for greater control of manner of production even though that increased control would mean slightly less income, since Moxon's 5 per cent of the gross sales would cut into Tennyson's share of the profits.[82]

With production costs now in his own hands, Tennyson felt freer than ever to ask for a trial edition. He did so in early 1850. "Usually Tennyson circulated these privately printed copies some months before publication and gave them prolonged study, and that may have been his intention now, for Patmore told William Rossetti [brother of Dante Gabriel and Christina Rossetti] on March 21st that *The Elegies* would probably not be published till about Christmas."[83] Unlike the trial edition for "The Lover's Tale," which resulted in Tennyson's withdrawing the poem altogether, the one for *In Memoriam* moved him to even earlier publication than at first intended. This may be a sign of Tennyson's increasing self-confidence. As usual, the enthusiastic responses of his friends — Drummond Rawnsley, de Vere, Charles Kingsley, Patmore, and especially Emily Sellwood — bolstered him. We can be sure, too, that Edward Moxon was most anxious to get the poem out of Tennyson's careless hands.

1500 copies of the volume, bound in deep purple boards, were readied for late May publication, at a sale price of six shillings a copy. In July Moxon printed 1500 more, and in August an additional 2000. For the Christmas trade he put out another 3000.[84] Tennyson's attempt to be anonymous by leaving his name off the title page seems half-hearted, since he inserted, opposite the first page, "In Memoriam /A. H. H. /Obiit MDCCCXXXIII." Most readers could have figured that out easily enough. Moxon, however, left nothing to chance: he took careful pains to insure that literary London knew who had authored the poem. And the *Publishers' Circular* for 1 June listed Tennyson as the author — which may have been an inadvertent admission, but, as Ricks notes, it was "a helpful error."[85] Amazingly enough, however, a number of reviewers were oblivious to the poem's authorship, one even asserting the presence of a female hand, without realizing that the previous week's column of new books had listed Tennyson as *In Memoriam*'s author.[86]

The critics, though praising the poem highly, suggested that the public would not take to it. In this they erred, for the coterie of ardent admirers, who had honored Tennyson before, was a coterie no longer: it was now the whole nation, or so it seemed, which proclaimed Tennyson's genius. Explanations for that sudden popularity have varied. George O. Marshall, Jr, for example, considers the poem's teachings the ground of its success:

> [*In Memoriam*] seemed to be such a satisfactory answer to the problems of existence, especially those raised by the struggle between religion and science, that the Victorians clasped it to their bosoms to supplement the consolation offered by the Bible. This wholehearted acceptance for its teachings went from the highest to the lowest. Prince Albert's admiration for *In Memoriam* was one of the reasons that Tennyson was appointed Poet Laureate. And Queen Victoria said to Tennyson when he visited her in April, 1862, after the death of the Prince Consort: "Next to the Bible 'In Memoriam' is my comfort."[87]

Sir Charles, on the other hand, attributes the poem's popularity less to its teachings than to its "warm humanity" and "touches of exquisite pathos." "Moreover," he observes, "every phase of the spiritual drama was reflected in the varying moods of the English countryside and the ever-changing beauty and majesty of English skies, and every section, stanza and line was, as always with Tennyson, wrought to the highest degree of effectiveness which his art could compass."[88]

Whatever the cause of *In Memoriam*'s popularity, brisk sales required another 5000 copies to be printed in November 1851. This printing supplied the need for only the next three years, however, for in 1855 and 1856 another 3000 were printed and sold. From then on, the poem sold at a steady rate and remained popular as a single volume even after various multi-volume collected editions of Tennyson's poetry became available.

Tennyson's steady income from *In Memoriam* – £445 for 1850, £273 for 1851, £133 for 1852, £175 for 1853, £150 for 1854, and about £100 each year for 1855 and 1856 – added to his regular income from *Poems* and *The Princess* – enabled the poet to live on the proceeds from his books. Of course, he had, too, his basic income of Civil List pension and investment interest, to which had been added in 1850 the Laureate's salary of £200 a year plus the traditional butt of sack!

For his immediate financial needs in preparation for marriage, Tennyson managed on the £300 advanced by Moxon, £300 from his savings account, and the provision of household furniture by Mr

Sellwood. Aunt Elizabeth Russell provided some funds for the wedding trip; Tennyson wrote to her from Tent Lodge, Coniston, in the Lake District, "I send you this little note just to tell you where we are, and how much your bounty has enabled us to enjoy ourselves among the mountains."[89]

On 13 June 1850, at Shiplake, Oxfordshire, where family friend Drummond Rawnsley was vicar, Emily and Alfred were finally wed. They had met in 1830 and had been in love for at least fourteen of the intervening years. Alfred may have had "black blood" and terrible "nerves," but never a faint heart. And judging from what he wrote in "Vicar of Shiplake," which was begun on his wedding day and finished six months later, his appreciation of Emily matched his perseverance in courting her:

> Vicar of that pleasant spot,
>   Where it was my chance to marry,
> Happy, happy be your lot
>   In the Vicarage by the quarry:
> You were he that knit the knot.
>
> Sweetly, smoothly flow your life.
>   Never parish feud perplex you,
> Tithe unpaid, or party strife.
>   All things please you, nothing vex you;
> You have given me such a wife.
>
> Have I seen in one so near
>   Aught but sweetness aye prevailing?
> Or, through more than half a year,
>   Half the fraction of a failing?
> Therefore bless you, Drummond dear.
>
> Good she is, and pure and just.
>   Being conquered by her sweetness
> I shall come through her, I trust,
>   Into fuller-orbed completeness;
> Though but made of erring dust.   (ll. 1–20)

These words, sounding as they do like the Prince's speech to Ida at the end of *The Princess*, imply that Emily provided fulfillment for Tennyson. James O. Hoge evaluates their relationship in this way:

She brought him a happiness and a completeness unknown during two decades of rarely relieved despondency. With her comfort and guidance he would indeed "gain in sweetness and moral height"; he would be spiritually healed and uplifted, and he would come to know "the peace of God," which, as he remarked many years later, "came into my life before the altar when I wedded her." Emily shielded and supported Tennyson, and she lessened the vexations he had formerly suffered. But more importantly, she freed him from the prison of selfhood and enabled him to bear the responsibilities of a less alienated existence than that in which he had long indulged. She helped him to survive the pressures and conflicts of a materialistic age which challenged his most cherished beliefs and to attain a position of comparative confidence and tranquility.[90]

Hoge also notes, "There is no dearth of testimony about the effect Emily Tennyson's understanding, her protection, and her wide and loving attention had upon her husband's troubled spirit." But he summarizes, too, the statements of those later critics such as Harold Nicolson who "characterize[d] Tennyson's wife as a 'wistful lady' who bound 'what was most wild in him and most original' and passed 'timid but appropriate criticisms' upon the 'tender little things' she encouraged the Laureate to write."[91] These conjectures are worth examining, I suppose, but the game of imagining what Tennyson's poetry would have been like had he *not* married Emily Sellwood I leave to those who prefer conjecture to fact. The *fact* is that his closest friends thought him well blessed to have her, he thought the same, and, most importantly from a literary perspective, after his marriage he produced the two great long poems, *Maud* and *The Idylls of the King*, many shorter ones having the same power as those published in the 1842 *Poems*, and a number of poetic dramas, which, though not to modern taste, are comparable to those written by Shelley and Browning. There was some change of tone, to be sure, as Tennyson settled into family life and grew older, but a diminution of artistry and emotional force? No.

One more benefit was in store for Tennyson as a direct result of publishing *In Memoriam*. Wordsworth's death on 23 April 1850 had made available the Poet Laureateship. Although the Queen first offered it in May to Samuel Rogers, he refused because of his advanced age, forcing the Queen to reconsider. Elizabeth Barrett Browning and Leigh Hunt then became the favorites of the press, though Tennyson was mentioned along with Professor John Wilson, Sheridan Knowles, and Henry Taylor. The Queen decided on Tennyson once she found that Prince Albert's admiration for *In Memoriam* was matched by Samuel Rogers's estimation of the poet's character. On 19 November Tennyson was appointed officially; his acceptance was attended by the usual indecision, as he told his friend James Knowles:

> The night before I was asked to take the Laureateship, which was offered to me through Prince Albert's liking for my *In Memoriam*, I dreamed that he came to me and kissed me on the cheek. I said, in my dream, "Very kind, but very German." In the morning the letter about the Laureateship was brought to me and laid upon my bed. I thought about it through the day, but could not make up my mind whether to take it or refuse it, and at the last I wrote two letters, one accepting and one declining, and threw them on the table, and settled to decide which I would send after my dinner and bottle of port.[92]

The honor brought with it occasional duties — a poem for this or that christening or wedding — and increased invasions of Tennyson's privacy, the latter so irksome already that he wrote, "I was even told that being already in receipt of a pension I could not gracefully refuse it: but I wish more and more that somebody else had it. I have no passion for courts but a great love of privacy: nor do I count having the office as any particular feather in my cap."[93]

Alfred settled into his Laureate position well enough, nonetheless. In May 1851 he attended the Queen's Ball — declining, however, Rogers's offer of "the old Laureate suit," which may have been a Wordsworth hand-me-down. (Moxon was sent to Rogers with the message about the suit since Tennyson was ill.)[94] Moreover, Tennyson's first separate publication after *In Memoriam* was a Laureate poem: "The Ode on the Death of the Duke of Wellington," November 1852. The Duke had died on 14 September 1852; on 6 November Moxon wrote to Tennyson: "For an edition of 10,000 copies of your Ode on the Death of the Duke of Wellington I beg to offer you two hundred pounds, the amount to be paid at Christmas, or, should you wish it, on the day of publication."[95] The poem appeared in slate-colored paper wrappers, at one shilling per copy, on 15 November, two days before the Duke's funeral; all 10,000 copies were quickly taken up by the memento-hunting nation. A second edition was issued in early 1853, with the poem first appearing in a volume in *Maud and Other Poems* (1855). Tennyson's unusual haste in composition resulted in his first effort being castigated by the press, so much so that he feared for Moxon's possible financial loss. Tennyson therefore advised his publisher: "If you lose by the Ode, I will not consent to accept the whole sum of £200, which you offered me. I consider it quite a sufficient loss if you do not gain by it."[96] (Those who call Tennyson's dealings with his publishers only "shrewd" overlook evidence such as this which points to his sense of fair play.) For the second edition of the "Ode," three months after the first, Tennyson revised and improved the poem, drawing upon his experience in seeing the funeral procession and reading about the burial in St. Paul's.[97] Although Ricks objects to the poem's "failures of conviction which lead to failures of impression," most readers today who can enter into the sprit of this public, occasional poem also recognize its dignity and nobility. The metrics cannot be appreciated when the poem is read silently. Tennyson liked to read it aloud, as he did a number of other poems that would lose much of their force without the proper cadence imparted by impassioned reading. Sir Charles, in fact, highly praises the poem's conclusion, saying that "certainly [Tennyson] had never used language, rhyme and rhythm with greater power and freedom."[98]

During his first years as Poet Laureate Tennyson published a few poems in periodicals or annuals, later including them in new volumes. He also regularly added new compositions to each new one-volume edition of the old 1842 *Poems*. For example, in the seventh edition (1851), the first Laureate Edition, he included a new blank verse English idyl, "Edwin Morris," and "The Eagle," and "To the Queen" ("Revered, beloved"), which later served as a general dedication to the collected editions. That seventh edition also included "Come not, when I am dead," first published in *The Keepsake* for 1851.

On the personal side, Tennyson's life after his marriage became quite settled and orderly, a veritable change indeed from his chaotic bachelor days. Even with the arrival of children – Hallam on 11 August 1852 and Lionel on 16 March 1854 – and a house often hectically full of visitors, Tennyson soon established a regular daily schedule which was hardly changed throughout the rest of his life except when he was away from home. He rose early, breakfasted alone, and worked until eleven in the morning. From eleven to one he walked, regardless of the weather, his wide black hat and black cape

keeping off showers and intruders alike. After a family luncheon he
played with his children, gardened, talked with guests, helped Emily
in her household planning. He walked again from five to six, dined
with his family and guests, and devoted some time each evening to
reading aloud to Emily, listening and performing music, or convers-
ing. In the evening, also, he habitually took to his smoking and
writing once more. Sir Charles, the grandson, comments, "The half-
hours after breakfast and dinner were usually set aside for meditation
over his pipe, for it was then that ideas came to him most readily.
These were assembled and elaborated on his walks about the downs
and lanes and the results jotted down at leisure, often quite
disjointedly, in the notebooks which Emily bound up for him."[99] To
which Hallam Tennyson, the son, adds,

As he made the different poems he would repeat or read them. The
constant reading of the new poems aloud was the surest way of
helping him to find out any defects there might be. During his
"sacred half-hours" and his other working hours and even on the
Downs, he would murmur his new passages or new lines as they
came to him, a habit which had always been his since boyhood, and
which caused the Somersby cook to say, "What is master Awlfred
always a praying for?"[100]

By the fall of 1852 the Tennysons found Chapel House at
Twickenham, which they had been leasing, ill-suited to their
increased needs for space and privacy, and Alfred began the job of
house-hunting. A year later he found what was to be their new home:
Farringford on the Isle of Wight.[101]
The income from his poetry, although varying somewhat from
year to year as his own productivity and outside influences dictated,
proved substantial enough for Alfred to lease the house and park with
an option to buy.[102] Knowing, however, that he had no new volume
ready to offer the public during 1854 may have made Tennyson more
amenable to Moxon's suggestion, proffered during January 1854,
that the publisher issue an *Illustrated Edition of Tennyson's Poems*,
particularly when he promised at least a £2000 profit, which
Tennyson could put towards the purchase of Farringford. That year,
"owing to the depressing influence of the Crimean War, [the receipts
from Moxon's] fell away to under £500."[103] Yet Tennyson had
prepared for just such a fluctuation in his income by investing wisely

the fall before while planning to lease Farringford. On 14 November 1853 he recorded,

> I wrote on Friday to accept the house (Farringford), I also wrote to-day to Moxon to advance one thousand pounds, four hundred pounds he owes me, the odd six hundred to be paid if he will in March when I get my moneys in. Why I did it? Because by buying safe debentures in the East Lincolnshire Line for two thousand five hundred pounds, with that and five hundred a year [income from his books] I think we ought to get on.[104]

With his income and housing thus established, Tennyson settled once more into his work. In late 1854 he composed another Laureate poem even more quickly than he had created the Wellington "Ode." His famous "Charge of the Light Brigade" was written on 2 December "in a few minutes, after reading the description in the *Times* in which occurred the phrase 'some one had blundered,' and this was the origin of the metre of his poem."[105] John Forster published the poem on 9 December in the *Examiner*, with the initials "A. T." under it. The first two stanzas read:

> Half a league, half a league,
> Half a league onward,
> All in the valley of Death
>   Rode the six hundred.
> 'Forward the Light Brigade!
> Charge for the guns!' he said:
> Into the valley of Death
>   Rode the six hundred.
>
> 'Forward, the Light Brigade!'
> Was there a man dismayed?
> Not though the soldier knew
>   Some one had blundered.
> Their's not to make reply,
> Their's not to reason why.
> Their's but to do and die:
> Into the valley of Death
>   Rode the six hundred.

For the version published in *Maud and Other Poems* (1855) Tennyson excised the "some one had blundered" line at the insistence of "some friends of excellent critical judgment," including the young American poet, Frederick Tuckerman. Tennyson quickly decided he himself had blundered by being so misguided. John Ruskin, by then gaining prominence as a literary critic, urged the line's reinstatement: "I am very sorry you put the 'Some one had blundered' out of the 'Light Brigade,'" he advised Tennyson in a 12 November 1855 letter. "It was precisely the most tragical line in the poem. It is as true to its history as essential to its tragedy."[106] One of the objections to the line by Tuckerman and other purists was the rhyming of "blundered" and "hundred"; but Lincolnshire natives such as W. F. Rawnsley asserted that in that county the number is pronounced "hunderd" and therefore was heard thus by Tennyson.[107]

The *Examiner* publication of Tennyson's celebration of such a disastrous event from the Crimea created heated controversy, some readers complaining of the poem's statement and others ridiculing its rhymes and meter. Such a reaction depressed Alfred, who was already upset over the course of the war. "My heart almost burst," Sir Charles quotes him as writing, "with indignation at the accursed mismanagement of our noble little Army, the flower of our men." The biographer continues,

It was therefore with particular satisfaction that he received a message from a chaplain serving in the military hospital at Scutari, saying that the greatest service which could be done at the moment would be to send out copies of *The Charge of the Light Brigade* on printed slips for distribution among the soldiers. It was, said the writer, the greatest favourite of the men. "Half are singing it and all want to have it in black and white, so as to read what has so taken them. . . ." Alfred immediately wrote to Forster, sending him a revised copy of the ballad, practically in the form we know today. . . . he now realized that his second thoughts [for the *Maud* volume version] had (an unusual thing with him) not been improvements on the first, and this impression was confirmed by the report of the poweful effect which the original version had made upon the soldiers. Two thousand copies of the slip were printed [by Moxon] and sent to the chaplain before the end of August.[108]

"Some one had blundered" thus regained its rightful place as the poem's keynote. Tennyson added "The Charge of the Light Brigade" to his growing list of poems most suitable for reading aloud to his family and friends. In fact, his reading of the poem, with its gripping opening repetition "Half a league, half a league, /Half a league onward" rolled out, exists for us to listen to, though as from a distance, on a recording made from one of Thomas Edison's original waxed cylinders.

Beyond the sound and emotive pull of the poem, however, lies its "shape." Tennyson once likened the shape or the curve of the action of short poems to the double curve which the rind of an apple makes when thrown upon the floor;[109] he molded such a shape in "The Charge of the Light Brigade" as well as in some of the Arthurian poems, "The Golden Year," "Crossing the Bar," and others. It is this "shape" which Ricks delineates:

> How characteristic, not only of the movement of Tennyson's mind but also of the movements of his verse, this thrusting forward which then wheels back. The repetitions in the poem (there within the opening line, "Half a league, half a league") epitomize the outward—homeward curve; "Cannon in front of them," then "Cannon behind them"; "Into the mouth of Hell," then "Back from the mouth of Hell." Like the sword Excalibur, rising from the lake and at last returning to it; like the coming and the passing of Arthur, "From the great deep to the great deep he goes"; like "The Golden Year,"
>
> > The dark Earth follows wheeled in her ellipse;
> > And human things returning on themselves . . .
>
> —like these, "The Charge of the Light Brigade" advances and wheels. At the very end of his life, Tennyson was to envisage such a curve more truly, as something other than a heroically fatuous reversal:
>
> > But such a tide as moving seems asleep,
> >   Too full for sound and foam,
> > When that which drew from out the boundless deep
> >   Turns again home.[110]

Tennyson's publishing method for this poem — first issuing it in a periodical, then in a book, then on single sheets — epitomized his

newly acquired flexibility and increasing attention to appealing to a
wider audience through diversity of media and greater topicality.
Tennyson, in other words, took to his Poet Laureate occupation
seriously enough to let it affect the vehicle in which he presented his
poetry to the public, but not so seriously that he let it detract him
from continuing to experiment with his art itself. Thus, a highly
experimental poem, his first extended effort since *In Memoriam*,
tested his powers of composition throughout the summer and fall of
1854. *Maud, or the Madness*, as it was first entitled, was written
"Morning and evening" as Alfred sat "in his hard high-backed
wooden chair in his little room at the top of the house."[111] Its origin
and composition he himself called "singular":

> He had accidentally lighted upon a poem of his own which begins
> "O that 'twere possible," and which had long before been
> published in a selected volume got up by Lord Northampton for
> the aid of a sick clergyman. It had struck him, in consequence, I
> think [observes Aubrey de Vere], of a suggestion made by Sir John
> Simeon, that, to render the poem fully intelligible, a preceding one
> was necessary. He wrote it; the second poem too required a
> predecessor; and thus the whole work was written, as it were,
> *backwards*.[112]

But, backwards or forwards, *Maud* actually proceeded more in
Tennyson's usual fashion than did the hastily written Wellington
"Ode" and "Charge of the Light Brigade," with the exception of the
mad scene, which Hallam Tennyson records as having been written
in "twenty minutes."[113] Although Hallam also writes that by 10
January 1855 his father had "finished, and read out, several lyrics of
'Maud,'" the poet did not really complete the poem for another six
months.[114] In February he added the mad scene; in April he started
copying out the poem for the press, probably for the trial edition, of
which he wrote to Tuckerman in July: "These poems [*Maud* and the
others for the volume], when printed, I found needed considerable
elision and so the book has hung on hand."[115] Finally, in July, "the
last touch was put to 'Maud,' before giving it to the publisher."[116]
One can well imagine Moxon's joyful anticipation of this new
publication by Tennyson. After the popular success of *In Memoriam*
five years before, after the Laureateship, after the notice paid to the
Wellington "Ode" and Crimean "Charge," after the recent honor of
Tennyson's being turned into "Dr Tennyson," through Oxford's

conferring of a degree, *honores causa*, here at last was a new Tennyson book. The publisher's high expectations are reflected in the size of the first edition – 10,000 copies, selling at five shillings each. From the first, sales were excellent: shortly after publication Moxon wrote to Mrs Tennyson, "I drop you a line to say that as we have already received orders for upwards of 3,000 copies of *Maud*, I have requested the Printers to strike off immediately 2,000 copies more, & to keep the type standing." A second edition was required before the end of the year. Receipts of over £2000 from Moxon in 1856, plus the expectation of another £2000 at least from the *Illustrated Edition* in process, encouraged the Tennysons to buy Farringford once an agreement could be reached on a price for house, park, timberland and orchard.[117] Tennyson's financial stability, however, was threatened that summer by bank failure. Hallam Tennyson explains,

In June [1856] news came that R's bank would probably break and that all my father's little savings might be lost. On July 2nd my mother wrote: "A. showed a noble disregard of money, much as the loss would affect us." That evening, so as to give her courage, he asked her to play and sing the grand Welsh national air, "Come to battle": and afterwards, to divert themselves from dwelling on the possible loss, they hung their Michael Angelo engravings round the drawing-room.[118]

After a few suspense-filled weeks Emily and Alfred were relieved to find that the failure took only a few hundred pounds of their savings.[119]

This danger to Tennyson's bank account was matched by the danger to his reputation which *Maud* was creating. The virulence of the criticism which greeted the poem's appearance is unmatched in Tennyson's long career. The Liberal press inveighed against the poem's politics, the ordinary reader found its form incomprehensible, and the critics castigated it for almost every conceivable reason. Sir Charles relates the responses:

Poor *Maud* was received with almost universal reprobation. Even Patmore thought its publication a hideous mistake which he would have tried to prevent had he been given the chance, but Alfred had only read him a passage here and there, "and his reading magnifies everything, it is so grand." "Obscurity taken for profundity," "the dead level of prose run mad," "rampant and rabid bloodthirstiness of soul," were a few of the descriptions lavished on it by the reviewers. One critic commented that one of the two vowels should be omitted from the title, and that it didn't much matter which was chosen for the purpose. Another said: "If an author pipe of adultery, fornication, murder and suicide, set him down as the practiser of those crimes," [to which Alfred] replied: "Adulterer I may be, fornicator I may be, murderer I may be, suicide I am not yet."[120]

But most of the criticism Alfred could not dismiss so lightly. He even seemed upset over what one might call a "crank" letter – anonymous, of course – which shouted, "Sir, once I worshipped you – now I loathe you! So you've taken to imitating Longfellow, you BEAST!"[121] A few years later Tennyson said earnestly to Mrs Browning, "You must always stand up for 'Maud' when you hear my pet bantling abused. Perhaps that is why I am sensitive about her. You know mothers always make the most of a child that is abused."[122] Some of this sensitivity must have mellowed by a decade later, though, for he said jokingly to Allingham in 1865, "Allingham, would it disgust you if I read 'Maud'? Would you expire?"[123]

Moxon tried to mitigate the effects of the negative responses to *Maud* by passing along praise to Tennyson whenever he could. In August 1855 he wrote to Alfred and Emily saying "that Browning considered *Maud* a great poem and had already read it four times."[124] It is no accident that Browning could read *Maud* appreciatively where others could not, for his own convoluted poetry, with its intensive probings of the "abysmal deeps of personality" (Tennyson's term in "The Palace of Art") and impassioned exploration of madness shared Tennyson's interests in *Maud*. Browning, too, suffered from much greater critical disfavor than did Tennyson, and without the palliative of popular success.

What seemed to confuse readers most was *Maud's* "mono-dramatic" form. Tennyson clarified the form's significance to the work by changing the title from *Maud, or the Madness* to *Maud: A Monodrama*, but this he did in 1875, long after the confusion had begun. Few readers in 1855 apprehended that his "monodrama" was an effort to render credible both movement and progression of psychological states within a single character. The speaker's state in Part III is normative for him, acting as a guide to both the jubilation of Part I and the madness of Part II – but this, too, the poem's first readers had difficulty understanding, especially as the poem was not divided into sections until later: into two sections in 1859 and into three in 1865. What Tennyson apparently desired was to reach a broad public while having an undercurrent which appealed to the informed, but he underestimated the difficulty of getting even the informed to do their job. "Like *The Princess* in which the reader was invited into an active role in the formulation of the poem's meaning," suggests Catherine Stevenson, "*Maud* obtrudes particular fragments of experience upon the reader, requiring *him* to work out their unity and meaning under the impetus provided by the poem. At each stage in the poem the reader must reassess the character of the speaker, must evaluate anew the meaning of his actions in terms of his previous psychological states or behavior."[125] Most readers, however, remained confused and assigned the disordered state of *Maud*'s erratic, disturbed speaker to Tennyson's supposed confusions and personal life. Though the "facts" of Tennyson's experience with women, particularly Rosa Baring, Sophia Rawnsley and Emily Sellwood, and the "facts" surrounding his father's disinheritance became in *Maud* "integral parts of an aesthetic construct"[126] and not autobiographical statement, most readers, then as now, needed guidance before apprehending this kind of subtle artistic experience. Yet, although Tennyson did not provide early on guidance in the form of a fitting subtitle or division into sections, he did say a number of things relative to *Maud* which are illuminating. Of the autobiographical confusion he said,

> In a certain way, no doubt, poets and novelists, however dramatic they are, give themselves in their works. The mistake that people make is that they think the poet's poems are a kind of 'catalogue raisonné" of his very own self, and of all the facts of his life, not seeing that they often only express a poetic instinct, or judgment on character real or imagined, and on the facts of lives real or imagined.[127]

Furthermore, he called *Maud* "a little *Hamlet*," "a drama where successive phases of passion in one person take the place of successive persons," and "a Drama of the Soul."[128] The modern reader needs all of this background in order to read with the constant activity Stevenson suggests – but, once that is done, few will fail to appreciate why *Maud* holds its current high position in the Tennyson canon.

In spite of all the misunderstandings and consequent critical abuse, *Maud and Other Poems* (the others were "The Brook," "The Letters," the Wellington "Ode," "The Daisy," "To the Rev. F. D. Maurice,"

"Will," and "The Charge of the Light Brigade") attracted many buyers and cemented even more firmly than before Moxon's reputation as "publisher of poets." While Alfred Tennyson had been regulating his own life and working at his trade, Edward Moxon had been similarly tending to his own personal and business affairs. His family responsibilities were large, including as they did not only his own wife and seven children but also some support for his brothers and sisters. At first the family lived in the upper stories of the bookshop at 44 Dover Street; later, when finances had steadied and Moxon's health partially failed, they moved to Tudor Lodge, on Putney Heath, which had been built by Edward's brother William.[129] Moxon's most trying business years, the early 1840s, were long past, but his lung condition kept him from fully enjoying his new prosperity. Moreover, the firm's future was to be under-mined by his ill health:

> His last eight or ten years of publishing, which were financially comfortable, show Moxon adding only three or four new names to his list of authors and devoting his energy, which was on the wane from ill-health, to reprints of his favorite writers and to new volumes by those who were still living. By the mid-fifties his closest friends had died – Lamb, Rogers, Wordsworth, and Talfourd. Leigh Hunt was in his seventy-seventh year. Sheridan Knowles, who had become almost fanatically religious, had dropped his earlier friendships. Sir Henry Taylor, Monckton Milnes, and Tennyson were almost the only survivors of the friends whom Moxon had made through publishing. He had neither the heart nor the energy during his last years to expand the business. It had risen to its height; he would merely maintain it there with the well-known Moxon names. . . . This failure to add new names partly accounts for the instability of the firm after its founder's death.[130]

Moxon's last project with Tennyson added nothing to the firm's profits and in fact precipitated the only period of major conflict which Tennyson ever had with his publishers. The story of the beautiful, though ill fated, *Illustrated Edition of Tennyson's Poems* (1857) centers on the firm after Edward Moxon's death in June 1858, though Edward himself initiated, prepared and published it.

Edward Moxon, then, died at his height as publisher, leaving behind an established, well-respected firm and an estate of £16,000, which "if distributed equally over his business years [represents] an annual profit of nearly six hundred pounds."[131] And all of this came out of a business which was entered in debt and dedicated to the publishing of poetry, hardly the market's most lucrative commodity, even in Tennyson's heyday.

4 Troubled Years with Moxon & Co. (1858–68)

A decade of difficulty, centering first on the celebrated *Illustrated Edition of Tennyson's Poems* (1857) and then on others, followed Edward Moxon's death in June 1858.[1]

By 1854, the year when the *Illustrated Edition* was first mentioned between them, Moxon had issued for Tennyson five different volumes, which ran to numerous editions: *Poems* (1832), *Poems* (1842), *The Princess* (1847), *In Memoriam* (1850), and the "Ode on the Death of the Duke of Wellington" (1852). *Maud and Other Poems* was in the works and would be out by 1855. "Every volume, except possibly the first, had been a money-maker."[2]

The *Illustrated Edition* was a beautiful one-volume edition of the 1842 *Poems* with fifty-four wood blocks drawn by eight leading artists, the most famous of whom are the three Pre-Raphaelites Dante Gabriel Rossetti, William Holman Hunt and John Everett Millais. Moxon had written to Tennyson on 11 January 1854 proposing such an edition:

> As you have an idea of purchasing your house if you can get together the requisite amount, you cannot in my opinion do better than allow me to bring out an illustrated edition of your poems. I could by this means I am almost sure, & within a very short time too, put into your pocket at least a couple of thousand pounds. But as soon as the days are a little longer, and the weather . . . somewhat more settled, I will come over to the Isle of Wight and talk the matter over with you. I will at the same time bring with me a copy of an illustrated edition of Keats. . . .[3]

Moxon's successes with illustrated Samuel Rogers editions added to his confidence.

Tennyson, however, was reluctant to bring out such a volume, for at least two reasons that we know of: (1) he generally disliked illustrations to his own poems, because "they never seemed to him to illustrate his own ideas," and (2) he preferred the simplest style of publication – plain covers, good print, no artwork. [4]

On the first point, Tennyson did not dislike pictorial art in itself, as some have maintained. [5] During the 1850s, for instance, he took his children regularly to the National Gallery and attended other exhibitions to see specific works; these visits indicate more than passing interest in pictures. Each year, according to Hallam Tennyson's recollection of his childhood, on the way through London to Lincolnshire, Tennyson would take the boys to the National Gallery, in which he "much delighted and would point us out the various excellences of the different masters; he always led the way first of all to the 'Raising of Lazarus' by Sebastian del Piombo and to Titian's 'Bacchus and Ariadne.'" [6] In the summer of 1857, on the way to the Lakes, the whole Tennyson family "visited Manchester, where Alfred was very anxious to see a great exhibition then on view, with a particularly fine collection of pictures." [7] Hallam Tennyson specifies, "Much time [was] spent in studying Holman Hunt's pictures, the Turner sketches, Mulready's drawings, and various fine Gainsboroughs and Reynolds." [8] Furthermore, Tennyson's friends included a number of artists, particularly Thomas Woolner, a frequent visitor at Farringford. Another apparently forgotten part of Tennyson's life by those who accuse him of disliking art was his own painting. In 1858, for example, Tennyson had built for himself a summer house at Farringford – built, that is, "to his own designs and decorated with [his own] elaborate paintings of kingfishers flying through screens of reed, and wonderful dragons. The execution of these decorations," writes Sir Charles, who saw his grandfather's paintings before dampness and rough handling almost obliterated them, "was most imaginative and skilful, and Holman Hunt had admired them greatly." [9]

Thus, Tennyson seems to have expressed in various significant ways an active appreciation for art. Nonetheless, much as he might enjoy pictures in themselves, he found the illustrations to his own poems at best irrelevant, usually distracting, and at worst downright deceiving, as we shall see in further detail later.

Tennyson's second objection to Moxon's proposal – that is, its departure from his preferred style of publication – can be inferred by looking at the major editions of Tennyson's poetry over which the poet exercised greater control: plain cloth binding, usually green; clear type; well-spaced lines; relatively inexpensive selling prices; no advertisements, and no puffing. The *Illustrated Edition* turned out to be a thick book bound in bright blue silk-like cloth with gilded edges and with a gilt urn on the cover, and sold for a guinea and a half. It was – and still is – an expensive and beautiful book, but Tennyson knew full well when Moxon suggested the project that his own ideal of utmost simplicity in publication would be compromised by it.

By this aversion to illustrated and fancily bound "coffee-table" books, Tennyson dissociated himself firmly from the predominant taste of his times. Those who make a case for the independence of Tennyson's poetry might well add to their argument his refusal to gratify the tastes of his audience when it came to even the visual side of his publications. Aesthetic principles usually overruled the law of the marketplace.

Nevertheless, on this occasion, Tennyson denied his own convictions and accepted Moxon's enthusiastic proposal. He did need the money to purchase Farringford, and he realized that such an edition would require from him no new poems, thus freeing him for a project already under way which required the full use of his creative powers – the composition of the *Idylls of the King*. He did not, however, avoid participating in Moxon's project once it got started. As he said, "When I had once consented to the thing being done I on many accounts urged its speedy completion." He visited some of the artists; he invited Millais to Farringford so that young Hallam could be used as a model for a design for "Dora"; he went to London during the actual publication month to assist Moxon.

The financial agreement struck by the two men differed from their usual one in that the publisher apparently volunteered to bear the costs of publication himself. Emily Tennyson wrote, "In conversation Alfred stated that it was impossible for him to furnish funds to pay the artists and I think, as far as I can remember, Moxon said, 'Oh, we can manage all that.'" The rest of the agreement seems to have been the usual division of profits: one-third to Moxon, two-thirds to Tennyson.

Within two months of proposing the edition to Tennyson, Edward Moxon had begun his arrangements. Apparently the choice of artists was his: he mentioned on 27 February 1854 already having seen Landseer, Mulready, Creswick, Millais.

> . . . as soon as the above artists have selected their subjects it is my intention to call upon Stanfield, Maclise, Horsley, and Frost – all excellent in their respective lines, and all men who can draw on

wood. From the cordial manner in which those artists to whom I have spoken appear to enter into the matter, I shall, I have no doubt, be able to produce a first-rate book, — one in fact which will command a large sale.

In May Tennyson went to London to consult with Moxon about the volume and himself "went round" to several of the artists. Although Moxon chose the artists, Tennyson apparently recommended several quite strongly. His new friendship with Ruskin, who was himself advancing the members of the Pre-Raphaelite Brotherhood, no doubt influenced him to suggest Dante Gabriel Rossetti and Holman Hunt; the influence of his wife made him recommend Lizzie Siddall. Emily wrote to Moxon that "she had rather pay for Miss S's designs herself than not have them in the book."[10] Miss Siddall, on her part, was an enthusiastic Tennysonian; Alfred "had heard that, ever since finding a poem of his on a printed sheet wrapped round some butter, she had become his ardent admirer."[11] Moxon, as usual, saw in his relationship to Tennyson enough of a partnership to honor his recommendation of Rossetti and Hunt, but he drew the line at Siddall. In the same letter in which he rejected her, however, he welcomed the Tennysons' suggestion that a print of Thomas Woolner's medallion of the poet be used as frontispiece.

Whereas the publisher (with help from the poet) chose the artists, the artists themselves chose their subjects and had a free hand in interpreting them, a freedom Tennyson regretted in the case of Rossetti. At one point Rossetti exclaimed, "T[ennyson] loathes mine [i.e. my designs]."[12] The artist's brother, William Michael, explained Tennyson's "loathing" in this way: "It must be said that himself [Dante Rossetti] only, and not Tennyson, was his guide. He drew just what he chose, taking from his author's text nothing more than a hint and an opportunity. The illustration of St. Cecilia puzzled Tennyson not a little, and he had to give up the problem of what it had to do with his verses."[13] Dante Rossetti's own testimony is even more clear: he wanted, he said, to choose subjects such as "The Vision of Sin" and "The Palace of Art" — "those where one can allegorize on one's own hook on the subject of the poem, without killing for oneself and every one a distinct idea of the poet's."[14] But, by the time the lackadaisical Rossetti got to work, he found his favorite subjects already taken.

Only Millais of the three Pre-Raphaelites stuck close to the text with his designs, which may explain Tennyson's preference for his work over Rossetti's and Hunt's. As early as 1850, long before Tennyson and Moxon planned such an edition, Tennyson had said, when he had seen some of Millais's illustrations for poetry, "I wish he would do something for me."[15] Before Millais went to Farringford to sketch Hallam as a model, he wrote to Tennyson, "[I have] some questions I wish to ask you about the poems I am to illustrate." That he would seek the author's interpretation separates him at once from Rossetti, who sought none but his own. Fifteen years later Tennyson still thought so well of Millais's work that he asked him to do illustrations for a volume of songs, an offer Millais refused owing to other work pressing.[16]

The engravers for the *Illustrated Edition* were some of the best available in England and ones Moxon had used before — the Dalziels, W. J. Linton, T. Williams, and John Thompson.[17] Up to about 1850, the engraver's hand was pre-eminent in the production of book illustrations, with the artist supplying only the basic idea. But then artists such as Rossetti and Millais insisted on drawing right on the wood block itself, leaving the engraver simply the task of cutting the lines in. For the Tennyson book, both methods were used: some artists drew on paper and had the engraver transfer the idea to the block; others, in the newer style, drew directly onto the wood themselves. In the latter case the originals were necessarily and irrevocably lost in the process itself, so it is difficult now to see how well the engraver preserved the flavor of the drawing.[18]

Rossetti complained, "I find the work of drawing on wood particularly trying to the eyes," yet this physical difficulty was not Rossetti's only distress: the engravers exasperated him. To Allingham, in a letter postmarked 18 December 1856, he wrote,

> But these engravers! What ministers of wrath! Your drawing comes to them, like Agag, delicately, and is hewn in pieces before the Lord Harry. I took more pains with one block lately than I had with anything for a long while. It came back to me on paper, the other day, with Dalziel performing his cannibal jig in the corner, and I have really felt like an invalid ever since. As yet, I fare best with W. J. Linton. He keeps stomache aches for you, but Dalziel deals in fevers and agues.[19]

Rossetti, who dawdled, was also complained about; at one point he caused Moxon to apply to another artist, Ford Madox Brown, to do one of the subjects which Rossetti had failed to complete, and that one, "The Vision of Sin," was a subject he had particularly favored! Also, "In 1856 Moxon visited Holman Hunt 'with many repinings that the book was so long delayed' and 'a sore heart about Rossetti, who having promised, had not sent any drawing, and now, when Moxon called, was "not at home."' Hunt undertook to speed Rossetti up."[20]

In addition to being late with his own designs, Rossetti added further delay by his fussiness over the engravers' work. His brother described him as "very fastidious, and therefore somewhat dilatory over his own share in these designs . . . he corrected, altered, protested, and sent back blocks to be amended. My brother was, no doubt, a difficult man with whom to carry on work in cooperation; having his own ideas, from which he was not to be moved."[21] Somehow, though, one would have expected Edward Moxon to have handled Rossetti more efficiently, since the artist's fastidiousness about wood blocks was like Tennyson's about proofs – and that fastidiousness Moxon had been dealing with successfully for twenty-five years.

These and other delays so plagued the *Illustrated Edition* that the pre-Christmas 1856 publication date was missed and a May book issued instead. In February Emily anticipated the slow sales which would result: she entered in her diary: "The illustrated edition will be a failure – and from the money point of view." No doubt these feelings were communicated to Moxon, for a letter from him to Emily that spring, before Tennyson's May visit to London, sounds quite defensive:

> I am sorry to hear that with few exceptions you would not care to have the illustrations at [*sic*] a gift. All I can say is that neither labour nor expense has been spared in the getting up of the book – the best artists have been employed, and for the designs and engraving alone I have paid upwards of £1500. The price of the book will be either 30/- or 31/6. Mr. Routledge it is true makes the price of his annual volumes a guinea, but your friends should bear in mind that he pays *nothing* for copyright.
> I shall be glad to see Mr. Tennyson.

Moxon had indeed spared no expense. "According to Holman Hunt the price to be paid for each drawing was £25, but Rossetti exacted the stipulation that 'he should be paid five pounds more than any other designer was receiving.'"[22] A list made up by Charles Moxon, the publisher's son, shows that the price for each engraving was £12 minimum, with Green receiving a whopping £42 for two designs. The paper, binding and printing, moreover, were the best to be had.

Moxon printed in the first edition 10,000 copies (as he had printed 10,000 of *Maud* in 1855). *In Memoriam*, on the other hand, had had an 1850 first edition of only 5000, so Moxon seems to have been increasingly confident of Tennyson's popularity. But, at one and a half guineas (31s.6d.), the book was too expensive for Tennyson's usual readers, who were used to paying five or six shillings per volume at most. Had it appeared at Christmas time the book might have done well as a gift book, but its deferred arrival in May made disappointing results almost inevitable. These poor sales may have been caused, too, by the diversity of the schools of art represented in it. One of the artists, Holman Hunt, "noted later that people who liked the work of the artists long established in favor felt that the pages of Pre-Raphaelite designs destroyed the attractiveness of the volume and the few who liked the latter 'would not give the price for the publication because there was so large a proportion of the contributors of a kind which they did not value.'"[23] Perhaps, too, the public was eager for new work from Tennyson — as the amazing sales of the *Idylls of the King* proved two years later — and found the old 1842 *Poems*, even with illustrations, unexciting, especially at a guinea and a half.

Before 18 July 1857, Moxon had sounded relatively sure about good sales, for he had written to Emily, "We have sold 1300 of the illustrated edition, which is I think a fair number to begin with." Yet that expectation quickly dwindled, for by 22 July 1857 Moxon had offered Tennyson a flat sum to relieve the poet

> from all further anxiety in regard to the book. . . . As the illustrated edition of your poems will I am afraid have a much slower sale than I expected, I beg to make you the following offer: —
> I am willing to give you for your interest in the edition the sum which I originally said I should be able to realize for you, namely £2,000. . . .

By making this offer, which Tennyson quickly accepted, Moxon was admitting he had made a mistake. And he had indeed. In 1863, only six years after publication, 5000 unsold copies were remaindered to Routledge, and we know that, of the other 5000, Moxon had actually sold only 2210.[24]

In June 1858, about a year after this disastrous venture, Edward Moxon died. With his death Tennyson lost not only a business associate of more than twenty-six years, but also a good friend with whom he had enjoyed innumerable London dinner parties and comradely smoking into the wee hours (apparently Moxon could stand Tennyson's vile-smelling, strong tobacco better than others could). Thereafter Tennyson entered into many years of unpleasant squabbling with Moxon & Co. These same years, paradoxically enough, also brought the Poet Laureate his greatest sales, with both the *Idylls of the King* (first series) and *Enoch Arden* far surpassing all expectations.

The publishing business after Edward Moxon's death was managed by Bradbury & Evans, Printers, the trustees of the will. Moxon's younger brother William, a prominent barrister, had some hand in it too, for it was he who precipitated the long haggling with Tennyson over the terms of a new written agreement which had been drawn up to replace the previous verbal one. Charles Weld, Emily's brother-in-law, was appointed by Tennyson to deal with Moxon; he found huge difficulties in this task, as he explained in a letter to Alfred on 27 October 1858:

[William Moxon] informed me that . . . the estate of the late Mr. Moxon had claims on you to the amount of £8886. 8. 4 – on my demanding how this could possibly be he proceeded to tell me that in consequence of *your* earnest solicitations his late brother had embarked in the unfortunate speculation of publishing an illustrated edition of your Poems of which he printed 10,000 copies and that 7790 copies remained unsold. . . .

Tennyson's ire over this announcement may be perceived from the note he rushed off to Bradbury & Evans on 29 October 1858: "After my weary waiting for months & rejecting splendid offers from first-rate publishers because I chose to stick by the house of Moxon, I am treated at last discourteously & untruthfully by W. Moxon. . . . I decline entering into any business till all this is explained & apologized for. . . ." (The "first-rate publishers" to whom Tennyson referred were Macmillan, Chapman, and Smith.)

In reply, Bradbury & Evans, according to Sir Charles, "Urged that [Tennyson's] works were the keystone of the arch of the Moxon business."[25] Their dependence on Tennyson, his many years of friendship with Edward Moxon, and his growing concern for the possible financial straits of Emma, Moxon's widow, to whom he had made a present of £1500 or more and was now anonymously giving £300 a year, kept Tennyson from leaving the firm. (Tennyson was always reluctant to change publishers, because of his fear that the public might think him fickle.)²⁶

Another bone of contention between Tennyson and the Moxon firm was the illustrated edition of *The Princess* which the firm now wanted to produce. Alfred was so exercised about both these editions that, although he did not want to leave the firm, he had to draw up the following "Statement of facts," which Emily transmitted to John Forster on 31 October with the note, "Alfred desires that there should be a stop put to the illustrated edition of *The Princess* until something concerning it can be decided. I enclose a statement of facts respecting the illustrated editions. They must be taken as *mine* in which he as far as he remembers concurs."²⁷ (The statement given below is also in Emily's hand and was probably written shortly after 29 October 1858.)

A statement of facts respecting the Illustrated Edition of my poems. The Illustration of the Poems was entirely the late Mr. Moxon's own proposal on occasion of the encouragement given him to mrk. a publication by different book sellers with whom he had transactions respecting the Illustrated Edition of Keats (they would take 2000 but if they had [?] Tennyson they would have taken many more)

That I objected at first is implied by the promise of 2000 which is referred to in the letters & which he engaged to make for me by the Illustrated Edition within a short time, I think, three years. When I had once consented to the thing being done I on many accounts urged its speedy completion & for Moxon's sake I am heartily sorry if the speculations have proved a failure. That I accepted the 2000 in lieu of the much larger sum I had reason to expect proves that I was not greedy of gain. [On an inserted page Tennyson himself adds: "My banking book proves that I accepted the 2000 for the Illustrated Edition according to the arrangement in Edward Moxon's letter. The absence of any notice of the Edition in my Christmas bill confirms this. William Moxon paid the last installment of the 2,000 himself. I gave him a stampt receipt."]

As to the Princess, I was one day astonished by hearing that Maclise was in Italy or had been in Italy (I forget which) making drawings for an Illustrated Edition. Having to the best of my belief never had a word with Moxon on the subject except that he once said in a casual manner "We must get Maclise to illustrate the Princess" to which I as casually answered "Oh ho" & thought no more about it — until the news of Maclise came. Neither did Mr. Forster communicate with me on the subject.

Not long before Moxon's death I through my wife remonstrated and suggested that the Illustrations might be published separately. This is the first I have seen of the Illustrations. [The inserted page then has this note of Emily's: "Alfred is certain he never agreed to the Princess unless it were by silence.

I will of course copy anything answer anything do anything I can to lessen your trouble dear Mr. Forster. Between ourselves I will even come up to Burlington House alone if it would be desirable to question me personally."]

Because the firm had already invested so much in *The Princess* venture, Tennyson capitulated and allowed that illustrated edition to be published. But on the charges made against him for the *Illustrated Edition* of the *Poems* he remained adamant. It took several weeks of lengthy correspondence and even legal opinion before the fallacious claim of £8886 8s. 4d. was withdrawn and the Tennysons became willing to enter into a new agreement with Moxons & Co. Tennyson ultimately emerged with a formal apology from Charles Moxon (the eldest son of Edward) and a new contract, which gave the firm only 10 per cent on books sold. Since Edward Moxon had usually taken a full third of the profits plus 5 per cent of the gross amount of sales, Tennyson was clearly the victor over the heirs in this battle, which was to be a prelude to later skirmishes with Moxon & Co. (The 5000 copies of the *Illustrated Edition* remaindered by Routledge Warne and Routledge in 1863 at a guinea a volume brought Tennyson a royalty of four shillings per copy, for a further income for him of £923 4s. 0d. on the original Moxon edition. Routledge in 1865 issued a new impression of 5000, giving Tennyson again the same royalty. And the same again in 1869. All in all, then, Tennyson made a total £4769 12s. 0d. on the *Illustrated Edition* — not a bad sum, even considering all the trouble it cost him.[28])

In spite of the awkward beginning, the five years under the management of Bradbury & Evans were otherwise smooth and prosperous. The first Tennyson publication under the new imprint, "Edwrd Moxon & Co., Dover Street," was a startling success: in July 1859, *Idylls of the King*, consisting of "Enid," "Vivien," "Elaine" and

"Guinevere," "appeared on the familiar green Boards, at 7 /-, and no less than 40,000 copies were printed and 10,000 sold in 6 weeks. Indeed, so great was the demand that a second edition had to be issued within six months."[29] Moxon & Co. issued six more editions before the 1869 second series of *Idylls*. Emily Tennyson's handwritten list of income from the *Idylls* shows payments averaging over £2300 a year for the first five years. No doubt this success, coming after anxiety over the *Illustrated Edition*, buoyed up the flagging spirits, not to mention the flattened pocketbooks, of both poet and publisher alike.

Tennyson must have been elated to find that his reshaping of the Arthurian legend, "a kind of literary second coming of Arthur, a resurrection in Victorian England of the long sequence of Arthuriads extending back before Malory and forward through Spenser, Dryden, [and] Scott" met with such popularity.[30] Yet being successful with the reading public did not mean sacrificing his own aesthetic judgment, for Tennyson had found a means whereby he could contribute to the popular culture while still standing outside of it, sometimes as judge, often as commentator, always as insightful poet. In the *Idylls of the King* he created a poem which in itself evolves truth and which demonstrates the confusion of illusion and reality. He allowed no one idyll, no one person's point of view, no one person's story to predominate. Reading the *Idylls* as a continuous whole is an experience in the epistemological process, for, as Rosenberg observes,

> The *Idylls of the King* is not only explicitly and constantly *about* the hazards of mistaking illusion for reality; it *dramatically enacts* those dangers, ensnaring the reader in the same delusions that maim and destroy its characters. Nothing in the poem is as it seems, and nothing seems to be what it is, with the possible exception of Arthur, who may himself be the most dangerous of illusions, the *homme fatal* of the *Idylls*. One passes through hundreds of lines of some of the most beautiful blank verse in English, green glades and shimmering towers, knights and maidens displayed in a rainbow pageant of music and color; yet the verse, fair as it is, at once unfolds and conceals a world of the rankest treacheries and vilest horrors: brothers murder one another, sadistic ladies drive their obsessed lovers impotent and insane, the King himself is a cuckold, and the faces of his traitor-knights are ground into featureless slime. The verse lulls and seduces at the same time that the events appall; grotesque sights entwine themselves upon a back[g]round of

excruciating clarity and beauty. . . . Tennyson forces his reader to a dramatic recognition that he has mistaken fair for foul, foul for fair, indeed that it is the human condition inevitably so to err, and perhaps most to err when most seeking to avoid such error. Holding a mirror up to itself, the poem is nowhere what it seems to be – a medieval charade – but rather the subtlest anatomy of the failure of ideality in our literature.[31]

Tennyson's first audience, however, was unable to realize this subtlety.

The *Idylls of the King*, complete and in the sequence in which we read it now, did not appear for Tennyson's readers until 1891. Such fragmentary composition and publication, from the "Morte d'Arthur" in 1833 to a final line about Arthur added fifty-eight years later, confused those who sensed that Tennyson had some great plan in mind but who, through no fault of their own, could not see its shape, because of its piecemeal delivery to them. The "idyll" form itself proved puzzling to an audience which was used to neatly pigeonholing works as "epic" or "allegory" or "drama." Up to and including our own day, the position of the poem in relation to traditional genres and the extent of its dependence on previous tellings of the tale have been elusive – and for good reason. As Rosenberg points out,

> Like every great long poem, the *Idylls* draws on traditional forms and *is itself a new genre* [emphasis added]. Shakespeare had Seneca and Marlowe; Milton had Homer; but tragedy and epic radically redefine themselves in their works. Tennyson bears this same innovative relation to tradition, but we have yet to assimilate into our literature this poem which is at once epic and lyric, narrative and drama, tragedy and romance. Our difficulty with Tennyson's "medieval charade" is not its derivativeness but its novelty.[32]

It may be that eventually readers will value the *Idylls of the King* as a great symbolist vision, "a journey through the dark night, ending on the uninhabited verge of the world, where Arthur's kingdom meets its apocalyptic doom in the 'last, dim, weird battle of the west,' " but the fact remains that for its original audience the poem seemed a comforting return to the certitudes of the Middle Ages.[33] Reviewers of Tennyson's day concerned themselves, therefore, with the standard questions applied to narrative: characterization and dramatic power. A sample serves to illustrate the variance in their evaluation. Two well-known writers, Walter Bagehot and W. E. Gladstone, published reviews in October 1859 in the *National Review* and the *Quarterly Review*, respectively. Whereas Bagehot observed, "It appears to us that the Idylls are defective in dramatic power," for Gladstone, "The grand poetical quality in which this volume gives to its author a new rank and standing is the dramatic power: the power of drawing character and of representing action."[34] The evaluation of ordinary readers must have been close to Gladstone's, for, as we have seen, they flocked to buy copies of the first four *Idylls* published by Moxon & Co.

In these years, too, Moxon & Co. brought out numerous new editions and reprints of Tennyson's old volumes: *Maud, In Memoriam, The Princess* and *Poems*. To top it off, *Enoch Arden, Etc.*, published in August 1864, sold 17,000 on the day of publication, 40,000 by November and the whole first impression of 60,000 by the end of the year. Tennyson's half-yearly payment from Moxon for *Enoch Arden* in January 1865 was £6664 4s. 2d., with £1400 17s. 8d. more coming in June 1865. Such huge sales and profits reflected the public's appreciation of Tennyson's handling of a theme current in both non-respectable "sensation novels" and respectable fiction, ballads, and melodrama: the bigamous marriage. Tennyson's own reading of popular fiction by Miss Braddon, Mrs Oliphant, Rhoda Broughton and Ouida, and his attending the popular melodramas of his day probably contributed to his use of what P. G. Scott identifies as "the common narrative tradition," that is, set-pieces, shared moral sentiments, and dramatic irony. But Tennyson employed these standard techniques with greater power and artistic skill than was typical.[35]

Most reviewers shared the public's appreciation of the poem, so much so, in fact, that modern readers become uneasy over the praise they lavished upon it. What are we to make of a comment such as "There is no nobler tale of true love than this," or "No other of his poems can reach above it"? Even Tennyson's fellow poets lauded *Enoch Arden* in a similar vein: Browning called it "A perfect thing" and Swinburne considered it "a new triumph worth any of the old."[36] The only dissonant note in the chorus of praise was sounded by those who questioned the morality of the poem. Out of its Wesleyanism the *London Quarterly Review*, for example, saw fit to moan, "It is a pity that the poet has left [Phillip and Annie] committed to that form of bigamy of which Miss Braddon's heroines are so fond, but here rendered more mischievous by the actors being portrayed as innocent, and protected by the silver shield of a great poet."[37] *The Times*, the *Athenaeum* and the *British Quarterly Review* shared these sentiments. Our age, of course, has no problem with the bigamous marriage in *Enoch Arden*, but rather finds the poem's sentimentality often oppressive and fails to identify with the "strong, heroic soul" who sacrificed his own happiness for those he loved.

A new edition of *Enoch Arden* appeared in 1866 with drawings by Arthur Hughes. Two recorded comments by Tennyson, one uttered in public at Payne's house after Alfred first looked at the proofs of the drawings, and one written in private indicate that Tennyson still found illustrations to his poems, even when relatively close to the text, as Hughes's were, annoying. Of one proof he said, "This is not right. 'There came so loud a calling of the sea.' The man cannot have lived by the sea; he does not know what a 'calling' means. It is anything but a great upheaval such as is here represented." To his wife he wrote, "I met Joseph Hooker who told me my tropical island was all right; but Arthur Hughes in his illustrations has made it all wrong, putting a herd of antelopes upon it, which never occurs in Polynesia."[38]

The next year, Gustave Doré having finished his illustrations to *La Fontaine* and turned his eye and hand towards Tennyson, although he could read the poems only in translation, Moxon & Co. began publishing folio editions of his steel engravings illustrating the *Idylls of the King*. By Christmas 1867 the "Vivien" and "Guinevere" volumes had reached the public. Although errors of proportion and detail abounded, probably as a result of Doré's quick production of the drawings, these Romantic illustrations captured for much of the nineteenth-century audience the essential mood of the *Idylls*. Sales were excellent. Though priced at one, three and five guineas, these were "the books most looked for in each year of their issue."[39]

All these successes added to Tennyson's income so substantially that he was at last able to boast to his friend William Allingham, "My whole living is from the sale of my books"[40] — momentarily forgetting his continuing Civil List pension and Laureate's salary. That Tennyson was content with this income is easily demonstrated: in 1861 he refused an offer of £3000 for an all-expenses-paid reading — lecturing tour of America; and in 1863 he refused a £10,000 offer for the same. No matter whether his refusal stemmed from his abhorrence of public demonstrations of himself or of the American spirit of enterprise, I doubt that Tennyson, had he needed or even wanted more money for his family, would have refused such offers.

Between 1859 and 1864, then, at least from the records I have seen, Tennyson had no financial difficulty with the Moxon house under the management of Bradbury & Evans. But "in 1864," as Harold Merriam explains in his biography of Edward Moxon, "Mrs. Moxon appointed as manager of the business, at a salary of £400 J. Bertrand Payne, who, for several years, had been a clerk in the employment of the firm. Soon she and her son Arthur, who had taken a share in the business, made Payne a partner and assigned to him a share in many of the company's copyrights."[41]

Tennyson's first publishing venture under Payne's aegis brought renewed conflict because of the manager's abrasive business tactics. In the late summer of 1864, Tennyson, as Sir Charles puts it, "settled down to carry out a scheme suggested to him by the success of *Enoch Arden* and the title 'Poet of the People,' which some of the reviewers had given him. He made up his mind to issue a selection of the more popular of his poems in sixpenny parts, hoping that these would reach the working men of England, to whom he dedicated the selections."[42] But for Payne a cheap paper series was not lucrative enough. Therefore a one-volume, five-shilling edition called *A Selection from the Works of Alfred Tennyson* in Moxon's Miniature Poets series was issued in 1865. Though the *Selections* brought Tennyson *in toto* £2210 4s. 2d. in 1865 and over £3500 in 1866, the project rankled with him, for he had been "persuaded, against his will, to issue the volume in a more ornamental style than his severe taste generally admitted."[43]

The strain between Payne and Tennyson increased in 1867, because of the firm's "uncertain financial condition." Tennyson wrote indignantly,

> I did not choose to bother you, but when it came to a rumour that your house had actually failed I considered that my best and handsomest course was to apply directly to yourself – seeing that I had stuck to the house of Moxon from the beginning thro' evil report and good report, and *really have been and am the main pillar of it*, it seems to me – that I should be fully informed of the state of affairs.[44]

Tennyson, incidentally, was right to be worried, though the news of the Moxon demise was premature – the firm did not actually collapse until a year or so later.

Other annoyances in 1867 are suggested by one of the few letters extant from Tennyson to Payne (the poet had been upset about the manager's error in his last account and further disturbed that Payne had misinterpreted Tennyson's previous note about it):

> You draw your own inferences from what I say & wrong ones. I never accused you of trying to overreach me. I merely asked a question or two — growlingly, perhaps. Certainly the £74–2 inserted as omitted, without a word of apology or explanation seemed to be a liberty; & you must recollect that in the accts of your house some few years ago there was an absolute error to a much greater amount. Which proves that you are not always so accurate as you suppose. . . .

A postscript to this 17 April 1867 letter introduces yet another area of contention: Tennyson had himself sued for breach of copyright and collected from some Glasgow booksellers £500 in damages. But "soon afterwards he discovered that Moxons, without his permission or knowledge, had been launching other actions and had recovered £75 from the Religious Tract Society, who had, without any wrong intention, reprinted one of his poems."[45] Tennyson addresses himself in his postscript to this: "I said nothing in my last about arrangements with individuals respecting the poems. I merely said that I could not accept anything from God nor I think can I directly or indirectly."

To some extent because of these annoyances with his publisher, during the winter and spring of 1868 Tennyson once again offered some poetry to periodicals. In January "The Spiteful Letter" appeared in *Once a Week* and "The Victim" in *Good Words*; "Wages" was printed in February in *Macmillan's Magazine*; "1865–1866" made the pages of *Good Words* in March; and in May "Lucretius," in its bowdlerized version, reached the English audience through *Macmillan's Magazine*, and, in its full version, the American audience through Ticknor & Fields's *Every Saturday*.[46] Though *Good Words* paid Tennyson £700 for "The Victim," only seventy-nine lines long, Emily Tennyson discouraged Tennyson from further periodical publication. On 20 November 1868 she wrote to him from Farringford:

> Pray do not let the poems go into "Good Words." As to people having no reason to complain if they were, there I differ, for part of the object of those who have the other poems would of course be to

have these as a volume in the series. And when it is taken into consideration that *Enoch Arden* in one year brought in about £6,000 it is perfectly absurd to think of £700. . . . Make a stand at once; it may save future trouble. Do thou not think so? Put it on me if thou wilt, for I do entirely object not only on these grounds but on the ground of the unpleasant position it puts thee in with regard to other magazines. There is now for instance an entreaty from Dallas through Mrs. Cameron. He says he will give anything asked by thee for "Property" for *Once a Week* this Christmas. . . .
Better give the poems to the edition allowing the single volume a start than let them go into *Good Words* in a money point of view. But I don't suppose it is in this point of view one so liberal as Chatham regards them. It is probably only as a tribute to his own fondling.[47]

Other reasons for Tennyson's periodical publication of these poems are offered by Leonard M. Findlay in his paper "Swinburne and Tennyson": "Tennyson felt the urge to go before the public as soon as possible after 1866 [publication of Swinburne's *Poems and Ballads*], both to remind them that he was still an active and accomplished poet, and to register his disgust with Swinburne."[48] Swinburne himself apparently felt wounded by what he considered to be intended barbs in these poems, for he forcefully suggested to Lord Houghton, "Cannot you, as a friend of Mr. Tennyson, prevent his making such a hideous exhibition of himself as he has been doing for the last three months? I thought there was a law against 'indecent exposure'?"[49] Findlay's point is well taken: at this point in his career, Tennyson may have added worries about increasing competition from Swinburne to his burden of worries about what his own publisher was doing.

Tennyson's exasperation with Payne reached its peak over the advertising done in 1868 for the Standard Edition in four volumes. This edition had been announced publicly before Tennyson had even agreed to its publication – and the advertisements implied a "newness" which was not there. Such dishonesty towards the public distressed the Tennysons no end. On 6 March Emily lamented in her journal, "We are sorely troubled by Mr. Payne's advertisement of a new edition, we don't know how to divide the poems into 4 volumes & there are not many new poems & the whole affair is hateful. Ally will have to go to town to consult his friends about it." And on 10 March she wrote a lengthy journal note suggesting counter-action:

The exceeding annoyance has made us both ill & wretched at times. What I do really care for is that my Ally should stand before the world in his own child-like simplicity & by this he would be made to appear a mere cunning tradesman. He hates it all as much as I do – only he does not see the consequences as clearly perhaps not having turned his mind to the subject. The first thing is to insist that there shall be no new bargain, so that this edition shall go in the old plain sailing fashion. The next [is] that we must insist on a little volume of the new poems in the same type as the old, for those who have the old edition. Mr. Pollock thinks that even from the money point of view it is a bad bargain. Mr. Payne it seems has pledged himself so far to paper makers [and] printers so that he cannot draw back.

Tennyson himself penned his annoyance to his friend Alexander Macmillan: "Payne has put me into a great perplexity by advertising the Standard Edition in his tremendous style – before any agreement was signed & before I had made up my mind as to whether I would have one at all. I expect now that if I do not publish this edition (and I have little desire to do it) the sales of the old one will fall off in expectation of this." Tennyson was not persuaded, however, and the Standard Edition was never published. But in this complaint one can sense Tennyson's exploration of what other publishers' ideas on advertising were, for Macmillan, though a friend, was pre-eminently a publisher. Tennyson was beginning, in other words, to look for Moxon & Co.'s successor. And by the start of the new year he had indeed made his move. On 15 January 1869 Emily recorded, "Today the Moxon connection of 37 years ceased. A. however anonymously still allows the widow (Mrs. Moxon) and her daughters a considerable sum a year. We would that the necessity for leaving had not arisen."[50]
The Tennyson copyright went to Alexander Strahan,

after a discussion at Farringford lasting till four in the morning . . . [He] offered £5,000 a year for five years. New works he offered to publish for nothing, but Alfred would not agree to this, and a commission of ten per cent was fixed. Alfred was rather staggered by the £5,000 offer, and told Strahan that he could not possibly make a profit on it. However, the publisher stuck to his point, and the bargain was struck to the satisfaction of both parties.[51]

(Macmillan had offered only £3000 for the old works and thus lost out once more. He did finally get the copyright in 1884.)

While Strahan was jubilantly celebrating his victory, rumor has it, J. Bertrand Payne, in addition to arranging for hostile attacks in the press and perhaps writing one himself for *The Queen's Messenger*, affixed a pair of ass's ears to the portrait of Tennyson which hung in the Moxon headquarters in Dover Street. Tennyson, we can be sure, had *he* owned a portrait of Payne, would have returned the favor.

In 1871 Ward, Lock and Tyler bought Moxons, paying creditors fifteen shillings in the pound.[52] Earlier predictions had been right: once their so-called "keystone" withdrew, the Moxon publishing arch fell.

5 Successors:
Strahan, King, and
Kegan Paul (1869—83)

I ALEXANDER STRAHAN (1869—73)

"In 1869 Strahan rushed into [William] Tinsley's office 'all excitement because he had signed an agreement with Tennyson to publish his books for a certain number of years, and boasted he had gained the blue ribbon of the publishing trade.'"[1] The terms, however, were so heavily in the poet's favor that Tinsley, a friend of Strahan's, failed to share the publisher's excitement: "If any future relation or descendent of Lord Tennyson ever imagines that his poet relation was not well paid for his work, and could not guard his own monetary interest in his books, let him beg of more than one publisher to show him how shrewd the poet was."[2] Tinsley, writing after he had seen Strahan's financial difficulties in the early 1870s, no doubt attributed his friend's losses to the high royalty paid Tennyson, but in fact no evidence exists to suggest that the Tennyson agreement was in any way the cause of those difficulties. Exactly the opposite seems to have been true. The sales of Tennyson's old and new books were astonishingly good, with at least one reliable source recording that "Strahan made a profit on the £5,000 contract."[3] (After Strahan had recouped the yearly £5,000 paid Tennyson for the old copyrights, full profits from sales of the old books went to the publisher. We have no records of those profits, but they were undoubtedly substantial, inasmuch as Tennyson's popularity was enormous. We can estimate, moreover, profits for a new book — the *Holy Grail* volume. On a sale of 40,000, at seven shillings a copy, Strahan would have received £1400 in commission on gross sales. Tennyson would have received about three shillings a copy after paying all costs of publication and Strahan's commission, giving him a total of £6000. (And, in fact, in Tennyson's receipts record appear three entries for the *Holy Grail* in 1870: £5000, £837 and £367 — total £6204.)

Alexander Strahan's relationship with Tennyson began under both the auspices and roof of James Knowles, in November 1868. Knowles himself had entered the Tennyson circle half a year before, when he took charge of the architecture of the Tennysons' new home, Aldworth, on Blackdown, Sussex. Knowles's architectural work pleased the family very much, even down to the luxurious novelty of a hot bath. "Tennyson, we are told, would at first take it four or five times a day, conceiving in the rapture of the new experience no higher pleasure in life than 'to sit in a hot bath and read about little birds.'"[4] But designing houses with baths was not Knowles's only forte. According to Emily Tennyson, Knowles's "active nature . . . spur[red] A. on to work when he [was] flagging." Thus, Knowles joined the list of friends which began with Arthur Hallam and included Edward Moxon, friends who persuaded the poet to produce. Tennyson himself once "pointed his finger at Knowles and with a grim smile said, 'I was often urged to go on with the *Idylls*, but I stuck; and then this beast said, "Do it," and I did it.'" Beyond this, Knowles actively encouraged Tennyson to publish with Alexander Strahan. Knowles's enthusiasm for Strahan's publishing was based on personal experience, for his own book *Legends of King Arthur* was then on Strahan's list.[5]

The mid-November to mid-December 1868 visit of Tennyson at Knowles's house in Clapham included conversation with F. D. Maurice, Tennyson's old friend from Apostle days and his son Hallam's godfather. It was actually Maurice who introduced Strahan to the poet. The time was propitious for such an introduction, for the dispute with Moxon & Co. had come to a head, and Tennyson had some new publishing projects on his mind. He read "The Holy Grail" twice to assembled guests, the usual benchmark on the road to publication, and he also wrote to his wife telling her he had sent "the whole of *The Lover's Tale* to the press."[6] Most of the Clapham conversation, however, centered on Knowles's idea of a Theological Society for discussion of "the speculative aspects of morality and the theological questions of the day." The agreement of Charles Pritchard, the man of science, and Tennyson, the man of letters, encouraged the energetic Knowles. Soon Dean Arthur Stanley of Westminster, Dean Henry Alford of Canterbury, Archbishop Henry Manning, the Rev. James Mortimer Ellicott, the Bishop of Gloucester and Bristol, Dr W. G. Ward, R. H. Hutton, and others joined forces to found the Metaphysical Society, the wider name having been suggested by Dean Stanley to aid in bridging the gap between religious and scientific thinkers. Ten of the sixty-two eventual members were editors of reviews, and two of them, Alford and then Knowles, edited Alexander Strahan's own *Contemporary Review*. The *Contemporary*, begun by Strahan in 1866, represented in general the Broad Church position, but it was never parochial. Neither, however, was it really belletristic, for the only names of literary note to appear on its pages were Tennyson himself (once, with "The Last Tournament" in 1871), Walter Besant, Augustine Birrell, John Newman and Edmund Gosse. The main emphasis seems to have been on social reform, which placed it firmly in the liberal tradition. The following titles appearing in the 1870 *Contemporary Review* suggest its scope: "The Science of Morals"; "Mr. Mill on the Subjection of Women"; "The Church and the Age"; "Mendelssohn's 'Elijah': A Study"; and "Dr. Pusey and the Ultra-Montanes." Under Knowles's editorship, 1870–7, the journal moved into increasingly rarified liberal positions, which ultimately caused Strahan, its publisher, and some new owners, described as "a group of sectarian nonconformists," to come into acrimonious dispute with the editor.[7] In 1877, therefore, Knowles left to found his own review, the *Nineteenth Century*, which was to feature poetry and articles of a more general nature. We have no comments in Tennyson's letters or Emily's Journal about this split between Strahan and Knowles, a division otherwise written about and discussed widely in intellectual circles, yet, when Knowles asked him to do so, Tennyson did write a sonnet which was published without title in the first number of the *Nineteenth Century*, March 1877. In it the Metaphysical Society members, "our true co-mates," were seen "leaving to the skill /of others their old craft seaworthy still [the *Contemporary Review*]." They embarked on a new vessel (the *Nineteenth Century*) "to put forth and brave the blast." But they were joined by some

> wilder comrades, sworn to seek
> If any golden harbour be for men
> In seas of Death and sunless gulfs of Doubt.[8]

Thus, by combining the two groups, Tennyson took a moderating position between the otherwise rival camps.

Alexander Strahan's piety led him into conflict with the open-minded Knowles, but it also led him, oddly enough, into a likemindedness with Tennyson on the matter of providing relatively cheap editions for the masses. Strahan firmly believed that the masses needed strong literature to wean them from vapid reading matter. "Such literature," he said he himself wanted to supply, "as will not ignobly interest nor frivolously amuse, but convey the wisest instruction in the pleasantest manner." To carry out these intentions, Strahan founded and published a series of magazines: *Good Words, Sunday Magazine, Good Words for the Young*, and the *Argosy*, in addition to the *Contemporary*. The benevolence behind these ventures is evident in an article Strahan wrote for the *Contemporary Review* in 1870. He began by proposing to review some "very cheap literature, purchased at random, with names such as *Ferret, Every Week, Life and Fashion*, and *The Novel Reader*."⁹ Strahan declared them to be rubbish, and asked, "Looking back even upon the best portions of the periodicals we had waded through, we cannot help asking ourselves what good can they do to anybody?" He decided, sensibly enough, that the working people read such drivel only because they had nothing else within their means and managed to derive a modicum of pleasure from it.

> If then, we would generate a taste for reading, we must, as our only chance of success, begin by pleasing. . . . Furnish the people liberally with literature – not written expressly for them as a class, but for all alike – and that the best of its kind. [They will want more.] . . . We shall find that in the writings of our best authors we possess all we require to strike our grappling-iron into the working people's soul, and chain them, willing followers, to the car of advancing civilization.

Whatever those painfully dragged by "advancing civilization" might think of it, Strahan, in his zealotry, was convinced that "no publisher could enter on a more glorious work" than to publish for the proletariat. However, this interloper of socialism was met by the publishing tribe with great suspicion which stemmed from a very reasonable fear of bankruptcy, as witnessed by the following account:

> Hanging over the publishing profession in particular was the traumatic example of Constable. And Constable, it was re-membered, had dreamed of bringing fiction to the millions. Again and again in literary and publishing circles one comes across a fear of cheap literature because it is thought that it will somehow release forces which will be beyond the trade's control: "our cheap literature," wrote Lever in a letter, "and our copious [?] writing –

like our low priced cottons and our cheap pen knives – will ultimately disparage our wares, both at home and abroad." In this the publishing trade's apprehensions were rather like those of otherwise liberal politicians of the age who feared universal suffrage – these were the edged tools that wise men did not give away too lightly.[10]

Strahan suffered from no such fear and neither did Tennyson, who himself had actively sought to provide cheaper editions of his poems, editions suitable for a "Poet of the People." Tennyson's plans with Strahan included a one-volume edition, the first "collected edition," at a moderate price. (As his business began to falter, Strahan could not fulfill this project himself, so he passed it on to Henry S. King, Tennyson's next publisher, who also delayed on it, and finally passed it on to Kegan Paul. The edition was issued in 1878.) This bond apparently cemented the poet's halcyon relationship with Strahan, which is never described as anything but personally pleasant and economically successful by both Alfred and Emily. Strahan himself, from the shadowy glimpses which emerge from the thickets of publishing histories such as Mumby's, was appealing. "With all his unbusinesslike habits," Mumby writes, "Strahan seems to have been a lovable character. Although somewhat reserved he drew men by a fascination all his own. . . ."[11] Fascination, however, could not sustain the firm for long. Strahan's business foundered in 1872–3 for reasons which are generally unclear, although Mumby hints at too rapid expansion as a possible cause: "Sanguine and buoyant to a degree," he writes of Strahan, "he never seemed to fear any exhaustion of resources."[12] Another contributing factor may have been a certain fecklessness towards the less lofty details of business, indicated by the fact that it was found necessary for Tennyson's solicitors, White, Broughton and White, to write to Strahan in 1870 reminding him of the exact amount he owed Tennyson.

Unbusinesslike though he may have been, Alexander Strahan published Tennyson's two important additions to the first four *Idylls of the King*, which had appeared in 1859: *The Holy Grail and Other Poems* (December 1869) and *Gareth and Lynette, Etc.* (December 1872), both of which took advantage of the Christmas season by selling very well.

Almost everyone Tennyson knew, including the enterprising publisher George Smith, had been trying for ten years to persuade him to publish more *Idylls*. Smith, as Mumby puts it, made "a record offer for English poetry up to that time," one which the publisher himself described as "extravagant."[13] Tennyson himself was not moved, as the following description of Smith's visit makes abundantly clear:

> Shortly after the appearance of the [1859] book, George Smith went down to Farringford and offered the poet five thousand guineas for another volume of "Idylls" of the same length as the first, Smith, Elder & Co. to have the right of publication for 3 years, with liberty to print in the Cornhill. Tennyson made no comment on this suggestion, but sat on smoking and chatting quite unmoved. Shortly afterwards his wife came into the room, whereupon he said to her, "My dear, we are much richer than we thought." He then told her of the offer made and continued "Of course if Mr. Smith offers me 5,000 guineas for the book, it is worth 10,000."
>
> Probably Tennyson was annoyed with Smith for trying to take him away from the firm with which he was under contract. In any case, [Tennyson's] estimate of the value of the book was a sound one. . . .[14]

Actually, Tennyson waited for ten more years before giving more *Idylls* to the public. During the 1868 stay at Knowles's house, when the Metaphysical Society was formed and the agreement reached with Strahan, Tennyson, as mentioned before, read "The Holy Grail" aloud several times to get his friends' opinions. They, too, encouraged him to bring out another section of "his projected scheme," but, although Tennyson did have Strahan print up a trial edition, he waited still another year before publication.[15] (Tennyson always worried about the trial editions getting into the wrong hands. In late December 1868, for example, he wrote to Francis Palgrave chiding him for passing on a copy of this latest *Idyll* to a friend.[16] When we consider the use Richard H. Shepherd and, later, Thomas J. Wise made of some of these trial editions, passing them off as fugitive first editions, Tennyson's fears appear particularly well grounded.)

In September 1869 Emily Tennyson read in sequence all eight *Idylls*: "The Coming of Arthur," "Enid," "Merlin and Vivien," "Lancelot and Elaine," "The Holy Grail," "Pelleas and Ettarre," "Guinevere" and "The Passing of Arthur." Once his wife's reading was completed, Tennyson was finally able to send the poems to press. This coincided with the usual pattern: (1) his friends heard him read

the poems; (2) his publisher produced a trial edition so the poet could
see the poems in print and spend the next year or so tinkering with
them; (3) Emily read the poems and called them good; (4) the poems
were published.

In time for the gift-book trade at Christmas time, Strahan
published *The Holy Grail and Other Poems* (December 1869, with title
page dated 1870), a volume which included, besides the title *Idyll*,
"The Coming of Arthur," "Pelleas and Ettarre" and "The Passing of
Arthur." These were subtitled for the first time "The Round Table."
In addition, a number of other poems were included, to flesh out
the volume: "The Victim," "Wages" and "Lucretius" (previously
printed in periodicals); a Lincolnshire dialect poem, "Northern
Farmer, New Style" (which became his most popular dialect poem);
"The Golden Supper," a blank verse sequel to "The Lover's Tale"
(then still unpublished); "Flower in the crannied wall"; and "The
Higher Pantheism" (which James Knowles had read at the first
meeting of the Metaphysical Society on 2 June 1869). A second
volume, containing all eight *Idylls* and entitled *Idylls of the King* (dated
1869), was published at the same time. This double publication
enabled Tennyson to attempt to satisfy both those who had copies of
the 1859 *Idylls* and wished only the new ones – and those who
wanted all eight together in one volume. In early November Emily
described this arrangement to her son Hallam and added that
"twenty-six thousand of this last volume [the new *Idylls*] are
bespoken, thirty-one of the other."[17] The *Holy Grail* volume
appeared in the usual green cloth boards and sold for seven shillings.
Tennyson received over £10,000 for it during 1870, far and away
his biggest yearly income to date.[18]

The critics received the new *Idylls* with almost as much enthusiasm
as the public. Two articles seemed to Tennyson the best. He
appreciated Dean Alford's essay in the *Contemporary Review*, which
refuted the argument offered earlier that year by Alfred Austin. (In
The Poetry of the Period Austin would not grant to Tennyson a place
even with third-rank poets, because he felt the poet had not
constructed a unified whole out of his Arthurian poems.) Tennyson's
other favorite, a letter to the *Spectator* (1 January 1870) by his friend
James Knowles, emphasized the increasing symbolism inherent
in these poems "shadowing Sense at war with Soul" ("To the
Queen," l. 37), "which, while it never interferes with the clear *melody*
of the poem, or perverts it into that most tedious of riddles a formal
allegory, gives a profound *harmony* to its music and a prophetic strain

to its intention most worthy of a great spiritual Bard."[19] Later, Tennyson, in reaction to excessive allegorizing about the *Idylls*, qualified his praise of Alford and Knowles's statements: "They have taken my hobby, and ridden it too hard, and have explained some things too allegorically, although there is an allegorical or perhaps rather a parabolic drift in the poem."[20] Further comments along these lines on the *Idylls* are among Tennyson's most significant critical statements:

> The Bishop of Ripon (Boyd Carpenter) once asked him whether they were right who interpreted the three Queens, who accompanied King Arthur on his last voyage, as Faith, Hope, and Charity. He answered: "They are right, and they are not right. They mean that and they do not. They are three of the noblest of women. They are also those three Graces, but they are much more. I hate to be tied down to say, '*This* means *that*,' because the thought within the image is much more than any one interpretation."
>
> As for the many meanings of the poem my father would affirm, "Poetry is like shot-silk with many glancing colours. Every reader must find his own interpretation according to his ability, and according to his sympathy with the poet."[21]

"By 'parabolic drift' and 'thought within the image,'" Rosenberg explains, "Tennyson means precisely what we [in the twentieth century] mean by *symbol*, the antithesis of the reductive, this-for-that equivalence which his commentators have found in the *Idylls*. The point is not that allegory is simplistic — a patent absurdity — but that the *Idylls* is not an allegory and that those who so read it are forced into simplistic conclusions."[22]

For the next installment of the *Idylls*, Tennyson took an unusual publication route: after his usual trial edition he published "The Last Tournament" in the December 1871 *Contemporary Review*, which Knowles was then editing for Strahan. Subsequently that *Idyll* was added to "Gareth and Lynette" and both published in the volume *Gareth and Lynette, Etc.* (December 1872). "That edition," explains John Pfordresher, "contained an explanatory paragraph which, in its proof state, indicated that these two poems concluded the *Idylls*. This was corrected before the book was published, but it indicates the possibility that Tennyson may not have been completely sure of the final shape of the poem, even at this late date." Other evidence suggests that he was already working on "Balin and Balan."

2. Emily Tennyson's handwritten list of semi-yearly income from *Idylls of the King, Enoch Arden* and *Selections*

1. Proof page of "Book-making" (later entitled "Poets and their Bibliographers"), showing Tennyson's extensive corrections, revisions and additions

4. "The Lady of Shalott" illustration by Dante Gabriel Rossetti for the *Illustrated Edition of Tennyson's Poems* (Moxon, 1857).

> *But Lancelot mused a little space;*
> *He said, 'She has a lovely face;*
> *God in his mercy lend her grace,*
> *The Lady of Shalott.'*

3. Alfred Tennyson's handwritten letter (17 April 1867) to J. Bertrand Payne, partner in Moxon & Co.

6. Alexander Macmillan, Tennyson's publisher from 1884 to 1892. From the photograph by O. G. Rejlander, taken between 1860 and 1870.

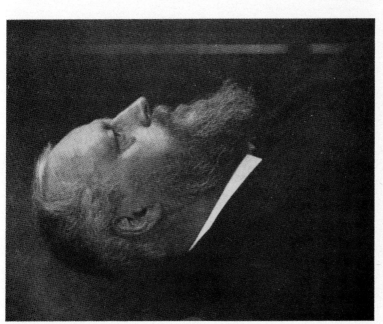

5. Charles Kegan Paul, Tennyson's publisher from 1879 to 1883.

7. Alfred Tennyson. From a photograph (1888) by Barraud's

8. Emily Tennyson with sons Hallam (left) and Lionel (right). From a photograph (circa 1864) by W. Jeffrey

9. Aldworth, Tennyson's home in Blackdown, Sussex. From a photograph (circa 1897) by Poulton & Son

THE HOLY GRAIL

And other Poems

By ALFRED TENNYSON, D.C.L.

POET LAUREATE

"Flos Regum Arthurus."
JOSEPH OF EXETER

STRAHAN AND CO., PUBLISHERS
56 LUDGATE HILL, LONDON
1869

11. Title page to trial copy of *The Holy Grail and Other Poems* (Strahan, 1869)

10. "Merlin and Vivien" illustration by Julia Margaret Cameron for *Idylls of the King* (Cabinet Edition, King, 1874). Merlin is posed by the photographer's husband, Charles Hay Cameron

12. The parting of Lancelot and Guinevere. "Guinevere" illustration by Gustav Doré for the folio edition of *Idylls of the King* (Moxon & Co., 1867)

> *And then they rode to the divided way,*
> *There kissed, and parted weeping.*

13. Guinevere's last meeting with Arthur. "Guinevere" illustration by Gustav Doré for the folio edition of *Idylls of the King* (Moxon & Co., 1867).

> *. . . she fell,*
> *And grovelled with her face against the floor:*
> *There with her milkwhite arms and shadowy hair*
> *She made her face a darkness from the King.*

Pfordresher contends that "this idyll was composed early in the 1870's, probably after 'Gareth and Lynette' and was contemporaneous to the additions being made for 'Merlin and Vivien' for the collected editions of 1874."[23] "Balin and Balan" did not see publication until 1885, the year in which *The Idylls of the King* can be considered complete, except for the line in which Arthur is described as being "Ideal manhood closed in real man," which was written in 1891 and added to the "Epilogue" for the 1899 Edition Deluxe.[24]

By publishing first in a periodical, then in a book, Tennyson garnered his usual book profits plus £500 for the *Contemporary* appearance, and an additional £150 from the American firm J. R. Osgood and Co. (Ticknor & Fields's new name) for their 1872 edition of *Gareth and Lynette*.[25]

A slight difference between the first version of "The Last Tournament," in the *Contemporary*, and its book form a year later indicates one of Tennyson's responses to public prudery. He felt compelled to tone down the passage

> He rose, he turn'd, then flinging round her neck,
> Claspt it, but while he bow'd himself to lay
> Warm kisses in the hollow of her throat

into a more chaste

> He rose, he turn'd, then flinging round her neck,
> Claspt it, and cried, "Thine order, O my Queen!"
> But while he bow'd to kiss the jewell'd throat,
> Out of the dark . . . .[26]

Tennyson created difficulties in preparing the *Gareth and Lynette* volume for press with his oft-mentioned carelessness in writing up a fair copy. He wrote to Emily in July from London, "I have sent 'Gareth' to press this morning. The MS is so ill-written that I expect much confusion,"[27] but by the end of September he had received his first set of proofs from Strahan, corrected them, and sent them back.[28] The revises, however, were slow in coming, so much so that Tennyson's presence was finally required in London. Typically enough, Emily ignored all her husband's delays with proof and complained only about the printers' when she wrote to Robert Browning on 3 November 1872, "My husband's patience having been tried beyond endurance by certain proof sheets he has rushed off with Mr. Knowles to look after them from his house."[29]

Gareth and Lynette, Etc., a relatively small book of 136 pages, did make the booksellers in time for the Christmas trade in spite of these proof delays. It sold for five shillings in the normal binding. All we can say for sure about sales and profits is that Tennyson's account with White, Broughton & White records two payments from Strahan in 1873, the year immediately after publication – one for £4300 and the other for £2774 0s. 3d.[30]

A sidelight on Tennyson's earning power at about this time comes from the extraordinary payment of £1000 by the *New York Ledger* for the privilege of publishing any poem of Tennyson's of three stanzas. He sent them "England and America in 1782," which appeared in that newspaper on 6 January 1872. (The poem was first published in a book in King's Cabinet Edition of 1874.)

Knowing that the poet's work had reached sufficient magnitude and popularity, Alexander Strahan began in the early 1870s to issue collected editions of Tennyson. He opened with the Miniature Edition (ten volumes, later expanded to thirteen) in 1870. For this, the first collected edition, some of the *Idylls*, occupying volumes IV, V and VI, had title changes, with Tennyson adding the male names: "Geraint and Enid," "Merlin and Vivien," "Lancelot and Elaine." In 1872 Strahan initiated the Imperial Library Edition (usually called the Library Edition).

Tennyson seized on the event to further develop his *Idylls*. This would be the first edition to contain all of the poems he had finished (including the *Gareth* poems), and so he decided that it would also be a good moment to take a second look at the poem as a whole. Consequently, he began work in 1871 and continued emending the text into 1873. Tennyson made hundreds of minor alterations, expanded four earlier poems, and wrote an "Epilogue."[31]

Along with the *Idylls*, Tennyson added in this edition "Alexander," "The Bridesmaid," "The Third of February, 1852," "Literary Squabbles" and "On a Spiteful Letter," the last three having been first published in periodicals.

Another Strahan publication was a song-cycle called *The Window or, The Song of the Wrens*, with twelve poems by Tennyson, music by Sir Arthur Sullivan, and a single illustration by John Everett Millais. The idea of collaborating had first been suggested by Sullivan and George Grove, the musicologist. Although Tennyson consented and wrote the poems, allowing Sir Ivor Guest to print them privately in

November 1867, he felt them to be below his standard and tried to withdraw from the bargain, even offering Sullivan £500 to drop the project. When Sullivan refused, Tennyson was forced to allow publication of the book of songs but included a preface which, justifiably, incurred Sullivan's anger. In it Tennyson wrote,

> Four years ago Mr. Sullivan requested me to write a little Liederkreis, German fashion, for him to exercise his art upon. He had been very successful in setting such old songs as "Orpheus with his lute made Trees", and I drest up for him a puppet in the old style, a mere motif for an air, indeed the veriest nothing unless Mr. Sullivan can make it dance to his instruments.
>
> I am sorry that my four-year-old puppet should have to dance at all in the dark shadow of these days [the Franco-Prussian war] but the music is now completed and I am bound by my promise.
>
> A. Tennyson.

I suspect that Tennyson was using the "dark shadow" as an excuse to protect his reputation, for his introduction seems intrinsically designed to keep the public from giving too much weight to the poems. Emily, in her Journal entry for 4 November 1870, seizes upon the unfortunate timing and even conveniently forgets that Tennyson had tried very hard indeed to sidestep his promise. She writes, giving only the best interpretation to her husband's action, "Mr. Arthur Sullivan, Mr. Knowles, and Mr. Strahan came. Mr. Sullivan wished to publish the 'Window Songs.' A. did not like publishing songs that were so trivial at such a grave crisis of affairs in Europe; but he had given his promise to Mr. Sullivan about them, and 'He that sweareth unto his neighbour and disappointest him not' determined us." She added that they would be published with Tennyson's protest. Strahan issued the volume to the public in December 1870. The financial arrangement seems to have been that Sullivan be paid £500 by Tennyson and the collaboration then treated as a commission book, with Strahan receiving his usual 10 per cent on net profits and Tennyson getting the rest.[32]

During the Strahan years, 1869–73, Tennyson also experienced other problems connected with publishing, not the least of which was a lawsuit initiated by Mrs Moxon against J. Bertrand Payne and the other partners left in Moxon & Co. Tennyson came to her aid once again. (It is to be remembered that Tennyson had been paying her an anonymous annuity of at first £300, than £100 a year, which ended in 1879.) On his own behalf he still had lawyers trying to get settled the final accounts with Moxon & Co. His solicitors, White, Boughton & White, kept up extended correspondence and meetings on these matters during 1870, with only threats finally enabling them to get their due. For example, though Tennyson's cash account for 1870 records £400 paid on 20 January, the payment of £338 13s. 11d. paid on 20 February is called by White "the alleged balance of account"; a further £100 seems to have finished up the Moxon business on 14 September. Strahan and Routledge, who had some remaindered stock from Moxon & Co., were conducting their own proceedings and threatening litigation − with considerable success, it appears, for one witness remarked in March 1870, "Things appear to be telling heavily against Payne. Routledge particularly fiery and no wonder."[33]

Another anxiety for Tennyson at this time, a difficulty encountered by most popular authors before international copyright agreements were reached, was the pirating of his works by unscrupulous book publishers and sellers. Tennyson suffered from three variations: (1) his own former publisher issued an unauthorized work; (2) foreign-published editions of his poems were sold in the British Isles; and (3) foreign-published editions were sold in other countries. From all such sales Tennyson received nothing.

Less than a year into the contract with Strahan, Tennyson discovered that none other than his old adversary, J. Bertrand Payne, had authorized the inclusion of the privately printed "The Window" in D. Barron Brightwell's *A Concordance to the Entire Works of Tennyson* (London, 1869), a volume published without Tennyson's knowledge, much less permission. Emily recorded, "A. annoyed by the concordance of his works. It seems to him that the world must think it an assumption to have one published during his lifetime but he knew nothing about it. He finds 'The Window' in the concordance published by Moxon, another breach of trust on Mr. Payne's part." To her son Lionel she was even more blunt: "Papa went to town yesterday on account of that wretched Payne."[34]

Such piracy close at hand was matched in equal strength by that farther afield. Often foreign publishers prepared an unauthorized edition, shipped copies over, and had them sold in the British Isles. Tennyson was so distressed by this practice that he wrote to Prime Minister Disraeli in April 1868 "begging him to try and stop this illicit trade" of smuggled editions in England.[35] Even when a foreign publisher conducted himself properly, as Baron von Tauchnitz did in

1868 when he paid for the right to produce an edition of Tennyson's poems in Germany, a letter to the Baron betrays Tennyson's sustained fear of piracy:

> I am quite aware that I made rather a bad bargain with you, in selling the continental copyright for so small a sum, and my publisher affirms (whether rightly or not) that I annually lose some hundreds of pounds by this transaction. I am also aware that the royalty you offer me now is all of your free grace, and that I have no claim upon you. I can only hope that my accepting this offer will not be made a pretext by sellers (of course I am not including yourself) and buyers for introducing more copies into England. Accept my thanks therefore.[36]

The flow of pirated volumes from America cut into Tennyson's income. In particular, in Scotland certain Glasgow booksellers were dealing briskly in American Tennyson editions. Early in 1870 the White firm decided to start civil proceedings to stop them. An injunction was obtained in the Edinburgh County Session; and thus when "one of them (Forrester) continued this trade, Tennyson & Strahan sued him & recovered £500 damages."[37]

About the sale in America of pirated editions issued by American publishers he could do little. Some years before, in March 1856, he had appointed Ticknor & Fields in Boston as his "official" American publisher, yet, although they paid him for copyrights and provided royalties, sales of *sub rosa* editions were high, as almost any book table at an American church rummage sale these days will show.[38]

The distress of litigation and piracy, however, never detracted from the cordiality based on mutual respect which characterized Tennyson's relationship with Alexander Strahan. The pious, generous Strahan was far from the "vulgar Mr. Payne," as Emily called him. Therefore it was with regret that Tennyson had to make another change of publisher, when Strahan's business failed in 1873.

II HENRY S. KING (1874—8)

The person to whom Tennyson turned next, Henry Samuel King (one of those Victorian specialties — a self-made, self-educated man), had been originally a bookseller from Brighton. Until 1868 he had been a partner in Smith, Elder for a quarter share of the profits, proving there his literary mettle by editing Frederick Robertson's *Sermons*, a task made extremely difficult by the great preacher's extemporaneous delivery. King worked assiduously from Robertson's manuscripts, which were written after delivery and therefore not reflective of that delivery's power – and conflicting first-hand notes made by hearers. Yet King produced "an example of almost perfect editing. And the work was done quietly, and, as it were, in secret; no editor's name was known: Mr. King effaced himself for his friend."[39] These four successive volumes of sermons were "perhaps the most widespread literature of the kind ever issued from the press."[40]

King took over Smith, Elder's Indian agency and banking business in 1868. Three years later, after the required hiatus required by the terms of his separation from the publishing end of Smith, Elder was completed, he returned to his first love – books – and began publishing under his own name. "The business increased with rapidity and success," reports Kegan Paul, who was King's reader for many years and literary advisor from 1871 to 1873.[41]

The backbone of King's publishing business was the International Scientific Series, an attempt, as Kegan Paul describes it, "to bring so much of each separate science as might be thought necessary for the ordinary layman within the compass of a single volume." Paul notes, though, that King's terms to the contributors were "too liberal indeed to make the 'Series' a great financial success." Owing to his firsthand knowledge of problems with the translators, Kegan Paul knew that the accuracy of the series was to some extent undermined – but, when the venture fell completely into his own hands some years later, the firm of Kegan Paul kept it going well into the twentieth century.[42]

King was also active in publishing *belles lettres*. In 1875, for example, in addition to Tennyson's poetry, he also published books of poems by William Cullen Bryant, Robert Buchanan, Aubrey de Vere, and a translation of *Faust* by Kegan Paul himself, who was by then King's manager.

The force of King's character was widely acknowledged. Kegan Paul epitomised it as

> great urbanity to all who were first introduced to him, unwearied attention to business, a large power of generalisation combined with extraordinary attention to details, an almost unexampled

memory, and an iron will. And under the urbanity this iron force was very apparent; not all were able to penetrate below it. Those who did so found an extremely tender heart, a most loving and lovable nature, a high and stern sense of duty for himself and others, with great toleration prevailing over a seeming intolerance.[43]

Tennyson's choice of King over other suitors for publishing rights to his works probably came from a combination of respect for his character, satisfaction with his business attitudes, and a feeling that continuing with someone who was a partner with Alexander Strahan would reduce the discomfort of switching publishers.

The arrangements for a new publishing agreement began in the spring of 1873, with James Knowles once again acting as go-between. James Virtue, who, along with King and Alexander Pollock Watt, had been among Strahan's partners, submitted a long letter to Arnold White outlining his own offer: "I presume that the result of the last four years arrangement has shown that the principle of giving a certain fixed sum per annum for the privilege of publishing Mr. Tennyson's work is not a sound one, as it is almost impossible to gauge the probable amount of the annual sales of the books and consequently the annual profits. . . . " Virtue then offered to publish all of Tennyson's works, both old and new, on a straight 5 per cent commission basis. A later paragraph jarred the Tennysons, for Virtue said, "I have no desire to found a claim upon Mr. Tennyson because the result [of the Strahan agreement] has been so disastrous." He concluded by suggesting that Tennyson aid them in recovering their losses by allowing them to sell the " 'pocket' [no doubt the Miniature] and 'Library' Editions (paid for by Strahan & Co.) for the next five years without royalty."

Arnold White told Knowles immediately that Virtue's statement about losses was "wholly unreconcileable with previous statements about *gains*"; Knowles conveyed that message to Tennyson along with his own judgment: "This may probably be no more than a quasi-American proceeding to influence the terms of a new bargain – but it does not at any rate seem to indicate much chance of a satisfactory proposal from them." In light of this, Tennyson informed White, "I, as you may well believe at once made up my mind to decline entertaining Mr. Virtue's proposal & suggestions. In fact his letter seems to me little short of an impertinence."

An informal competing proposal from King, however, which

Knowles copied and sent along to Mrs Tennyson with his own long letter about the merits of this offer and the demerits of anything from Virtue and Isbister, struck Tennyson as being just right. King offered £5000 a year for five years for old books, with only 5 per cent commission on new ones. (Since King offered even more liberal terms than Strahan had given Tennyson – and since King, as one of Strahan's partners, no doubt knew the ins and outs of Strahan's failure – it is reasonable to think that Strahan had not lost by Tennyson but rather by other aspects of his business. On the other hand, it is possible to surmise that King may have been willing to take on a potential loss in order to add Tennyson's prestigious name to his list.) Knowles pointed out the appeal of these terms and suggested further that, since King's name would soon be added to Strahan's anyway, "if a change were made by Mr. Tennyson to King the name of Strahan & Co. would still continue on the books instead of being replaced by Virtue & Isbister." King, as a further inducement, had mentioned that he contemplated a popular edition of the poems – that edition originally conceived in Strahan's mind, but never produced by him – to sell at "5/ for the whole works." All in all, Tennyson found the King proposal satisfactory and left the details to be settled by White.[44]

By the end of 1873 Emily Tennyson could reflect on King as follows: "We have been troubled again by publishing affairs. It is a pity that these splitting up of partnerships drive A. from one publisher to another. Let us hope however that he has found a steadfast publisher in Mr. King, with whom he may stay to the end. That he is most liberal there can be no doubt."[45] Nevertheless, for some reason, perhaps accumulated ill feelings about the need for switching publishers after Strahan's failure or the still rankling wounds inflicted by J. Bertrand Payne, Emily wrote to Alfred on 17 March 1874, "Assuredly the race of publishers cannot stand high with us as far as our experience goes. May better things be in store for the future. It is well that there is a prospect of something coming in at all counts. . . ."[46] (A week later Tennyson received his first payment from King: £1054 10s. 6d. for the stock turned over by Strahan.) Emily's strong statement about "the race of publishers" may also be accounted for by her failing health. Growing fatigue, caused by tireless handling of most business and personal correspondence, proof-reading, and household matters, forced her by the end of the summer of 1874 to cease her Journal entries and her secretarial duties for Alfred. At his mother's virtual collapse, Hallam Tennyson returned home from Cambridge and took over as his father's secretary. His later judgment of the appeal that King's personality and business methods had for Tennyson slips into a statement about Macmillan and bears more weight than does Emily's: "With none of the publishers into whose hands circumstances had thrown my father was the connection so uninterruptedly pleasant as with Messrs. Macmillan – unless perhaps that with Mr. Henry King."[47]

However, the contract with King, in spite of hopes and affinities, was to result in only two new publications, *Queen Mary* and *Harold*, and three more collected editions – the Cabinet, the Author's and the Imperial Library (a new edition of Strahan's 1872 publication). Moreover, King himself died before the five-year contract expired.

With King, Tennyson began a period in his career which was perhaps inevitable: he turned his attention almost completely to writing plays. The narrative impulse of the "middle" Tennyson was no longer primary once the *Idylls* were complete (except for a lengthy addition to "Merlin and Vivien," the publication of "Balin and Balan," and a few minor changes). The lyric impulse, so characteristic of the early Tennyson, had been set aside, to bloom once more in his last years; now the dramatic muse would take center stage.

Sir Charles gives this insight into his grandfather's new commitment:

> His attempt at the dramatic form was not generally popular with the public or the critics, who had come to regard him as a lyric and idyllic poet. But he no doubt felt that, though his fertility and power of attack were hardly impaired by age – he was now 65 years old – he was not likely to surpass or even to equal what he had already achieved in these fields. He had always been passionately fond of the theatre and was a profound student of Shakespeare and the Elizabethans (he had written blank verse plays at 14 years of age). He now set himself with characteristic courage and pertinacity to tackle a formidable task in this new field – to give a picture in dramatic form of the reign of Mary Tudor, which should illustrate the dying struggle of Roman Catholicism to retain its supremacy in England, its failure and with this, the final flickering out of the Middle Ages and the dawn of the English Renaissance under Elizabeth. No doubt it was also in his mind that his play would complete the great cycle of Shakespeare's historical dramas, which end with Henry VIII.[48]

It would have been surprising if Tennyson, of all major nineteenth-century poets, had *not* tried his hand at plays. After all, Shelley, Wordsworth, Byron, Coleridge and Browning had all done so. It would have been even more surprising had he succeeded at them. One wonders, actually, why Tennyson had not learned from the failures of his brother poets that stage requirements must be mastered before a successful play can be written and produced. By ignoring what Terry Otten in *The Deserted Stage* calls "the modest advances of the stage of his day," and by choosing "to write plays about England in a way which eclipses action in character with historical matter [in which] social and political material obscured individual internal conflict," Tennyson was dooming himself to failure.[49] He had the life-long interest in literary drama which might have sparked success; he had a strong dramatic sense which had evidenced itself in poems such as *The Princess* and *Maud* and The *Idylls of the King* and which Arthur Hallam had identified in 1831 as "a graft of the lyric on the dramatic"; he had, too, acquaintance with theatre people such as the Kembles, Macready and Irving — but these facets of his life, even when added to his habit of theatre-going, could not turn Tennyson the poet into Tennyson the playwright.[50] To explain Tennyson's failure in the drama, Christopher Ricks draws upon several outstanding critics. He mentions Henry James's

fine account of how Tennyson's verse moves, and of how "to produce his drama he has had to cease to be himself." Just what this means was made clear by Bagehot, before Tennyson ever set about these plays, in a discussion of dialogue (which "requires a very changing imagination") as against soliloquy ("steadily accumulating"): "His genius gives the notion of a slow depositing instinct; day by day, as the hours pass, the delicate sand falls into beautiful forms — in stillness, in peace, in brooding." Not in action or in dramatic outcome; Tennyson's essential genius is exploratory of the human situations for which there seems to be no denouement.[51]

The critical and stage history of Tennyson's plays has been given extensive treatment elsewhere, but a few brief comments on publication and sales are needed here.[52]

Queen Mary and *Harold*, the first two parts of an historical trilogy (*Becket* in 1879 would be the third part) appeared in May 1875 and November 1876, respectively, under King's imprint. The six-shilling volumes were bound in the dark green boards with gilt lettering now customary for Tennyson, no matter who published them. We cannot be sure how many copies of *Queen Mary* were printed that first year, for the accounts are not extant, but Sir Charles and others have noted that a second edition was required before the end of the year. Sir Charles adds, however,

> I expect that the first had been smaller than the first editions of Tennyson's recent works, as when "Harold" was published in November 1876 only 20,000 copies were issued, of which nearly 15,000 had been sold by the end of the year. The sales of these two volumes of plays fell away much more rapidly than those of the "Idylls" and "Enoch Arden" volumes had done. It was not necessary to reprint "Harold" or "Queen Mary."[53]

Marshall calls the sales of both "very poor."[54]

Apart from the ill-fated *Queen Mary* and *Harold*, King's major venture with Tennyson was the Cabinet Edition in monthly volumes, with illustrations and portrait. New poems in it included: "A Welcome to Her Royal Highness Marie Alexandrovna, Duchess of Edinburgh," a Laureate production first published in *The Times* on 7 March 1874, the day Alfred, Duke of Edinburgh, and his new wife landed in England after their January marriage in St Petersburg; "In the Garden at Swainston," written after the funeral of Tennyson's great friend Sir John Simeon; "The Voice and the Peak"; and "England and America in 1782," previously published in the *New York Ledger*. Also, Tennyson took this occasion to add lines 6–146 to "Merlin and Vivien."

For this Cabinet Edition, Julia Margaret Cameron, the photographer and close neighbor of the Tennysons on the Isle of Wight, contributed twelve illustrations to the *Idylls of the King* volumes. Her biographer writes,

> She was grieved at the loss of beauty when she saw her efforts diminished to small woodcuts in the pages of the book. "When I had achieved my beautiful large pictures," she murmured, "at such a cost of labour, strength and money, for I had taken 245 photographs to get these twelve successes, it seemed such a pity that they should only appear in the very tiny reduced form in Alfred's volume (where I gave them only as a matter of friendship, not that I would not gladly have consented to profit if profit had been

offered)." That was the bother. Everybody took her for an amateur and Julia herself generally behaved as one. Tennyson apparently accepted her work as a gift without further thought, and now, when she complained of the poor appearance of her photographic groups staged with such care, he suggested that she should bring them out in a large volume in their natural size – at her own risk.[55]

She did take this suggestion and produced, with King as publisher, a two-volume folio edition called *Illustrations to Tennyson's Idylls of the King, and Other Poems*, 1875, selling for six guineas. That same year she also had privately printed a "Miniature Edition" of the same photos, but in one volume half the size of the folio. The *Morning Post* gave high praise indeed to Mrs Cameron's work, but, as Hill concludes,

> To twentieth-century eyes, however, these carefully grouped studies of Victorian men and women, clad in fancy dress and composing their faces to convey an emotion they did not feel, inevitably look somewhat absurd. "High camp" is, I am afraid, the only adjective they evoke today. It is not for her illustrations to Tennyson's poems, but for her straightforward portraits of her contemporaries that Julia Margaret Cameron is praised today.[56]

One of her most famous portraits is that of Tennyson himself, the one he called the "dirty monk" picture.

King printed 12,000 of each volume of the Cabinet Edition the first year (1874) and set the selling price at 2s. 6d. per volume. The next year he put out the Author's Edition, with portraits, in six volumes. Although we have no information about the numbers printed or sold, for either Cabinet or Author's Edition, it seems that they were successful enough to encourage King to publish a new edition of the seven-volume Imperial Library Edition in 1877.[57] On at least one score Tennyson was displeased by the Imperial Library Edition. He wrote to King,

> Allow me to ask you why in the VIIth volume of your last & very handsome issue of my Poems you have not inserted the second & amended edition of Queen Mary about which I took some pains and which as you know was published by your firm. I cannot account for this substitution of the more perfect by the less perfect form of the drama; and I am sorry not only for my own sake – for

an author must needs have sympathy with his own work — but for yours also seeing that such a substitution must more or less tend to detract from the value of the whole Imperial Edition.

Throughout these years with Henry S. King & Co., Tennyson found more and more reason for disputation with Charles Kegan Paul, the firm's manager. The disagreements, never personally acrimonious, centered on three techniques of book marketing: advertising, illustrated volumes and annotated editions.

As an example of the first, Kegan Paul saw no reason why they should not advertise the lines added to "Merlin and Vivien" for the Cabinet Edition, and thus wrote to Tennyson on 12 October 1874,

> We are of course always anxious to comply with any request you may make, especially one made with such urgency, but I confess I am quite unable to understand *why* we should not say that Vivien has in it additional lines. Having written them and consented to their publication, it is to be presumed that you wish them to be known. There are hundreds, I may say thousands of people, who having already the Idylls of the King will not buy another edition of them, unless they know that there is in them something new, but who it may be hoped will do so if they have that knowledge. And advertising is simply the way of stating a fact, which we suppose you as well as ourselves wish to be known. While we endeavor as far as possible to put ourselves in your position, and look on these matters as you do, in which we have not always succeeded, I am sure you will forgive our asking you to remember that the success of literature has two sides, and that the trade element is an important one, nor if rightly considered is it, I think, a wholly prosaic one.

Tennyson, however, was not swayed by this line of arguing, and Kegan Paul was forced to give way, writing again to the poet a few days later, "I have read your letter to Mr. King, who says that since you put it on the ground you do, there is not a word more to be said" (14 October 1874).

A second difference of opinion then arose. Illustrations based on an author's life, Kegan Paul knew, appealed to the public and helped sell books. He lobbied for the engraving of a portrait of Arthur Henry Hallam, an engraving of Farringford, one of Aldworth, "a bit of M. S. . . . as an introduction to volume 4" of the Cabinet Edition.

But in doing so Paul ran up against Tennyson's notorious resistance to intrusions into his privacy and dislike of illustrations to his poems. The manager even had to remind the poet that illustrations could hardly "be considered other than a publishers' question." He understood Tennyson's objections very well and met them head on. To Hallam Tennyson he explained, "No one will consider him [Tennyson] responsible for putting two views of his houses before the world in any vain glorious way. . . ." He also asked them to reconsider their objection to a reproduced manuscript page:

> While I dislike as much as any one, anything like over curiosity about a man's private life, and would resent for my friends as for myself anything like impertinence, I must say that a desire to possess the *ipsissima verba*, or as near them as may be of one we love and respect seems to be a blameless little bit of the instinctive worship we pay to those we love. It would be much if your father could concede this point. (5 August 1874)

When Tennyson tried a counter-suggestion of less personal illustrations, Kegan Paul would not be persuaded:

> Your suggestion of pictures of Tintagel and Caerleon is, I am afraid, answered in anticipation by the reception by the bookselling trade of the illustration to the last volume. While the booksellers had been much pleased with the former ones, especially with the engraving of Farringford they have been thoroughly dissatisfied with the Swainston Garden. And this not only because the subject in itself is poor; though the best which could then be got, but because it was a sudden departure from the special personal interest which had been the feature of the work so far. (12 October 1874)

Kegan Paul's forcefulness in these dealings, though tempered by courtesy and tact, reminded Tennyson unpleasantly of J. Bertrand Payne. Henry King, however, understood the poet's objections and personal tastes well enough to insure that no open confrontation flared up between his manager and his leading writer. A case in point is the Annotated Edition, a single-minded attempt by the publisher to market something new in 1876 regardless of the fact that Tennyson had no new play or volume of poetry ready.

From August to October 1876 correspondence flowed in abundance between Hallam Tennyson, Arnold White and Kegan Paul over plans for such an edition. Tennyson, as we know by now, disliked any supplements to his poems, but somehow or other he carelessly allowed Kegan Paul to begin work on such a project. Only when he saw the kinds of notes being produced did he start the convoluted struggle to curtail further annotation.

The first letter on this matter, written on 18 August 1876 by Kegan Paul to Hallam Tennyson, foreshadows the coming storm. From it we learn that Hallam Tennyson had submitted "notes and criticisms" on the material Paul had prepared, and then had specified that the edition must clearly state that these notes were published on the publisher's initiative. Kegan Paul replied, however, that, although he would oblige, these additions would be "probably not in the words or in the place which you dictate." Furthermore, Hallam had passed along Tennyson's complaint that the notes so far were "inferior to those of the 'annotated Byron,'" a contention with which Kegan Paul did not agree with the exception of one particular: namely, that "Byron was reviewed with much better criticism than your father has been," so that perforce the Tennyson notes were weak in contemporary criticism. Also, he added, local color and biographical details, so vital to Byron's poems, were not so for Tennyson's; "Some of this could no doubt lend great interest and value to our book but it is just the element your father is always so anxious to exclude, while his life has had, happily, none of the stormy incidents which needed explanation in Byron's case, and which themselves explained his Poems." Finally, Hallam had asked for a delay, to which Kegan Paul replied,

> The work is not, and is not going to be "scrawled through". We shall use the utmost care as well as diligence in its preparation. We count very much on your cordial cooperation to enable us to secure as perfect a work as possible within the necessarily limited time at our disposal for its publication. . . . You are very good to say you advise delay in our interest; but these are in a measure commercial. And delay as it brings nearer the time at which our arrangement expires gives less time for such a work, and operates therefore with extreme unfairness on those interests. We have no wish to give a mere collection of various readings, and shall always wish to follow your father's advice about the old Poems Illustrated. . . .

Immediately upon receipt of this letter, Hallam must have dashed off an inquiry to the Tennyson solicitor, Arnold W. White, on the legal obligations of their contract with Henry S. King & Co. On 21 August White supplied the information in his usual clear way:

> The 2nd Clause of the Agreement with Messrs. King expressly provides that "no poem matter or words shall be inserted in any future Edition or Editions which is not contained in the Library Edition, without the written consent of Mr. Tennyson."
>
> It is clear therefore that Messrs. King cannot publish an annotated edition without your father's express permission. To avoid misunderstanding at a future time I strongly recommend that this permission (if given at all) should be embodied in a separate agreement supplemental of the existing one.
>
> We could then insist on the insertion of such conditions as you allude to.   (White to Hallam, 21 August 1876)

The Tennysons instructed White to meet with Kegan Paul "to put the extinguisher on the Edition, if it can be done fairly." White reported at length on the 2 October meeting, summarizing for Hallam and Alfred Tennyson his argument to Kegan Paul:

> In my opinion, I concluded, if Mr. Tennyson were to repay you the actual expenses out of pocket which you have incurred in connection with this project, he would be quite free from any implied obligation, & would be at liberty to use his power of veto without giving any ground of complaint. Mr. Paul winced at this. He admitted that the actual money payments up to this time had not been very heavy (he *guessed* about £150). But he said a very heavy pecuniary loss would fall on Messrs. King if they were not allowed to bring out the Edition. They had counted upon it to recoup themselves for their very small sales this year. I replied that if they had only looked into their agreement they would have seen that they had no right to count upon such an Edition. Paul admitted this: but said, "*he* had never seen the Agreement until recently, as Mr. King kept it locked up in his desk."
>
> I *pressed* the proposal of Mr. Tennyson repaying "all moderate and reasonable expenses incurred" on condition of the Edition being altogether dropped for the present: leaving Messrs. King to renew the proposal, entirely de novo, at some future time if they thought fit.

Paul retired to consult Mr. King, & thus the matter stands at present.

A second report from White to Hallam a few days later indicated that Kegan Paul advised King to drop the edition, no doubt because the agreement gave Tennyson veto power, but probably also because Paul could sense that a spirit of good will, so vital to such a cooperative project, was fast disappearing and might eventually mean that, at contract time again, Tennyson would flee King and his manager, Kegan Paul.

And King did drop the matter. No annotated edition was published by King or by his successor, Kegan Paul, or in fact, by anyone until long after Tennyson's death; and then, for the 1908–9 Eversley Edition, Macmillan & Co. used authorized notes prepared by Hallam Tennyson and the poet himself during his last years. A coda to the abortive King edition: Tennyson did pay a total of £159 14s. 8d. to Messrs King in 1877 for "expenses incurred on the Annotated Edition."

On 12 February 1877, in an otherwise insignificant letter from Kegan Paul to Arnold White, this snippet appeared: "Mr. King, who is at Cannes for his health." The illness alluded to so briefly forced King to give up the publishing and bookselling business later that year.

Tennyson found that, after the retirement of the publisher, with whom he had had pleasant personal dealings, misunderstandings with his manager continued. Alfred, for example, objected strongly to suddenly discovering via an advertising circular that he, too, along with bound stock and old stereotype plates, had been transferred to Kegan Paul, King's successor. He instructed White to ask Paul to withdraw the transfer announcement in the *Athenaeum* and other papers. White stated the grounds: "under the Agreement of the 15th January 1874 the exclusive privilege of publishing Mr. Tennyson's works is confined to Messrs. Henry S. King & Co. and that they have no power, during the continuance of that Agreement to sell or transfer that privilege to any other person or firm." Kegan Paul and other members of the King firm immediately responded with various explanations for the oversight, including the need for a quick transfer, owing to King's failing health (even adding to White, "We cannot but think that neither you, nor Mr. Tennyson would desire to impede, or render futile the efforts made for his recovery"), Paul's diligent preparation for the press of the Tennyson publications, and so on. White and Tennyson had no choice but to concur, though they did add the stipulation to their transfer instructions that the books advertised and published with Paul must have "added to the style of that firm that they are 'successors to Messrs. Henry S. King & Co.' Mr. Tennyson desires that this should appear, as he does not wish to have the appearance of unnecessarily changing his publishers." (Letters of 12, 13, 22, 23 October 1877.) In spite of this awkward situation, we know by the fact that on 3 November 1877 Hallam Tennyson sent Kegan Paul a congratulatory note full of good will that all ended amicably. Tennyson's publishing years with Henry S. King, which had borne little fruit, had come to a close. King himself died on 17 November the following year.

III CHARLES KEGAN PAUL (1879–83)

The friendship between Charles Kegan Paul, Tennyson's new publisher, and Hallam Tennyson, the poet's son, had its roots in Kegan Paul's early days as vicar of Sturminster Marshall, Dorset, from 1862 to 1874. While at this post, Paul kept a school in his home in Baillie. Although disappointed in his pupils on the whole, his letters indicate that he enjoyed at least two: Hallam and Lionel Tennyson, sent to him in May 1864 to spend a year being "coached in preparation for a public school."[58] From Baillie on 3 September 1866, a few months after Hallam had begun at Marlborough, Paul wrote,

My dear Hallam:

Since you are one of those who I think will judge of a book more by its contents, its print & its binding than its size, I make no apology for sending you one which is little in bulk as a memorial of your stay here, and of my sincere regard. I was delighted with the Edition of a beautiful book when I saw it in London, and trust you also may be pleased with it.

Heard you were all abroad, but presume you have now got back again. Write and tell me how you get on, and of your house party. I miss you much.

Ever yours affly,
C. Kegan Paul

The mutual regard of pupil and teacher continued for many years and may have helped temper the controversies which arose when Kegan Paul became Tennyson's publisher and Hallam his father's secretary and, in effect, business manager.

Kegan Paul's entrance into the publishing world came late, following on the heels of difficulties with Christian doctrine which affected his other careers, in Church and education. Before taking the Dorset position, he had been headmaster at Eton. His tract on the boundaries of the Church of England, however, advanced views too liberal for the Provost, who, according to Kegan Paul, "was in a great fright about orthodoxy and *Essays and Reviews.*"[59] By 1870 Kegan Paul was "practically Unitarian" and in 1874 resigned his living and went up to London to join Henry King's publishing firm. After a few years as literary advisor and manager (as discussed in the previous section), he purchased the publishing firm with a partner, Alfred Trench, son of Archbishop Trench of Dublin, Tennyson's fellow Apostle. Later the firm became Kegan Paul, Trench, Trübner & Co., which today exists as Routledge & Kegan Paul. This firm and Macmillan are the only two of Tennyson's publishers still operating.[60]

Kegan Paul's attitude towards his work is evident in this introduction to the section in his autobiographical *Memories* in which he describes his twenty-five years as managing director of the firm: "Publishing is not by any means the ready road to wealth that many people think it, and . . . it is very inexpedient for any one without a large capital and considerable literary skill to enter such a business. Supposing, however, any one to have the capital and the literary skill, I can imagine no more interesting work."[61] That "considerable literary skill" which Paul prescribed for such a career he had in great measure himself as writer, editor, and astute judge of literary value.

In addition to many tracts, pamphlets and articles, some of which are collected in *Faith and Unfaith and Other Essays*, Paul produced a volume of poetry (*By the Way Side*) and the autobiography (*Memories*) which tells the tale of his movement from Anglicanism through Comtism to agnosticism and finally to Roman Catholicism. The rest of his books are mainly either biographies or translations and include: *William Godwin, His Friends and Contemporaries; Mary Wolstonecraft, Letters to Imlay, with Prefatory Memoir; Biographical Sketches; Maria Drummond, a Sketch; Goethe's Faust, in Rime; Pascal's Thoughts; Thomas à Kempis's De Imitatione; and Huysmans's En Route.*

As publisher "Paul's own literary standard was fastidiously high," maintains historian Mumby. "Distinguishing the difference, in his own phrase, between what was clever and clever-*ish*, he would have none of the class of book known today as a 'best-seller.' " As proof of this, Mumby offers Kegan Paul's publication of "the early books of Robert Louis Stevenson, and other eminent authors years before the reading public recognized their gifts." Thomas Hardy, who had been published by King, continued with Kegan Paul. Mumby also notes that "the association with Tennyson, though a luxury beyond their means, brought the publishers [Kegan Paul and Trench] much of the best contemporary poetry," particularly that of Austin Dobson and William Barnes.[62] Other literary figures on Kegan Paul's list included Sir Richard and Lady Burton, Edward Dowden, Aubrey de Vere, Archbishop Trench, Sir Henry Taylor, Andrew Lang, Frederick Locker, Edmund Gosse and Wilfrid Blunt. And, though he never published them, he numbered among those who had given him "pleasant companionship" through literature George Eliot, George Henry Lewes, and M and Mme Renan.

The International Scientific Series begun under King was continued by Kegan Paul, with some of the volumes going into myriad editions. Herbert Spencer's *Study of Sociology*, for example, "went through more than twenty-two editions."[63] The major contributors to the Series were also actively writing for the *Nineteenth Century*, owned and edited at that time by James Knowles, and another facet of Kegan Paul's publishing.

Kegan Paul's "considerable literary skill" was heightened by visual sensitivity to the physical details of book production. He wrote, for instance, that his firm distinguished itself by the Parchment Library: "The intention of this series was to present in thoroughly good paper and print some of the most distinguished English classics, and we certainly set the fashion of really beautiful books."[64] In relation to the aesthetics of publishing he extended this challenge to the rest of the trade: "There could scarcely be a better thing for the artistic future of books than that which might be done by some master of decorative art, like Mr. William Morris, and some great firm of type-founders in conjunction, would they design and produce some new types for our choicer printed books."[65]

It had not been since Edward Moxon's death in 1858 that Tennyson had had as his publisher a person with such finely honed literary sensibilities. The records extant show no disputes on purely literary matters between Kegan Paul and his chief poet. Paul's business attitudes, however, proved uncongenial to the Tennysons, as attested to by his summing up, in his autobiography, of his publishing relationship with Tennyson:

> One who lived by literature alone is Lord Tennyson, who for many years was associated with us and with whom our relations were always friendly and pleasant. He was, however, a thorough man of business, and our final parting at the end of one of our periods of agreement was that we, as publishers, and he, as author, took a different view of his pecuniary value.[66]

(From the Tennyson perspective, it was Kegan Paul, no doubt, who was the "thorough man of business.") One senses Paul's feeling that Tennyson could live "by literature alone" because he received too much money from his publishers. On another level, an underlying tension in their relationship may have been caused by Paul's strong conviction that literature was not — and, perhaps even should not be — a well-paying profession in its own right. He once told a story which indicated the camaraderie he felt towards writers who were not entirely supported by their literary works, Tennyson, of course, *not* being among them:

> Not long before her [Mrs Proctor's] death Mr. Browning, Mr. Matthew Arnold and I were standing in front of the fireplace one Sunday afternoon, talking about the various incomes made by prominent persons, and Mrs. Proctor was giving her own reminiscences of barristers' and physicans' fees, and the sums obtained by literature by men known to her in her youth.
>
> Mr. Browning thereupon told how at the house of a distinguished surgeon he had met an exalted personage, who to much *bonhomie* joins an inordinate curiosity. He said to the surgeon, "I should like to know, of course I do not speak of present company, what a first-rate surgeon makes in his profession." "Well, sir," said the host, "I should say that about £15,000 a year would be the mark." "What," said the prince, turning to the then acknowledged leader of the English Bar, "what does a great barrister make?" "I suppose, sir, £25,000 would hit the mark." Sir John Millais was also present, and he was the third asked. "Possibly, sir, £35,000 a year." "Oh, come, come," said the questioner. "Well, sir," said Sir John Millais, rather nettled, "as a matter of fact, last year I made £40,000, and might have made more, had I not been taking

holiday longer than usual in Scotland." When he had finished speaking Mr. Browning put his arms through Mr. Arnold's and mine, and said, "We don't make that by literature, do we?"[67]

Furthermore, Paul objected to Tennyson's personality. For example, he made this comparison: "Certainly no one posed less as a poet in society [than did Robert Browning]. In his absolute simplicity he was a great contrast to Tennyson. . . . Tennyson always posed. Matthew Arnold did not pose as a poet, but he had a certain grandiose manner which he never laid aside. Browning was always the simple man of the world."[68]

Kegan Paul's response to Tennyson's poetry was mixed as well. While at Eton, he said,

> I read Tennyson for myself, learning by heart the greater part of the original volumes, and thinking, as I still think, that for subtle workmanship no one had at all approached the same perfection since Milton. I did not then recognise how little thought is contained in that pomp and melody of verse, still less how very little of what thought there is, is the poet's own.

To support this criticism, he enumerated illustrations of Tennyson's supposed "derivativeness," a charge very similar to that made in popular critical articles current at the time he was writing *Memories*.[69] Yet in his "Publishing" chapter he revealed that, since Robert Browning, Elizabeth Barrett Browning and Tennyson, no poet had been able to move him – and that the Laureateship should, in his opinion, have been "allowed to die out after it had been honoured by such names as Southey, Wordsworth, and Tennyson."[70]

Such ambivalence never characterized Alfred and Hallam Tennyson's and even Arnold White's attitude towards Kegan Paul: they thought him only "mean and tricky" when it came to business matters. Others in the publishing trade expressed similar views. At the beginning of the contract with Macmillan, "Kegan Pauls had caused some resentment by offering a large stock of the collected works which they had by them at half price – 'A Kegan Paully proceeding' G. L. Craik of Macmillan's called it.'"[71]

Such phrases, tantalizing though they be, do not reveal the full story of the Kegan Paul–Tennyson relationship; much of the correspondence which might do so was destroyed in the 1883 fire which completely destroyed Kegan Paul's premises at 1, Paternoster

Square. A close look at what remains, particularly the 1879 agreement and the correspondence surrounding it, when added to the struggle over the Annotated Edition during the time of Henry S. King (see previous section), nonetheless reveals the inherent differences of attitude between these two determined businessmen. Tennyson, on the one hand, had waited for his poet's laurels for a good many years, and, once he had grasped them, wore them proudly and used them for leverage in getting publishers to meet his terms. He was a commodity much in demand in the marketplace — and he knew what he was worth, even in name alone, to any publishing house. From this strong-willed position Tennyson entered negotiations with Kegan Paul for an agreement to cover the next five years (1879—83) at the expiration of the Henry S. King contract. But he no longer traveled light. With him he now brought the copyrights to old editions; old stock (bound and unbound); stereoplates; poems first published in periodicals; plays produced on stage but not yet published; and his own reputation for exasperating publishers by keeping proofs for lengthy periods and by making extensive revisions in proof, thus delaying the whole proof stage of an edition. Kegan Paul, on the other hand, had been working so closely on Tennyson's poems at King's for several years that he was well aware of the difficulties a new agreement with the poet could present. Added to his burden was the knowledge that Tennyson's sales of new books had been declining, *Queen Mary* and *Harold*, Tennyson's only new books with King, selling appreciably more slowly than, for instance, the 1869 *Holy Grail* volume with Strahan. Yet Kegan Paul was anxious for an agreement, probably because he expected that continued good sales of various collected editions, such as the Crown, would offset Tennyson's apparent drying up in the production of highly saleable new volumes of poetry.

Under the old agreement with King, but with the Kegan Paul name on the title page as King's successor, Kegan Paul brought out in 1878 the Shilling Edition in thirteen volumes. This was the cheapest edition so far, at one shilling a copy for the monthly, blue-paper covered volumes. Kegan Paul printed 55,000 the first year and sold 30,323. His account book shows a net loss of £235 15s. 9d. on this edition the first year, though by the end of the next year, when he printed over 100,000, he recovered more than the loss and made a profit of £1105 10s. 5d. Thereafter he simply held his own with the Shilling Edition.[72] His next venture, the Crown Edition, was slated for fine sales, too, because it was the first collected edition in one volume, always an important publication step in the life of a poet. He printed 75,400 in 1878 and sold 54,974 during the first six months. 100,000 copies of this edition sold over the years that Kegan Paul had Tennyson on his list. It was issued in three different bindings: the "Plain," at six shillings, the "Gilt," at 7s. 6d., and the "Roxburgh," at 8s. 6d., a diversity intended to suit the public's varying tastes and pocketbooks. Paul reprinted this good seller in 1880, 1881 and 1883. His net profits were suitably large: about £5000 the first year and an average of almost £2000 for each successive year.[73]

Some idea of the differing reading needs these multiple collected editions met can be learned from the special appreciation General George Gordon had for his very portable set. Tennyson had long admired General Gordon, had entertained him, had collaborated with him on plans for training-homes for young soldiers [plans carried out later as a memorial to Gordon]; and Gordon seems to have delighted in Tennyson's poetry, judging by what Lady Cardwell reported at the time:

> I often hear from him of his long solitary rides of hundreds of miles in the desert and wilderness, and wished to find the most acceptable companion I could send to him.
>
> It must be in a very small compass. Happily I found the beautiful edition of all your books in the small green case, and I sent it a few months ago.
>
> He is intensely delighted with it and mentions it in every letter. In his last, lately received from Khartoum, he says: "I find the reading of Tennyson is my great relief, and the volumes are so small and of such clear print that they will always go with me. I have long wanted a small copy, but never knew that he had published one. . . ."[74]

(Incidentally, one of Kegan Paul's great successes as a publisher was in outbidding rivals for Gordon's diaries and publishing them as *Last Journals of General Gordon*.)

Tennyson got a good start on negotiations for a new contract by instructing Arnold White on 14 April 1878 "to serve a notice tomorrow on Kegan Paul & Co. to the effect that the agreement between us is to terminate at the expiration of its current year. I would have you at the same time remind them of the clause by which they are forbidden to print any copies of my works after the date of this notice terminating the agreement." He would not be transferred without his permission again – and he would keep as much control of his books as he could.

Kegan Paul's first offer (7 June), which was presented to Tennyson via James Knowles, was unsatisfactory. Arnold White immediately began seeking other publishers, writing to Hallam that he would be "quite willing to open negotiations with Mr. Macmillan if such is Mr. Tennyson's wish, and, as it would contribute to your father's peace of mind to have the business settled at once, I see no sufficient reason for delay" (22 June 1878). With Tennyson's permission obtained, White began negotiations with Macmillan.

Various existing letters provide a glimpse of Arnold White at work on the Tennyson matter over a few days in July. Reconstruction of events might be as follows: At 3 p.m. on 11 July 1878, White wrote to Hallam that he was "daily in expectation of receiving an offer from [Mr. Macmillan]." But Kegan Paul had been by the office the day before saying that *he* had expected a "counter-offer" after Tennyson had refused his first one. When he was assured by White that there would be no such "counter-offer," Paul "begged permission to make another offer." But by 3 p.m. on the 11th White had not yet received it. Later that afternoon, however, the offer came, complete with this enclosure: "In either case we fully desire to remain Mr. Tennyson's publishers after the expiration of the agreement though the terms might have to be modified." White's report to Tennyson on 12 July said that Paul had come in person once more: "This morning, he has been with me to say that he is most desirous to continue your publisher, & if you assent to the general principle of his proposal, he will be prepared to modify the details as much as possible to meet your wishes." Enter another competitor, George Routledge, with what they thought would be a better offer than Kegan Paul's. White met with Tennyson to talk Paul's proposal over, and the poet decided to reject it. Enter James Knowles again. On 24 July White informed Hallam, "I was on the point of writing to Paul as we agreed when I had a visit from Mr. Knowles who said that he feared Routledge would not give anything like the sum expected for the Copyright & he strongly advised me to pause before absolutely rejecting Paul's offer. . . . Under these circumstances I think we must have a 'Congress' before going further." The "Congress" drafted a memo setting forth Tennyson's basic requirements in any new contract with Kegan Paul. And, with that document in hand, the negotiators could begin in earnest.

It is clear from this that Tennyson was reluctant indeed to go with

Kegan Paul. He tried two other possibilities, Macmillan and Routledge, the terms of whose proposals we are lacking, before entering into formal negotiations with Kegan Paul – who, on the other hand, very much wanted to keep Tennyson on his list, as we can surmise from his submitting two different offers and then twice stopping by at White's to reaffirm his interest. Tennyson was definitely Kegan Paul's choice poet, though Kegan Paul, it seems, was only Tennyson's third-choice publisher.

Four main issues complicated the Kegan Paul–Tennyson negotiations: (1) Tennyson wanted to keep the prices up by not allowing any special sales; (2) he also asked for proofs to be submitted to him without any time limit, while Paul demanded a clear limit to Tennyson's time with proofs; (3) Tennyson required an annual account of sales and stock (not surprisingly, Paul was agreeable to stock, but not sales, accounts); and (4) the two sides disagreed about the price at which Tennyson would purchase unsold stock and stereotype plates produced under the previous contract.[75] These disputed points were outlined in the memo mentioned above.

Kegan Paul responded personally to White on 26 August about these demands. He agreed to the sale-price item, qualified the corrections item, demurred on annual sales accounting and left the price of unsold stock and plates "for discussion between yourself and our lawyers." He added, however, a crucial condition: "We hope that if we make these large concessions, two of which at least are quite unusual – if the matter is looked at from a purely business point of view – that Mr. Tennyson will withdraw his objection to the publication of an Annotated Edition, of course on the understanding that no note shall be published which has not his full sanction." We can imagine the Tennysons' reaction to that.

By November, however, Paul was mellowing. He agreed to modify his conditions on corrections made to existing stereotype plates and to give Tennyson a yearly accounting of the number of copies of each edition sold. Yet the quibbling about the price of the plates themselves went on. Kegan Paul's intentions were viewed with great suspicion by the Tennyson side. For example, Hallam expostulated to White at about his time, " 'The new stereotypes' my father is 'bound to purchase at *cost* price' is plainly absurd – for Paul might make new stereotypes for everything *at once* – & make us pay double at the end. Judging from the outrageous amount of Editions now, there might be in fact no end to the new plates." Hallam then called the "cost price" clause "manifestly absurd," and ended with "You must settle as you think best. Arbitration is the only method it seems to me. . . . Please knock Paul's haggling on the head if possible. It worries my father."

In trying to settle the stereoplate matter, Kegan Paul supplied a list, at Tennyson's request, of who owned what plates, but the list was erroneous in that it listed all the plates (except *Queen Mary*) as belonging to Kegan Paul, when in fact all editions before Tennyson went to Henry S. King had been purchased by Tennyson. Finally, however, settlement was reached on ownership of the plates.

Somehow the entire agreement was ready for signature by very late November. But, to Kegan Paul's dismay, enter Routledge again. Tennyson had been negotiating with the Routledge firm about their reissuing the old Illustrated Edition, which had been remaindered to them after Moxons had folded. White wrote,

> On Thursday afternoon Paul called here in considerable agitation to say that he had learnt that a rival Publisher had gone down to see Mr. Tennyson, he wished to know if it implied any doubt as to carrying out the Agreement we were negotiating. He did not mention nor did I ask for the name of the Rival: but I assured him I know of no such visit & that I was not aware of any reason why the contemplated agreement should not be carried out. The next morning brought me your letter of the 28th mentioning Routledge's visit, to which, no doubt, Paul alluded.
>
> (2 December 1878)

Tennyson ultimately conceded that any arrangements for such a reissue must be arranged with Kegan Paul.

The legal agreement, dated 14 February 1879 (the full text of which appears in Appendix II), at last was sent to both parties — and Kegan Paul managed to sign in the wrong place. After it was re-executed, an appointment was set for the exchange of signed agreements, and thus the negotiations, which had taken from 15 April to 15 February, ten full months, were at an end.

In essence the terms of the new agreement differed considerably from Tennyson's previous terms with King. Kegan Paul agreed to pay Tennyson £2500 a year for the right to publish the existing works, except for *Queen Mary* and *Harold*. These two plays and all new works C. Kegan Paul and Co. were to have the right to issue on a 5 per cent commission basis, paying all costs themselves. Tennyson was thus reduced from a guaranteed £5000 a year to only £2500, a reduction warranted by declining sales, but he was relieved of production costs for new editions. One very clear Tennyson victory is evident in Clause 13: "C. Kegan Paul & Co. shall not advertise any of the existing or future works of the said Alfred Tennyson in any manner which may be distasteful to him and shall immediately withdraw any advertisement to which the said Alfred Tennyson shall signify his objection." The Annotated Edition, too, was finally laid to rest by Clause 8, which specified that Kegan Paul be prohibited from producing an annotated edition or from making any additions or alterations without the written consent of Tennyson.

Comparing these long, complicated negotiations complete with explicit legal agreement with the informal, verbal arrangement which Tennyson had had for so many years with Edward Moxon makes us inevitably conclude that Tennyson and his publishers had both learned by trying experiences. The Illustrated Edition struggle with Payne of Moxon and Co., Kegan Paul's attempts to get an annotated edition published by Henry S. King, the continuing problem of stereoplate ownership – all these had taught Tennyson to spell out everything in writing and, in general, not to trust his publishers. His publishers, on the other hand, had learned by one frustrating experience after another both to control closely Tennyson's penchant for extensive, cumbersome corrections to proofs, and to diminish, if possible, the amount they had to pay for the copyrights to the old works, in light of reduced sales. Gone was the camaraderie, gone the mutual trust, gone the gentlemen's agreement between poet and publisher, or even the notion of one. In their place now stood the usual reams of legal documents, solicitors, negotiations, and what Carlyle would have called the "Cash Nexus."

Under the new agreement Kegan Paul continued publishing the seven-volume Author's Edition started by King in 1875 and, of course, also his own Crown and Shilling Editions. In 1881 he came out with a Royal Edition in one volume, replete with illustrations and portrait. This sold well enough to require reprinting in 1882.

Tennyson, meanwhile, was still at work on plays, writing *The Falcon*, finished in November 1879, and *The Cup*, begun in that same month and completed towards the end of the following year. Both these plays were produced long before they were published. *The Falcon* ran for sixty-seven nights, beginning 18 December 1879, with Mr and Mrs Kendal as both producers and leading actors. For twenty-four performances of this one-act play, Tennyson received £48, at his usual rate of £2 per act per night.[76] When Henry Irving sought a

license for *The Cup* in May 1880, he requested these same terms and
asked for a five-year license plus the stipulation that the play not be
published until after its first run. As this was a two-act play, Tennyson
garnered £4 a night.

The play was produced at the Lyceum Theatre by Henry Irving on
January 3, 1881, and ran for between 125 and 130 nights. The
leading roles were played by Irving and Ellen Terry. Although this
was Tennyson's first real stage success, the author was dissatisfied
with the way Irving portrayed Synorix, the protagonist. Tennyson
said, "Irving has not hit off my Synorix, who is a subtle blend of
Roman refinement and intellectuality, and barbarian, self-satisfied
sensuality."[77]

Oddly enough, Tennyson and Kegan Paul did not see fit to publish
these plays, in spite of the stage success of *The Cup*. They did not reach
the public in printed form until Alexander Macmillan made them his
first Tennyson publication in February 1884. Kegan Paul, we can
presume, wanted no marginal publications on his hands.

Tennyson on his own initiative withdrew from publication
another play produced during the Kegan Paul years, the disastrous
The Promise of May. This prose attempt at a "modern village
tragedy" was refused by both Henry Irving and the Kendals, but
taken up by Mrs Bernard Beere, who directed it and played the role of
Dora Steer. It ran at the Globe Theatre from 11 November to 15
December 1882.

In her diary on November 11, 1882 Mary Gladstone recorded the
unhappy experience of attending the first night's performance with
the poet's two sons, Hallam and Lionel: "It was most painful, there
being a brutal Bradlaugh gallery and pit who jeered and hissed and
greeted with peals of laughter the special points of pathos, morality
or tragedy. . . . There are obvious defects in the play wh[ich]
w[ou]ld make it specially unacceptable to the 19th Century
audience. It was miserable work."[78]

(*The Promise of May* was published finally in *Locksley Hall Sixty Years
After*, 1886.)

Tennyson's first poetry publication with Kegan Paul under the
new contract was *The Lover's Tale* (1879), an old poem. The first
three parts of it had been composed in 1827–8; the fourth part, "The

Golden Supper," had been written much later and published by
Strahan in the 1869 *Holy Grail* volume. Tennyson's headnote to the
1879 edition sums up his reasons for finally issuing to the public a
work he had tried so hard to suppress:

> The original Preface to *The Lover's Tale* states that it was composed
> in my nineteenth year. Two only of the three parts then written
> were printed, when, feeling the imperfection of the poem, I
> withdrew it from the press. One of my friends however who,
> boylike, admired the boy's work, distributed among our common
> associates of that hour some copies of these two parts, without my
> knowledge, without the omissions and amendments which I had in
> contemplation, and marred by the many misprints of the com-
> positor. Seeing that these two parts have of late been mercilessly
> pirated, and that what I had deemed scarce worthy to live is not
> allowed to die, may I not be pardoned if I suffer the whole poem at
> last to come into the light — accompanied with a reprint of the
> sequel — a work of my mature life — 'The Golden Supper'?[79]

The 1467 lines of the blank-verse poem, after this checkered history
of clandestine distribution, piracy and forgery, became, in 1879, a
legitimate, authorized Tennyson volume, classically resplendent in
green cloth with gilt lettering. It sold for 3s. 6d., but the records of its
sales are gone.

In November 1880 Kegan Paul published Tennyson's only newly
composed book of poetry since *Gareth and Lynette* in 1872. *Ballads and
Other Poems* (with the title clearly echoing Swinburne's *Poems and
Ballads* of 1866), in the usual binding and selling at five shillings,
found an admiring public pleased at Tennyson's "return to lyric and
narrative verse." Their delight "found expression in a chorus of
praise, *Rizpah* and the two great fighting ballads being acclaimed as
amongst his finest work. The critics were, on the whole, delighted to
find him coming once more close to the problems of the time and the
emotions of common life — once more showing himself 'The Poet of
the People.'"[80] Today most readers of Tennyson esteem the gripping
ballads "Rizpah," and "The Revenge."[81] Some, like Ricks, recognize the "Battle of Brunanburh" as "probably the best verse-
translation of any Anglo-Saxon poetry;[82] some few others admire
"De Profoundis" for its forceful reassertion of the creed formerly
expressed in "The Higher Pantheism." The forms he choose to use —
particularly the ballad and sonnet — attest to Tennyson's continued

experimentation and building of his repertoire as well as his desire to reach the populace.

Ballads and Other Poems, though refreshing in its signalling that Tennyson's preoccupation with the drama might be over — which it was not, incidentally — was not enough of a success to make Kegan Paul anxious to continue as Tennyson's publisher after the contract's expiration in 1883. Like most of the public, Paul imagined that Tennyson, even though recently honored by the Queen and her government with a peerage, was a lordly swan who had now sung his last song.

6 Final Choice:
Alexander Macmillan
(1884—92)

Tennyson departed from the fold of Charles Kegan Paul at the expiration of the five-year contract in January 1884. The September before, he had received an offer from Macmillan & Co. which granted terms quite desirable. They offered, among other things, "to pay Mr. Tennyson a royalty of one third of the advertised price on all the books we print and sell" and "to pay in advance £1,500 annually on account of this royalty, but also as an absolute payment, in case the royalty any year did not reach this amount." With this financial guarantee also came the security of not having to change publishers again, for Macmillan offered a ten-year contract.[1] These two items — the change from a share in profits or a commission basis to this one-third royalty (very high, even by Tennyson's standards), and the move from the usual five-year to a ten-year agreement were the major points of interest in the new contract and represented Alexander Macmillan's attempt to win now by generosity what had before been lost by financial prudence.

Hallam Tennyson later that fall advised Alexander Macmillan on two matters:

> Let us advise you by all means to buy Paul's stock if you can. It will be a perpetual thorn in your side if he is always for years selling the books at low prices.
>
> In your seven volume Edition had you not better call the separate volumes by names e.g. "Enoch Arden etc." "The Idylls of the King" etc. and not number them? because we find that separate volumes are wanted for wedding & birthday presents etc. Of course *you* will know best about this point.[2]

This suggestion for naming the separate volumes shows the Tennyson family's awareness of the minutiae of the book trade, and their encouragement of Macmillan to buy Kegan Paul's stock reveals the deep distrust which had developed in the Tennyson–Kegan Paul relationship by the end of their five-year agreement. Hallam wrote to Alexander Macmillan in 14 January 1884, "We are very pleased to think that on the 16th if all be well, we shall really be under your protection." What, indeed, had been so dangerous about Kegan Paul that the Tennysons needed another publisher's protection?

A partial answer to that question is given by noting the elaborate lengths the Tennysons and Arnold White, their solicitor, had to go to secure Kegan Paul's stock of Tennyson editions. First, Paul's estimate of the stock's value depended on estimates of their production cost, which far exceeded Macmillan's estimates. The price, therefore, could not be agreed upon easily. In fact, it was only under threat of bringing in an outside arbitrator that the two companies came to terms. Secondly, Paul sent a check in partial payment of his regular 15 January accounting, to which White replied, "I confess I am somewhat surprised at your holding back any part of the payment due to [Tennyson] and which should have been made on the 15th inst. as that has nothing to do with the purchase of the stock." To Hallam on the same day White exploded, "The keeping back of part of the money is just one of Paul's mean & tricky ways. As we are so soon to get rid of him, it is not worth while making a fuss about it, but it paints the man" (29 January 1884). The strength of these words is uncharacteristic of the usually moderate White and suggests the depths of the resentment felt by both the Tennysons and himself. At a later point in the correspondence, White even went so far as to complain to Paul himself that he was both surprised and regretful "that a firm of your eminence should think it becoming, in dealing with Lord Tennyson, to adopt a course so narrow, and I may almost add, insulting," appending that such a course was "wanting in delicacy" (2 February 1884). Thirdly, Paul, as late as 1887, continued to show his cheek by still advertising and selling various copies of Tennyson's works with the Kegan Paul name in them. Thus he further threatened the Tennysons financially, since legally no payment had to be made to Tennyson for these sales. Finally, Paul also eroded the Tennysons' control over the timing and format of publication. For example, from 1885 to 1887, correspondence reveals that he wanted to reprint Tennyson's *Songs Set to Music*, but Macmillan would not allow it. Yet Kegan Paul advertised the work in the 18 November 1887 *Athenaeum*. The two firms eventually compromised on this matter, but the idea that an unauthorized edition or reprinting should appear was a forceful reminder to the Tennysons that piracy was not only an overseas act perpetrated by unscrupulous Americans but also one that former publishers might spring on the unwary author.

Such losses of control — even the specter of such potential losses — over his profession troubled Tennyson in much the same way that infringements of his sense of privacy did.

He chose to set a high-pitched standard easily followed by the rest of his family by his almost hysterical reaction to the tourists and his extreme recalcitrance to allowing personal illustrations or biographical references in his volumes. Yet Hallam Tennyson appears to have been even more concerned about complete control than Alfred himself. One may be tempted to call the son almost obsessed on the subject, particularly as his actions — the well-known excisions from his father's letters and his mother's Journal (what he could not cut out he inked over so heavily that even modern technology cannot restore the sense) and his labyrinthine protective procedures when giving the manuscripts of Tennyson's poems to Trinity College, Cambridge — have scotched much scholarly inquiry.

Therefore one could argue that the conflict between Kegan Paul and the Tennysons may have been based more on the latter's fear of personal exposure than on any ideological differences about the advertising and selling of books. Happily, all these squabbles, whatever their causes, were put behind him with Tennyson's going to Macmillan.

A letter Alexander Macmillan wrote to Lady Tennyson on 16 January 1884 evinces his genuine pleasure in his new position as Tennyson's publisher:

> I am sending you by this post a copy of our first book as Lord Tennyson's publisher. We have striven to keep it simple & as beautiful as the narrow conditions will allow. We hope by & bye to do worthier editions.
>
> It is just forty two years since I first read "Poems by Alfred Tennyson", and got bitten by a *healthy mania* from which I have not recovered and dont want to recover. I then tried to bite others, with some success. I have now *other*, I cannot say *deeper* motives for continuing the process. How much I owe to Alfred Tennyson for the increase of ennobling thought & feeling, no one can tell. Now our closer connection will not lessen my desire to repay the debt.

Part of Macmillan's delight came from finally having realized a dream; after all, three times before he had tried and failed to get the Tennyson copyright. In 1858, upon hearing that Tennyson might change his publisher after Edward Moxon's death, Macmillan had written to Franklin Lushington, Tennyson's friend, asking him to "say a word to [Tennyson] on our behalf." With typical reluctance to intrude, Macmillan also wrote, "As I don't know how exactly matters stand between Mr. Tennyson and any one else I will say nothing about terms . . ." (15 October 1858). But Tennyson, bound by his commitment to Moxon's widow and his normal reluctance to make unnecessary changes, stayed where he was. Then in 1868 Alexander Macmillan was outbid by Alexander Strahan, who offered £5000 for the right to publish Tennyson's old works, as against the £3000 offered by Macmillan. In 1878 Macmillan once again offered less than a rival, this time Kegan Paul. W. E. Cushon, a senior member of the Macmillan firm in our century, offered this sound explanation for why Tennyson took such a roundabout journey to get to Macmillan — roundabout that is, in the light of the poet's intention to do so and Macmillan's great wish to have him: Tennyson, according to Cushon, "wanted too much money."[3] But by 1884 Tennyson had moderated his pecuniary demands after learning from bitter experience with Kegan Paul that trust and respect in the author—publisher relationship were worth a great deal in themselves. Sales of his works had been tapering off, too, so Macmillan's guaranteed payment of £1500 looked all the more appealing and his one-third selling-price royalty even generous. No trace of the slightest disagreement can be found in Tennyson's years with Macmillan & Co.

The personal relationship began in 1859, the end of a decade in which Alexander Macmillan had had to witness his brother Daniel's slow death from consumption. The two Scots had begun their operation with a book shop at 57, Aldersgate Street in London, but soon moved to Trinity Street, Cambridge, and expanded into publishing itself. Daniel had been a man of "special gifts," as the *Dictionary of National Biography* observes. "No man who ever sold books for a livelihood was more conscious of a vocation. His strongly marked character — ambitious, devout but not austere, impetuous yet under constant self-restraint — produced a strong impression on all who met him." By 1844 Daniel and Alexander had begun publishing educational works, starting with A. R. Craig's *Philosophy of Training*. Soon the writings of F. D. Maurice and Richard Chenevix Trench (later Archbishop of Dublin) were added to the list. By the mid-1850s the firm was established as a publisher of all manner of literary offerings, including a few bestsellers, such as *Westward Ho!* and *Tom Brown's Schooldays*. Upon Daniel's death, Alexander, who had a wife and four small children himself, took under his own roof his brother's widow and four children, whom he and his wife later adopted. (Daniel's two sons, Frederick and Maurice, along with Alexander's own son George, were eventually to enter the firm.) Later, Alexander moved the main business back to London, leaving Robert Bowes, a nephew, in charge of Macmillan and Bowes Bookshop at Cambridge. Alexander, "a man of fine integrity, high ideals and sound common sense," was not short on success.[4] He served as publisher to Oxford University for many years, and branched out with firms in New York, India and Canada, to become one of the most highly respected publishers in the English-speaking world.

Alexander Macmillan had educated himself for the most part through the reading of superior literature. "His youthful enthusiasm for Carlyle and Coleridge, for Shakespeare, Burns, Shelley, Wordsworth, Tennyson, never changed or faded," maintained Canon A. Aingier in an article written after Macmillan's death. Plato (read in translation), the Psalms, George Fox, Bunyan, De Quincey, and especially Scott (but not Dickens, curiously enough) were favorites. These writers all "formed for him a secret standard and criterion of excellence which saved him in a remarkable way from false admirations."[5] Such a standard proved invaluable. For most of his active publishing life he was his own reader, somehow finding time to write both long explanations of rejections and to offer careful counsel on future writing projects as well as necessary repairs to manuscripts in hand.

His literary output was scanty: his only book, an anonymously edited selection from Shelley with brief memoir (London: Bell, 1840); a few anonymous verses in the *Christian Socialist* in 1850; a translation from Heine in *Macmillan's Magazine* in 1872; and some prose contributions to the same periodical under the pseudonym "Amos Yates." Macmillan himself once said, "I could not write a book myself to save my life," but had entertained the idea of writing on the topic of children, which he described in 1875 in a letter to F. W. Farrar, then headmaster of Marlborough: "I find my joints too stiff to attempt any literary work, and I have long given up the hope of doing this [book on children] or anything else, and must content myself with being a suggester and, perhaps, in some way a helper of literary work."[6] This quality of being literary dolphin to perpetually drowning sailors of prose and poetry and bringing them to safe harbor was profoundly appreciated by the writers and their families, as expressed by Mrs Green, wife of J. R. Green, the historian, who remembers

> many visits of my husband to [Alexander Macmillan's] office for the discussion of his books, their chances and their success; Mr. Macmillan never seemed hurried on such occasions. His interest in the books was always fresh and earnest, and his time and sympathy were always ready and given without stint. It was a part of his original genius to realize the value to an author of a publisher's genuine interest in his work, and this trouble he never grudged.[7]

Macmillan's own early poverty and his struggle to get a foothold in a profession made him especially sympathetic to other beginners. But, along with time, sympathy, generosity, enthusiasm and hospitality, came also a driven, overbearing intellect. His own children, it is reported, sometimes fell silent in the face of his ebullient conversation, and no doubt his innate Calvinism, nourished by reading Carlyle, disposed him towards working twelve hours a day in the shop, followed by several more late into the night, which did not always lie easily with his employees. Nevertheless his many friends and workers felt a genuine admiration and love for Alexander Macmillan – not all of it, fortunately, expressed after his death – and on balance the few reports of ill will are negligible.[8]

It was at Cambridge in the summer of 1859, when he and Francis Palgrave (later famous for the *Golden Treasury* series) were returning from a tour of Portugal, Spain and North Africa, that Tennyson first met Alexander Macmillan. Sir Charles Tennyson, the poet's biographer and grandson, reports that the two "took to one another immediately."[9] A long letter from Alexander Macmillan to Emily Tennyson in late September reveals more than could third-party description the sincerity of his admiration for Tennyson's poetry and his willingness to trust new acquaintances with his intimate feelings. Such lengthy and heartfelt communications, neatly penned on pale-blue paper, are indicators of Macmillan's enormous ability to set apart time from the business at hand to devote to matters of what he would have called "the soul." It is small wonder, then, that the author of "The Way of the Soul" (an earlier title of *In Memoriam*, you will remember) should have become his friend. Here is that letter to Emily in full:

Cambridge Sept. 29. 1859

Dear Madam,

I am afraid you will think that I am making a somewhat too rapid response to the kind invitation which you & Mr. Tennyson gave me. But you will not hesitate to say if you would rather not see me down at the Isle of Wight at present. The occasion of my proposing to come so speedily is that Professor Masson & myself had arranged to take a two or three days run together somewhere before our winter's work fairly begins, and on talking over the question of place today, it occurred to us that we could not do better than come to the Isle of Wight, especially if we had a chance of an hour or two with Mr. Tennyson and yourself. If you would kindly let me know if you are at home, and whether you could conveniently see us, we propose coming on Friday next week Oct. 7 & being about the Island up till Monday Oct. 10. Any time within these bounds we could call on you.

I cannot help telling you what deep joy Mr. Tennyson's visit gave & has left in our household. If you will pardon my intruding my private matters on you, I would like to tell you how Mr. Tennyson is linked in the minds of myself, my wife & sister-in-law who lives with us by bands deeper than as a writer of noble poetry, though as such he is indeed dear to us as to thousands of English speaking people. The two men who were nearest to me in relationship, were happily for me, also nearest to me in love and intellectual intercourse. My brother Daniel, who was my partner in all ways, for eighteen years of most blessed intercourse – (we had been separated by circumstances in earlier life –) was the first who introduced me to Mr. Tennyson's poetry. Ever since 1842, when the first 2 volume edition was published, there has been no book, but one, so often in our hands, or whose words have been so often on our lips. Each successive publication was hailed with a fresh joy & conned & discussed & read & re-read together till every sentence was familiar to us. Our most earnest aspirations after any nobleness in life or thought got its best verbal expression oftenest I believe in the words of these books. For the last few years of his life, he was a hopeless invalid. His disease – pulmonary – was one, we knew, that could not but take him from us very soon & he & we were both conscious for at least two years before he went, that any day almost might be the last of his own intercourse here. You may perhaps judge how in what spirit we read "In Memoriam" together. It & Mr. Maurice's books were the constant companions of our fireside or of any pleasure outing we had. Then besides my brother, my wife's brother George Brimley had been for some years before my marriage about my most intimate friend next to my brother. My marriage with his sister deepened this, of course. I need hardly tell you how he admired and, intelligently, Mr. Tennyson's poetry. The Essay which he published in the Cambridge Essays was written at a time when we were constantly together, and many of the points were discussed long and earnestly between us. He was naturally a man of keen critical faculty. I was by temperament more enthusiastic & the results arrived at in the Essay were not always what I sympathised with. But deeper and more important by far than any mere criticism, was the hold which Mr. Tennyson's poetry took on my dear friend & brother's feelings. He, like my brother Daniel, was under the influence of a fatal and most painful disease. His naturally critical and sceptical mind had led to a considerable extent to a loss of any distinct hold on things unseen. Mr. Tennyson's "In Memoriam", I have reason to believe, came home to him with great power & had a blessed influence on his whole life after. In a most beautiful article which he wrote in the Spectator, under the title of Christmas Thoughts for 1857, he manifested this influence strongly & I think every Christmas eve afterwards at our family gatherings that noble hymn "Ring out wild bells" was read.

In May 1857 dear George was taken from us, & in a month after Daniel took his last farewell of us too. Two nobler or braver or more loving men I cannot ever hope to know again in this world. Their memory is wound up in every act & work of my daily life; and so it is with my dear wife & sister. "In Memoriam" is still often read at our fireside & every line is linked with the memory of these two blessed brothers.

You will understand how when the man to whom we owe so much, that is thus deeply woven up with so precious memories, came among us, he came not alone, but seemed almost to give us back what we had lost, and when we found him so kind and genial, I hope he would forgive us if we seemed to treat him as an old & most familiar friend.

You will forgive me if I have written thus to you in a strain that is usually only permitted to intimate & long continued friends. But I could not refrain from expressing to you thus some of the deep debt of gratitude & love I and my household feel to your husband; and entering thus freely on the grounds of it.

Do not, I beg of you, hesitate to say if our coming to see you at this time would at all inconvenience you & I will willingly defer the pleasure I promise myself till some future & more convenient opportunity.

believe me dear Madam
most respectfully & gratefully yours

Alexander Macmillan

At the time of this letter — the fall of 1859 — Macmillan was working on plans for a shilling magazine which he thought to call "The Round Table."[10] It was his hope to have a Tennyson poem in an early issue. To James MacLehose, a fellow Scot and bookseller, he wrote:

We are progressing satisfactorily with *Maga* [*Macmillan's Magazine*]. Hughes's story opens brilliantly — quite Tom Brown himself. Masson says it could not be better. I think the other articles will follow suit — good stuff all. Don't whisper it to a soul, as it may after all come to nothing, but I am in hopes of a poem from Tennyson. He was down in Cambridge for two days, and spent the great part of them with us. He was most friendly. He said several times he wished we were his publishers, but he was so tied that he could not move at present. He is such a noble, kindly man. I could not help thinking how he and dear Daniel would have taken to each other. If he respects the Macmillan blood in so unworthy a representative as myself, what would he not have done in so noble a one as Daniel? May I never disgrace that noble and sweet memory. I could not help writing a long letter to Mrs. Tennyson [quoted previously] — she wrote one to me a few months since thanking me for a little interest I had taken in getting her husband's bust into Trinity, and invited me to come and see them. In my letter I ventured to tell her something about Daniel and George Brimley, and how they would bound up in memory with her husband's books. The result was a most warm repetition of her invitation, and Masson, who also has an old invitation on hand, and I are going

down tomorrow to spend two or three days with them, in the Isle
of Wight, giving Kingsley a look in on our way back.

My hope for Tennyson's poem is a half promise he made when
he was in Cambridge, which I mean to try and clinch – if I can do it
without obtrusiveness – when I am with him.[11]

Of these days at Farringford Macmillan wrote to George Wilson on
12 October, "We had three glorious days with Tennyson, whom we
found in all ways genial, manly, and pleasant. We talked and walked
and smoked and chatted with the ladies, and altogether were as happy
as we could be."[12] Macmillan followed up the visit with a long letter
to Tennyson accepting the "Seaside Idyll" (actually, "Sea Dreams:
An Idyll") for the *Magazine*, inviting him at the same time to a
literary dinner in November, and also noting the books he was
sending along to him (Maurice's latest and a novel by Henry
Kingsley). In short, Macmillan wasted no time in developing the
friendship and its attendant publishing connection. But the latter tie
posed a problem: Could Macmillan publish a Tennyson poem
without intruding on the Moxon rights? (This was a moral question
alone, as prior periodical publication was legally acceptable.) Emily
Tennyson must have expressed some qualms about such publication,
for Macmillan felt obligated to write to her,

I very deeply sympathise with your feeling about the unusual
arrangements, of which my own will more or less partake. The
only apology I have to make for it is that it is a single and complete
affair, and carrying with it no future harassing and unknown
responsibilities. I must frankly admit a double selfishness. It will be
an inexpressible delight for me to be in any way connected as a
publisher with Mr. Tennyson – gratifying my vanity I fear I must
honestly admit – perhaps a little of some better feeling mingles
with it, and commercially, I think it will do our magazine a great
deal of good. Yet I do hope you will not feel yourself induced by
instincts (which I cannot but admit to be most wholesome) to
persuade Mr. Tennyson to alter his mind, but that we may have the
poem for the magazine as he kindly promised. I think I am honest
in saying that so long as the Moxon family have any interest in the
publications I would not move a finger to induce their coming to
us; and I simply wish this *Idyll* for magazine purposes, and will
unrepiningly see it go back to its natural publishing channels.[13]

Tennyson was paid £250 for the 304-line poem which appeared in the January issue of *Macmillan's* and later in Moxon & Co.'s 1864 *Enoch Arden, Etc.*[14] The poem's most notable feature, in this writer's opinion, is the little nursery song "What does little birdie say," which captures, without moralizing, a simple truth about growing up.

In the December issue, Macmillan published pseudonymously a reply to the *Quarterly Review*'s recent article on Tennyson's *Maud*. He asserted that *Maud* is dramatic — that "the author was not speaking in his own person, but was, in fact, writing a long and sustained dramatic poem in a style striking and novel." Such a recognition of the *persona* was exceptional at that point in Tennyson criticism.[15] Macmillan's defense of *Maud* was rooted in his early enthusiasm for it after he had seen a copy at Moxon's in 1855. "Mr. Robert Bowes remembers how he [Macmillan] put the volume into his pocket and walked out to the village of Coton to read it undisturbed." Macmillan's first report of his response to the poem, as far as we know, appears in a letter to an unknown correspondent on 27 July 1855.

> The great event of this week has been *Maud*. I can tell you that in a word. Our sale has been 50 copies. I don't think this very bad for a long vacation day. . . . I cannot say what I think of it as a whole, except that the first impression is excessively painful. It begins to dawn on me as a kind of prophetic utterance — our selfish griefs and joys have to be swallowed up in a larger one by this war.[16]

On 1 September he wrote, "*Maud* is not according to Grundy in any sense seemingly. George Brimley tells me that I am the only one he knows who stands for it altogether."[17] By that clearly stated, however brief, article in his magazine, Macmillan set himself apart from all Tennyson's other publishers by being the only one to write any notable criticism of his works. He also showed his good critical sense and audacity in praising a poem which to this day has left many a critic confused, if not outright cold.

The years following their 1859 Cambridge meeting and Macmillan's subsequent visit to Farringford found Tennyson and Macmillan in frequent contact. Tennyson was part of some of the "Tobacco Parliaments" which met in Macmillan's Henrietta Street home in the 1860s. "The Round Table" had been thought of as the first name for *Macmillan's Magazine*, and, although King Arthur did retain some prominence on the cover as the top medallion of a series which also included those of Chaucer, Shakespeare and Milton, the Arthurian name itself was dropped. Macmillan contented himself with having in his home an actual round table of English oak around which the magazine's supporters and other friends met for their smoky discussions. Those who added their handwritten names to the table's edge included, in addition to Tennyson, F. D. Maurice, Thomas Huxley, Herbert Spencer, J. W. Blakesley, G. S. Venables, Franklin Lushington, Coventry Patmore, Francis Palgrave, F. G. Stephens, William Allingham and Thomas Hughes — a sort of "Who's Who" of literary and philosophical London in the 1860s, minus novelists such as Dickens, Thackeray and Trollope, for whom Macmillan had little enthusiasm.[18]

Other connections flourished between poet and publisher during this period. The Tennyson family seems to have ordered books from Macmillan's shop more than from Moxon's, probably because of the developing ill will between Tennyson and J. Bertrand Payne, Moxon's manager (see Chapter 4). Any number of letters from Emily Tennyson to Macmillan during this decade include thanks for books sent. For example, in September 1868, while Tennyson was negotiating for Moxon & Co.'s successor, Emily wrote, "Am I taking too great a liberty if pending a fresh publishing arrangement I ask you to procure me books which Lionel wants for Eton?" In the same letter she also asked about the date for taking Lionel up to school, since Macmillan also had a son enrolled there himself (BM, 13 September 1868). Shortly before this, Hallam had written to Macmillan himself about his own reading material for Marlborough (BM, 15 July 1868). No doubt Macmillan's deep-felt appreciation for Tennyson's poetry and his judicious publishing enhanced his position as friend to the family. Once, in an attempt to discourage W. Stigant from publishing too much too soon, he wrote,

> I feel sure that a publication of a poem or volume of poems that does not command public attention is an injury to a man's reputation. It almost secures indifference to his future efforts. See how slowly Tennyson publishes, and this not by any means because he could not produce more. He told me, and I am sure it was no mere boast, that he could write verse almost as fast as he could write prose if he liked to get at it. But slowly maturing everything he does to the very utmost of his power he never publishes now without at once commanding a large sale. . . .[19]

An important watermark in the Macmillan – Tennyson publishing relationship was the appearance in May 1868 of "Lucretius" in *Macmillan's Magazine*. (It appeared, too, in *Every Saturday* on 2 May 1868, and in the 1869 *Holy Grail and Other Poems* volume published by Strahan.) Only that past January Tennyson had read the 280-line poem to a small group at Knapdale, Macmillan's large home. But, before either having heard or read the poem, Macmillan had accepted it for the *Magazine*, and had assented to the terms which George Grove, editor from 1868–83, had worked out with Tennyson. Macmillan had also taken the initiative in getting American publication by Ticknor and Fields, leaving the terms up to Tennyson, to whom he wrote, "I have no sort of objection to your getting as much as you can from them, provided they don't anticipate us."[20] The Americans were permitted to see the full text of "Lucretius," but in *Macmillan's* the English had only an expurgated version. Lines 188–92, those allowed the American public, read in the full version,

> here an Oread – how the sun delights
> To glance and shift about her slippery sides,
> And rosy knees and supple roundedness,
> And budded bosom-peaks – who this way runs
> Before the rest. . . .

Apparently on Grove's advice, Tennyson, who liked the first version better, offered only this single line to the English: 'here an Oread, and this way she runs.' Two letters reveal Tennyson's own disposition to leave the full text: one to Grove on 3 March 1868 – "With respect to the Oread please yourself, but send the full passage to America. They are not so squeamish as we are"; and an undated one to an unknown recipient – "My wife is copying *Lucretius*. . . . *She* does not think it will shock people."[21]

This and other occasional publications in *Macmillan's Magazine* added one more strand to the tapestry of friendship being woven between Alexander Macmillan and Alfred Tennyson during the years of Tennyson's publishing contracts with Moxon and Co., Strahan, King, and Kegan Paul. Macmillan's descriptions of two Sundays spent at Aldworth in 1882 epitomizes the great pleasure all seemed to take in this bond: "The chats and chaff and play of wit, wisdom and rollick were delightful." Not all was lightheartedness, however; weighty matters of life and death were aired, too. On one of these Sundays a lengthy discussion on the Hereafter (of which Alfred was more sure than he was of this life) involved Alfred, Alexander, and James Spedding, another visitor. This particular talk remained long in both Tennyson's and Macmillan's memories, because Spedding, at one time a Cambridge Apostle and a long-time friend and an accomplished editor of the work of Sir Francis Bacon, was run down and killed by a hansom cab just a few weeks after the Aldworth visit.[22]

When Tennyson came to Macmillan & Co. in 1884, the firm was specializing in textbooks, scholarly works, and *belles lettres*, particularly older, established works. Its *Elementary Classics* Series, for example, was standard fare in schools of the day. The outstanding literary names on the list were Meredith, Pater, Saintsbury, Hardy, James, and, in the 1890s, Kipling. Names of a few contemporary novelists in a lighter style were present, too: Charlotte Yonge, Mrs Oliphant and Helen Hunt Jackson. Macmillan was gaining reputation, too, for his well-edited series: particularly John Morley's *English Men of Letters*, Palgrave's *Golden Treasury*, the *Cambridge Shakespeare*, the *Globe Shakespeare*, and the *Globe Library* itself. Grove's *Dictionary of Music and Musicians*, still a standard reference work, was also a Macmillan publication.

With this kind of diversified, first-rate list, Macmillan was in the enviable position of not really needing the Poet Laureate – which could not have been said of Strahan and King during their contract years with Tennyson. But Alexander Macmillan was eager to have him in any case. Consequently poet and publisher joined together out of their respective well-established positions, both able to prosper even more by that union and both free of the chains of monetary necessity.

Macmillan's business was hallmarked throughout its duration by his own personal qualities and quirks, all of which proved congenial to the Tennysons. First among these was his prudence in official agreements with authors but generosity with regard to ancillary money matters with them. For example, the firm "frequently advanced [Matthew] Arnold money to pay the premiums on his life insurance."[23] The story of J. R. Green's success with the *Short History of the English People* bears witness to this same spirit. Alexander Macmillan had bought the copyright for £300, in spite of the reservations expressed by Grove and other advisors.

Its success was instantaneous. After 8000 copies had been sold, Alexander decided that he had made too good a bargain, sent for the contract in which Green assigned his copyright, destroyed it, and substituted for it a royalty agreement greatly and continuously to the advantage of the author and his heirs. Thirty-five thousand copies were sold in the first year.[24]

Secondly, Alexander Macmillan attended meticulously to the whole life of a book, from reading the submitted manuscript himself, attending to the details of production – he even interested himself in stock quality and cover designs – to finally selecting the methods of promotion and distribution. This tremendous personal attention was mitigated somewhat, however, by his third significant business quality, that of having the ability to delegate. He willingly shared his reading work with a remarkable group which included John Morley, George Grove and Norman Lockyer. Early in his career, Alexander had taken on full working partners such as his nephew Robert Bowes in Cambridge and, in the 1860s, George Lillie Craik. Morgan, the firm's historian, describes the wisdom of the decision to hire Craik:

> It was a fortunate choice, for Craik, though he had an artificial leg and other physical disabilities, was precisely what Alexander needed as an administrator – a man full of energy and character. He stayed in the firm until his death forty years later and was still a legend among the elder members of the staff yet another forty years on. "Is your hearrt in your worrk?" he would demand of them [in his Scots burr] as he passed their desks.[25]

In addition to Craik, Macmillan took into the firm his own son George Augustin and his brother Daniel's sons, Frederick Orridge and Maurice Crawford, whom he had raised. Giving increasing responsibilities to these men, Alexander had arranged his business so that "by the time he was, in effect, out of the firm, his successors were experienced in the management of it."[26] This final quality of being a good administrator, added to his diligence in preparing for the transition of power tempered the impetuosity which marked Alexander Macmillan's speech.

By the late 1880s, Macmillan was no longer able to participate in the day-to-day affairs of the firm. A good deal of his spirit vanished after news came that his son Malcolm had disappeared while climbing Mount Olympus in 1889. But this loss served further to strengthen the bond between poet and publisher, for in 1886, three years before

Macmillan's son's death, Tennyson's younger son Lionel had died of fever on his way home from India. Craik and Frederick Macmillan became the correspondents of Hallam Tennyson, who had years before taken over the administration of his father's business. As Alexander started to withdraw, Tennyson grew closer to his primary advisor, Craik. During his last two summers, 1891 and 1892, Tennyson visited Craik at his home in London in July. Craik's closeness can be seen in the family's choice of him to handle the Laureate's funeral arrangements in Westminster Abbey.

Tennyson's first new publications with Macmillan & Co. continued his lack-lustre experiment with drama. *The Cup* and *The Falcon*, previously produced on stage and printed in a trial edition but never published, appeared together in the usual green boards in February 1884 at a sale price of five shillings. (In all likelihood, only 20,000 were printed during the first year of publication.) Accounts for 1884 are not extant, but, judging by the 1885 account, which lists 6674 copies on hand by the beginning of 1886 and only thirty-three copies sold during 1885, sales fell off very rapidly. A few years later, however, in August 1887, Mary Anderson, the American actress then playing in London in *The Winter's Tale*, was enthusiastic enough about *The Cup* to sign a contract to produce it. In the spring of 1888, she visited Tennyson several times to consult about the production as well as a production of *The Foresters*, but she never did do the plays: in 1890 she married and retired from the stage.

A new play, *Becket*, published by Macmillan in December of that first year fared a little better, and was ultimately Tennyson's most successful play. This volume, in the standard format, sold for six shillings. Although we do not know how many copies Macmillan printed at first (the figure was probably 20,000), we do know that he had to run off 2688 during 1885 to replenish stock. This seems like a very few, but perhaps the first month-and-a-half's sale, which would have been recorded on the missing 1884 accounts, was very large and the first printing was exhausted quickly. Twice Hallam wrote to Macmillan trying to influence *Becket's* reception. In October 1884 he simply said, "Get also a good review in 'Times' & 'Spectator' if you can." But in November he was more explicit: "By all means ask Burkie to get someone good to review Becket in the '*Times*' as it is one of my Fathers [*sic*] greatest works. They have been carping there lately." (BM, 24 October and 6 November 1884.)

The story of *Becket* on stage, though it breaks the normal chronology here, is worth examining for the light it sheds on

Tennyson's eagerness to get his plays produced. For over ten years
Tennyson tried to get Henry Irving to produce *Becket* at the Lyceum.
Irving considered it several times, but hesitated, and, on the whole
proved no easy man to deal with. In writing to Macmillan Hallam
frequently explained the difficulties encountered with the great actor.
After one telegram from Irving asking for a chance "to negotiate
archbishop," Hallam asked Macmillan, "Please advise me. Shall I pin
him in any other way because he is a most strange man and has bought
at least a dozen plays and has not acted them?" (BM, February 1883).
On another occasion Hallam complained to Macmillan, "The real
truth is that Irving telegraphed from America asking for leave to
produce 'Becket' on the Lyceum stage. We agreed to see if it could be
managed, but we have never heard a word from him from that time
to this. He is an odd fish, & perhaps he now desires the right" (BM,
January 1886). In light of Irving's shilly-shallying, Lawrence Barrett,
an American actor, was given both American and British rights in
July 1891. But Barrett died while the play was in rehearsal and
Tennyson once more looked to Irving, who examined Barrett's
adaptation "in earnest and with more confidence than ever before."[27]
Irving finally prepared an acting version. Sir Charles recounts the
subsequent events in this way:

> On April 19th Bram Stoker [Irving's manager] brought a sketch of
> this down to Farringford for approval and found the poet suffering
> from a bad cold. He asked him whether Irving might alter the play
> as he thought necessary. "Irving may do whatever he pleases with
> it," was the reply. "In that case," said Stoker, "he will do it within a
> year." The two went through Irving's draft, which had been made
> by cutting up two copies of the published play and sticking the
> pages on sheets of foolscap. In this way the reader could see the final
> result without having the actual omissions forced on his notice.
> Tennyson evidently knew the play by heart and recognized
> immediately every cut that had been made.
>   Omissions and rearrangements were drastic, but he seemed
> eager to accept Irving's decision in everything.[28]

Stoker paid a final visit to Tennyson on 25 September 1892, at which
time the poet, in his last days, found that "the sight of Stoker and the
mention of his play cheered him considerably, and he began to joke
again."[29]

On Monday, 3 October, when G. R. Dabbs, Tennyson's doctor, came home from a day trip to London with the news that he had seen Irving,

> the sick man roused himself at once and asked what was happening about *Becket.* Dabbs gave him what information he could. "It will be successful on the stage with Irving," said Tennyson; then: "I suppose I shall never see it." "I fear not," replied the doctor. "AH!" And then, after a long pause: "They did not do me justice with *The Promise of May,* but – with a flash of the old pugnacity, which had always so much impressed Irving – I can trust Irving – Irving will do me justice."[30]

And Irving did, though Tennyson never knew it. The *Becket* productions he gave in London in early 1893 and on tour in England and America during 1893 and 1894, and subsequent *Becket* productions up until 1905, when it was the last play in which he acted, proved thoroughly successful.[31]

In spite of the weak publishing sales of *The Cup and The Falcon* and *Becket* during 1884, Tennyson received a check from Macmillan for that year for £4148, about which Hallam wrote, "We thank you for all the care and thought that you have had for us in providing us with this good cheque. We rejoice that you think it satisfactory. It is most acceptable to us (BM, 16 January 1885). The various collected editions, plus sales of old stock bought from Kegan Paul, must have accounted for much of this profit.

The first collected edition by Macmillan, called *The Complete Works* (in one volume), and selling for 7s. 6d., was a significant one in that its sales indicated the continuing steady market for Tennyson's poems as opposed to that for his plays. "During the years 1885–8 sales averaged nearly 15,000 copies yearly and during the next three years the figure rose to about 19,000."[32] From that one book alone, in its second year, Tennyson received £1800 7s. 6d. in royalties on English sales and £31 10s. od. on the 1260 copies sold in America. (His American royalty was only six pence per copy, as opposed to his English royalty of 2s. 6d.) For the rest of his life, Tennyson's yearly royalties from that one book were always far over the £1500 total royalties that Macmillan were pledged to pay no matter how sales went.

Macmillan also put out a seven-volume *Complete Works,* which had much smaller sales. About both this edition and the 1884 School

Edition in four volumes, the Tennysons demonstrated a concern for an item usually important only to *readers*, namely print size. Hallam instructed George Macmillan in January 1884, "My father and mother would like as big print as you can allow in the new seven-volume Edition. They think that the Authors Edition [King, 1875] print is too small." And in March, after accepting a six pence royalty agreement on the seven-volume edition and agreeing to the same terms for the School Edition as for the Crown (Hallam's term for the 1 vol. *Complete Works*), Hallam wrote regarding the School Edition, "We hope that the book will be good large type for the boys" (BM, March 1884).

In 1887 Tennyson wrote to Albert Hamann in Berlin about another collected edition, "There is now a Miniature Edition published in 12 books the only perfect one, which I will send you. . . ." This 1886 publication, first in ten volumes selling for twenty-one shillings a set, was Tennyson's third largest royalty income during 1886, with £386 15s. od. coming from it. (*The Complete Works* in one volume sold 14,461 that year, with £1807 12s. 6d. royalty for Tennyson, and *Locksley Hall Sixty Years After* — of which more later — brought in £1429 6s. od. on its 14,293 copies sold.)

A New Library Edition, in nine volumes at first and eventually in twelve, at five shillings each volume, came out in 1888. Its significance lies in its inclusion of the full *Idylls of the King* — "Balin and Balan" had been added and the Enid poem had been halved, making a total of twelve "books," the standard epic number. In 1890 Macmillan published a Pocket Edition, printing 7000 and selling 3000 the first year at 7s. 6d.; a Parchment Edition (called in accounts, "Handmade Paper Edition") was available for the carriage-trade readers from 1884 and completed in 10 volumes in 1893. This full range of collected editions — complete in one volume, complete in matching volumes, miniature, large-print school texts, parchment paper, pocket size, etc. — illustrates Macmillan's ability to meet every possible reader's need as well as an ability to keep sales steady rather than simply dependent on new poems from an aging author.

But Alexander Macmillan was to be pleasantly surprised when Tennyson, his flurry of play-writing having ebbed, resumed writing lyric and narrative poetry.

The first result of this new creative activity was *Tiresias and Other Poems*, published in December 1885 to catch Christmas sales. Not since *Ballads and Poems* under Kegan Paul's imprint in 1880 had

Tennyson produced such a volume. The public seemed grateful for his return to early forms, buying 15,771 copies at six shillings each that first year. No doubt Emily was glad for the new book – and the concomitant income, for, although the Macmillan sales of collected editions and of Kegan Paul's old stock were good, she was feeling a pinch during 1885. On 15 October she complained in a letter to her sister Agnes Weld, "We are looking anxiously to know how Lionel will be able to meet these Indian expenses. This year I have been reduced to the purchase of 2 black woolen dresses, so you will divine that we are not very flourishing. Indeed I do not know who is, except it be Mr. Chamberlain."[33] Macmillan had again accurately estimated public demand, printing 20,000 the first year and not having to reprint thereafter. Several poems seen for the first time in this volume – particularly, "Tiresias," "The Wreck," "The Ancient Sage," and "Balin and Balan" – had the power of Tennyson's best verse and the full range of metrical forms he had developed through the years. Some poems in the volume had first appeared in periodicals. Of particular success among these were "Despair," "The Spinster's Sweet-Arts" (in Lincolnshire dialect), "The Charge of the Heavy Brigade at Balaclava," " 'Frater Ave atque Vale,' " and "Hands All Round," which Walter Savage Landor called "incomparably the best convivial song in the language."[34] The reception given the *Tiresias* volume by the critics matched that of the book-buying public, though some of the praise may have been predicated more on the premise that a seventy-six-year-old man should not have been producing new poems at all, much less such good poems, rather than on a true assessment of the book's quality. "Yet," as Sir Charles maintains, "there was some excuse for the critics; the new book was both strong and varied and showed that the poet's poems were as yet little affected by age, though naturally in tone and manner there was a change from the work of his youth."[35] The volume, dedicated "to Robert Browning, whose genius and geniality will best appreciate what may be best and make most allowance for what may be worst," included also a fifty-six line dedication of "Tiresias" "to Edward FitzGerald" and an epilogue in the same meter which completed the Fitz dedication. Since publication of the *Poems* of 1842, FitzGerald had not approved of Tennyson's poetry, but the friendship of the two, though limited by distance and ill health, continued and found expression in Fitz's lively and genuinely moving semi-yearly letters. "Tiresias" had been written in 1876 "after Tennyson and his son Hallam had spent several days with FitzGerald at his home 'Little

Grange' in Woodbridge, Suffolk."[36] That was to be their last visit. In 1883 Tennyson was

> much shaken by the sudden death, on June 14th, of his old friend — perhaps the dearest of his old friends, Edward FitzGerald. Less than two months before, the old man had written Hallam one of his delightful letters, in which he reported feeling "somewhat croaky," and chaffed Alfred about the authorship of a line parodying Wordsworth:
>
> A Mister Wilkinson, a clergyman.
>
> "One of the grandest lines in all blank verse, of which," said FitzGerald, 'I was the author . . . but which the paltry poet took as it fell from my inspired lips and has adopted for his own."[37]

Shortly after FitzGerald's death, Tennyson wrote to Sir Frederick Pollock,

> Dear old Fitz — I had no truer friend — he was one of the kindliest to me & I have never known one of so fine & delicate a wit — I had written a poem to him within the last week — a dedication — which he will never see.
> There are now left to me only two or three of my old college companions, & who goes next?[38]

Late the next year, in time for Christmas sales, Tennyson produced a second new volume of poems under the Macmillan imprint. Entitled *Locksley Hall Sixty Years After, Etc.*, it included, in addition to the title poem, "The Fleet," first published in the 23 April 1885 *Times* but changed considerably for book publication; "Opening of the Indian and Colonial Exhibition by the Queen," containing the refrain, "Britons, hold your own," first set to music by Sir Arthur Sullivan and sung at Albert Hall on 4 May 1886, shortly after news of Lionel Tennyson's death had reached the family; and *The Promise of May*, the only play of Tennyson's ever published in a volume of poems. It is, however, the title poem which has endured as the classic in this volume.

The dedication to Emily of *Locksley Hall Sixty Years After* sets out a point too often missed by readers, for Tennyson wrote, "To my wife I dedicate this dramatic monologue and the poems which follow."

The dramatic form, then, was underscored by Tennyson, no doubt because he was only too aware of the critic's and reader's penchant for identifying him with every major character he created, particularly one speaking in the first person. Tennyson guessed that the pessimism of the old man in "Locksley Hall Sixty Years After" would be read as *his* pessimism, just as the despondency which ends in a jingoistic faith in progress for the youthful speaker of "Locksley Hall" had been read as belonging to him also. Sure enough, Gladstone, in the January 1887 *Nineteenth Century*, rose to the defense of his government's policies, which he felt Tennyson was attacking in "Locksley Hall Sixty Years After." Walt Whitman, on the other hand, defended the poem on the grounds that its warnings "would be effective in curbing the excesses of democracy."[39] But neither statesman nor poet conceded Tennyson's point that it was "a dramatic poem, and Dramatis Personae are imaginary."

> Since it is so much the fashion in these days to regard each poem and story as a story of the poet's life or part of it, may I not be allowed to remind my readers of the possibility, that some event which comes to the poet's knowledge, some hint flashed from another mind, some thought or feeling arising in his own, or some mood coming — he knows not whence or how — may strike a chord from which a poem evolves its life, and that this to other eyes may bear small relation to the thought, or fact, or feeling, to which the poem owes its birth, whether the tenor be dramatic, or given as a parable?[40]

About all that can reasonably be said connecting the poet's life and his creation of the second "Locksley Hall" poem is that its tone is different from that of most of the poems written in Tennyson's youth. That the old poet could create with veracity an old speaker should not surprise anyone who knows what Tennyson did in his middle years with mid-life characters such as King Arthur, or in his early years with youthful speakers such as the young man in "Locksley Hall." But one must also remember that it was the *young* Tennyson who created Ulysses and Tiresias, two aged speakers. What can be said, then, except that Tennyson retained his original dramatic sense and even honed it well throughout his long career?

Sadly enough, in the same volume with the effective "Locksley Hall Sixty Years After" appears the disastrous *Promise of May*. It is strange to find Tennyson bothering to publish it at all considering its thoroughly unsuccessful stage production in November 1882 (see Chapter 5). However, even with the regrettable *Promise of May* taking up most of its space, the volume sold well. Macmillan printed 19,000 the first year and sold by its end, at six shillings each, 14,293 copies. Tennyson's royalties from it were £1429 6s. 0d. from English sales and £75 from American sales during that first year. During the second year, another 2290 were sold in England, bringing in £229, plus 104 sold in America, resulting in £17 15s. 0d. in royalties. By the third year, sales dropped to 101, with £10 2s. 0d. royalties from English sales — and no sales in America.

This mention of Tennyson's American royalties or lack thereof introduces his entire relationship with American publishers during the last eight years of his life. By the 1880s Macmillan's New York branch was thriving, particularly because young Frederick Macmillan, Daniel's elder son, had been there firmly establishing the New York trade. Early in 1884, Hallam had accepted for his father a mutually-agreed-upon six pence royalty per copy on all the Crown editions sold in America. In the same letter to Frederick Macmillan, Hallam wrote that Tennyson "will be glad to receive £75 for 'The Cup' etc. from you, as he wishes to be free from all haggling with Americans." Hallam added this suggestion: "Surely your American copies ought to have some special mark on them to prevent their being sent over or back and sold in England" (BM, 8 January 1884).

These three points are typical of Tennyson's concerns with American publishing: (1) he agreed, usually, to the royalties his English publishers suggested and accepted the money gratefully, knowing full well that legally no overseas publisher need have paid him anything at all; (2) he disliked the complications involved and wanted "to be free from all haggling with Americans"; and (3) he feared continued piracy. On this last point, it can be noted that, although Tennyson was pirated extensively, he also received the first American payment to an English author — the $150 payment from Ticknor for the 1842 *Poems* — and continued to receive royalties thenceforth where legally none had to be paid.

One surviving letter suggests that Tennyson's connections with literary and theatrical worlds in America was much more amicable than his "haggling with Americans" phrase intimates. George Parsons Lathrop, for example, wrote to the Laureate requesting permission for a London adaptation of "Elaine," the American production having been successful "artistically, but not financially," according to Lathrop.

. . . my return in money was but nominal.

Had it been otherwise, I should have directed that a proportion of the proceeds should be sent to you, as a formal acknowledgment at least of the great obligation which I owed to the creative source. . . .

I formed the Copyright League, in the United States, which is now extending all over the country, & for six years has toiled ardulously & unceasingly to establish by law the recognition of the rights of all authors in this country — whether they be natives or foreigners.

Hence I wish it had been in my power to make a definite recognition of what should be your rights in this country, in the case of the play "Elaine." Mrs. Langtry offers me very fair terms for the play in London; but wishes to bring it out, first, as a matinee performance.

Should you agree to her doing this, & should she continue to play the piece; — I would very willingly state to you the terms of payment which she proposes to me, & would arrange that such proportion as you might think proper should be paid to your account; not because I believe you care anything about such a small sum of money, but because it would be a fitting procedure.

(BM, 31 March 1890)

Fairness seemed to prevail, too, when it came to payments Tennyson received for publication of his poems in American periodicals. The poet knew, too, that, had he desired it, he could have netted a fortune from an American reading tour. On 1 October 1885, to cite one instance, he had been offered $50,000 for fifty readings of his poems in America. But Tennyson eschewed such a public display of himself, and chose to retain his privacy.

Unfortunately, American tourists as well as English ones continually intruded on that privacy. One day in July 1891 "an American artisan suddenly appeared at Aldworth. He had worked his way over to England on a cattleship in order to recite *Maud* to its author. Though he suffered acutely from the recitation, Tennyson sat through it and paid his admirer's fare back to the United States."[41] No wonder, in the light of such persistent adulation, that Tennyson tried to keep his tie to America limited to the receipt of royalty checks and the entertainment of genteel visitors such as James T. Fields, Frederick Tuckerman and Henry James.

Tennyson's third volume of new poetry with Macmillan, *Demeter and Other Poems*, reached the public in 1889, at the usually propitious time – December. Marshall notes heightened interest in it because of two events: Tennyson's "serious illness with rheumatic gout in the fall of 1888, and his recently celebrated eightieth birthday four months before the volume was published. Twenty thousand copies were sold before publication."[42] Macmillan printed another 20,000 in 1889 and sold 13,211 by the end of that year. Tennyson and Macmillan arranged for a flat payment of £75 for the American royalty, the same as they had done for *Locksley Hall Sixty Years After*. By the end of 1890, its second year, only 423 copies remained in Macmillan's stock. *Locksley Hall* and *Tiresias* both had more than 1000 left by then, out of their original 20,000, so *Demeter* became Macmillan's most successful new book of Tennyson's poems to date.

The most significant poems in this well-received volume are "Demeter and Persephone," a framed, blank-verse handling of the classical myth, and "Crossing the Bar." The story of Tennyson's inspired writing of this hymn is too well-known to be repeated here,[43] but its reception bears emphasizing. Sir Charles writes of it,

> Probably no poem in our language ever created so profound an impression on its first appearance. During the weeks succeeding its publication, it was quoted in countless newspapers and periodicals, and read from thousands of pulpits in church and chapel throughout the country. In all the years during which he had been the acknowledged poet of the people, no poem of his had spoken so directly and so intimately to the hearts of his countrymen.[44]

Even today "Crossing the Bar" is probably Tennyson's most well-known poem.

Tennyson's final play, *The Foresters*, subtitled *Robin Hood and Maid Marian*, with incidental music by Sir Arthur Sullivan, was published by Macmillan in April 1892. Suggested originally by Irving, the subject when produced on stage never had the success in London which it had in America, perhaps because, as Marshall suggests, "The Americans liked a pastoral and the English did not."[45] Augustin Daly wanted the American rights and presented Tennyson with Ada Rehan, who was to play Marian. Later, Tennyson wrote for Irving's opinion of her, but, instead of writing back, Irving decided to send R. D. Blumenfeld down to Aldworth to convey his opinion. The details of this visit indicate once again the privacy mania which afflicted the poet:

Blumenfeld wrote to suggest [the visit] and was in due course invited to lunch. When he arrived Tennyson was out walking, and the butler suggested that the visitor should go to meet him along a path which he was certain to take on his way home.

Blumenfeld set out and before he had gone far, saw the tall, imposing figure, with cloak and wideawake and a grey shawl over the shoulders, stumping down the path. He approached and commenced a speech of explanation. The poet was evidently day-dreaming and had no idea of his visitor's identity. "What's that? Who are you?" "I'm Blumenfeld, come down to lunch . . .' The old man raised his stick threateningly, evidently taking the stranger for an importunate tourist or pressman. "Go away! I don't know who you are. What do you mean by coming here to molest me?" Blumenfeld thought it hopeless to explain, withdrew hurriedly and returned to London, — nor in spite of telegrams of explanation and apology did the interview ever take place. Soon afterwards Daly and Ada Rehan came down to Aldworth together, and an agreement for the New York production was signed.[46]

In spite of the frightful start to the relationship, the play went on and Daly wired a friendly telegraph to Hallam shortly after its opening: "I think the play has made a very great success repeated recalls after each act — first and third acts especially liked. Miss Rehan in fine spirit — her song encored — sleep song and fairy scene had to be repeated most brilliant audience everyone pleased."[47] Hallam quickly wrote to Frederick Macmillan in London a few days later, "I should publish on Saturday if I were you before the Yankee papers appear or any pirated copies (from the prompt-copies)" (BM, 22 March 1892). To protect his stage copyright in England, Tennyson was encouraged by legal advisors to have Irving produce the play simultaneously with the American production. Irving quickly put together a morning read-through at the Lyceum, telegraphing later, "Your beautiful play has been successfully performed by younger members of the Company before an enthusiastic audience of actors." Hallam reciprocated with presents — he asked Frederick Macmillan to send the Library Edition to Irving and forty-five copies of the Pocket Edition to the entire company (BM, 18 March 1892). But the *Daily News* was not enthusiastic about this circumventing of the spirit of the law and stated so in strong terms, calling it "a representation stealthily prepared and studiously kept secret with the avowed purpose of baffling curiosity and making this 'public performance' public only in

name." Even Frederick Macmillan's defense of this production
sounds like that of a man defending a shady action. In his letter to
Hallam on 22 March 1892 he writes,

> I do not think you need be in the least uneasy — there is no doubt
> that it *was* a public performance in the legal sense & the stage
> copyright or right of representation is fully secured (the book
> copyright is secured also, but there is no question about that).
> The Theatre was opened at 9.45 a.m. on Thursday; a bill was
> displayed in a conspicuous place outside the doors & the box office
> was open for the sale of seats. Several persons paid for their seats,
> one of whom was an absolute stranger unconnected with the
> theatre. His name and address were taken so that he could be called
> as a witness if necessary _ ____[?] Thomas could have been there
> himself if he had been sharp enough to be at the theatre at the right
> time.

In any event, the published version of *The Foresters* appeared when
Hallam had suggested it should, but Macmillan cautiously printed
only 12,500 for England and 3780 for America. By the end of the
year 6333 had been sold in England and 2987 in America, sales which
justified their caution. By the end of the next year, however, after
Tennyson's death, the stock of *The Foresters* in both countries was just
about depleted.

Sir Charles records that in September 1892 Tennyson's "mind was
as active as ever, and he was finishing off the poems for a new volume
which was to come out before the end of the year."[48] Early in
October "Craik was with him, going carefully through the proofs of
the miscellaneous volume, which he was on the point of issuing."[49]
On 5 October, the day before he died, "the poet asked if his book had
come — thinking of the proofs, which Hallam put into his hand."[50]
This final volume of poetry, *The Death of Oenone, Akbar's Dream and
Other Poems*, which Tennyson himself prepared for the press, was
published posthumously on 28 October 1892 within two weeks of
the Poet Laureate's funeral. Macmillan printed 30,000 in a six-shilling
edition, 500 in a large paper edition, and 4100 in a $1.25 American
edition — with 230 in large paper for the Americans, too, at $3.00.
Sales, as we should expect for such a final volume by a popular literary
figure, were exceptionally good, with over 26,000 copies sold in a
few months. Slightly fewer than 1500 sold in 1893, leaving about
6600 for the firm to dispose of in the following years.[51]

Of all the volume's varied poems, which range from lyric to Lincolnshire dialect humor to metaphysical and religious statements, the most important, critically, is the title poem, "The Death of Oenone." In it Tennyson captures the tone of the character he had first created in the 1830s, but now the heroine has grown older. Oenone's dreams, in which "Her Past became her Present" (l. 14); her progress down to Paris's pyre, where

> She rose and slowly down,
> By the long torrent's ever-deepened roar
> Paced, following, as in trance, the silent cry.   (ll. 84—6)

and her ultimate death:

> she leapt upon the funeral pile,
> And mixt herself with *him* and past in fire.   (ll. 105—6)

— all are cast in an effective dramatic mode and wrought by a powerful craftsman who for the most part managed to keep the debilities of age out of his art.

Although we do not have the figures for Macmillan & Co.'s profits on these years of publishing Tennyson, we can surmise from the monies paid to Tennyson and later to his heirs (an accounting of which is extant) that Alexander Macmillan's willingness in 1884 to make an agreement which others in the book trade thought reckless proved to be a lucrative venture for the firm. Macmillan must have heard in Tennyson's only new poetry with Kegan Paul, *Ballads and Other Poems* (1880), distant heraldings of *Tiresias, Locksley Hall Sixty Years After, Demeter,* and *The Death of Oenone* — four new, intrinsically worthy volumes which vindicated the faith the publisher had placed in the poet.

Appendixes

I TENNYSON EDITIONS

First Editions

Date	Title	Publisher	Price
20 Apr 1827	*Poems by Two Brothers*	J. and J. Jackson	5s., 7s.
June 1830	*Poems, Chiefly Lyrical*	Effingham Wilson	5s.
Dec 1832	*Poems*	Edward Moxon	6s.
14 May 1842	*Poems* (2 vols)	Edward Moxon	12s.
Dec 1847	*The Princess*	Edward Moxon	5s.
May 1850	*In Memoriam*	Edward Moxon	6s.
16 Nov 1852	*Ode on the Death of the Duke of Wellington*	Edward Moxon	1s.
July 1855	*Maud and Other Poems*	Edward Moxon	5s.
July 1859	*Idylls of the King*	Edward Moxon & Co.	7s.
Aug 1864	*Enoch Arden, Etc.*	Edward Moxon & Co.	6s.
Dec 1869	*The Holy Grail and Other Poems*	Strahan & Co.	7s.
Dec 1872	*Gareth and Lynette, Etc.*	Strahan & Co.	5s.
June 1875	*Queen Mary*	Henry S. King & Co.	6s.
Dec 1876	*Harold*	Henry S. King & Co.	6s.
May 1879	*The Lover's Tale*	C. Kegan Paul & Co.	3s. 6d.
Dec 1880	*Ballads and Other Poems*	C. Kegan Paul & Co.	5s.
Feb 1884	*The Cup and The Falcon*	Macmillan & Co.	5s.
Dec 1884	*Becket*	Macmillan & Co.	6s.
Dec 1885	*Tiresias and Other Poems*	Macmillan & Co.	6s.
Dec 1886	*Locksley Hall Sixty Years After, Etc.*	Macmillan & Co.	6s.
Dec 1889	*Demeter and Other Poems*	Macmillan & Co.	6s.
Apr 1892	*The Foresters*	Macmillan & Co.	6s.
28 Oct 1892	*The Death of Oenone, Akbar's Dream and Other Poems*	Macmillan & Co.	6s.

Other Significant Editions

Date	Title	Publisher	Price
May 1857	Illustrated Edition of Tennyson's Poems	Edward Moxon	31s. 6d.
Jan 1865	Moxon's Miniature Poets: A Selection from the Works of Alfred Tennyson [first selection]	Edward Moxon & Co.	5s.
1870	Miniature Edition (10 vols) [first collected edition]	Strahan & Co.	[?]
1874–81	Cabinet Edition (10 vols, with illustrations)	Henry S. King & Co.	2s. 6d. per vol.
1878	Crown Edition [first collected edition in one volume]	C. Kegan Paul & Co.	6s., 7s. 6d., 8s. 6d.
1907–8	Eversley Edition (9 vols) [first annotated edition]	Macmillan & Co.	4s. per vol.

II DEED OF AGREEMENT, 14 FEBRUARY 1879, BETWEEN ALFRED TENNYSON AND C. KEGAN PAUL & CO.

(From a copy in the Tennyson Research Centre, Lincoln.)

(1)

THIS INDENTURE made the 14th day of February 1879 BETWEEN ALFRED TENNYSON of Farringford in the Isle of Wight Esquire Her Majesty's Poet Laureate of the one part CHARLES KEGAN PAUL and ALFRED CHENEVIX TRENCH of No. 1 Paternoster Square in the City of London reading as C. Kegan Paul & Co. (successors to the publishing Department of H. S. King & Co.) of the other part WITNESSETH that it is hereby agreed and declared between and by the parties hereto for and on behalf of themselves and their respective heirs executors and administrators that the said Charles Kegan Paul and Alfred Chenevix Trench trading under the name and firm of and hereinafter referred to as Messrs. C. Kegan Paul & Co. shall be the Publishers of the said Alfred Tennyson from the 15th day of January 1879 upon and subject to the terms and conditions expressed in the following articles (that is to say)

1. ALL the unsold stock of the following works of the said Alfred Tennyson named "Poems" "The Princess" "In Memoriam" "Maud" "The Idylls of the King" "Enoch Arden" "Selections" "Gareth" "Holy Grail" "Songs" and "The Window" remaining in the hands of the said C. Kegan Paul & Co. are the property of the said C. Kegan Paul & Co. and may be sold by them under this Agreement.
2. ALL the unsold stock of the following works of the said Alfred Tennyson as published in separate volumes namely The Original Editions of − "Queen Mary" and "Harold" remaining in the hands of the said C. Kegan Paul & Co. are the property of the said Alfred Tennyson subject to the right of the said C. Kegan Paul & Co. to sell the same on commission as herein after is provided.
3. THE stereotype plates mentioned in 1st part of the schedule hereto are the property of the said C. Kegan Paul & Co. and the stereotype plates mentioned in the 2nd part of the said schedule are the property of the said Alfred Tennyson and the said C. Kegan Paul & Co. shall have the exclusive use of the last mentioned plates during the continuance of this Agreement.

4. DURING the continuance of this Agreement the said C. Kegan Paul & Co. shall have the exclusive privilege of printing and publishing at their own costs all the works mentioned in Article 1 & of including in any general and complete edition of the works of the said Alfred Tennyson the said 2 works called "Queen Mary" and "Harold" subject to such right (if any) as Messrs. Moxon & Co. of Dover Street Piccadilly the former publishers of the said Alfred Tennyson or any person claiming under them now have to sell the stock printed before the 15th day of January 1869 of any such works in an illustrated form and subject also to the provisions hereinafter contained.

5. IN consideration of the aforesaid privilege the said C. Kegan Paul & Co. shall on the 15th day of January 1880 and the 15th day of January in every successive year during the continuance of this Agreement pay to the said Alfred Tennyson his executors or administrators the sum of £2,500 clear of all deductions whatsoever and all the expenses of or connected with the printing, binding, publishing, registering, insuring, advertising and selling of the said works shall be paid by the said C. Kegan Paul & Co.

6. THE said C. Kegan Paul & Co. shall continue during the existence of this Agreement to sell in separate volumes the said works called "Queen Mary" and "Harold" on the terms of their being allowed a commission of 5 per cent on the proceeds of the sale thereof and they shall always keep in stock a sufficient quantity of these volumes to answer the demand which may be made for them.

7. BEFORE publishing any future edition of any of the works to which this Agreement relates the said C. Kegan Paul & Co. shall give notice of such intended publication to the said Alfred Tennyson who shall be at liberty at any time within one calendar month after receiving such notice to make any corrections or alterations in the work or works to which such notice shall apply provided that no existing poem shall be withdrawn and that if such new Edition shall be printed from the existing stereotype plates the paging of the present edition shall not be interfered with. The corrections and alterations to be made at the expense of the said Alfred Tennyson except so far as such corrections and alterations are rendered necessary by the neglect or default of the publishers or printers.

8. NO annotated edition of the said works or any of them shall be published without the written consent of the said Alfred Tennyson his executors or administrators and no addition or alteration shall be made to or in the text of the said works or any of them without a similar consent in writing.

9. No edition of the complete works of the said Alfred Tennyson shall be published at less than 6/- per copy being the present published price of the Crown Edition.

10. THE said C. Kegan Paul & Co. shall on or before the 1st day of March in every year furnish to the said Alfred Tennyson his executors or administrators an account of the number of copies of each of the several works and each edition thereof sold during the preceding year and also of the number of copies of each such work and edition remaining in their hands at the date of such account.

11. THE said Alfred Tennyson shall be at liberty to publish any poem or poems which he has already written or may hereafter write (other than those included in the above mentioned works) in any magazine or other periodical first offering the same to the said C. Kegan Paul & Co. for that purpose but if the said Alfred Tennyson shall be desirous of publishing any poem or poems in a separate form then during the continuance of this Agreement he shall first offer the publication thereof to the said C. Kegan Paul & Co. on the terms of the said C. Kegan Paul & Co. being allowed a commission of 5 per cent on the proceeds of the sale thereof but in case the said C. Kegan Paul & Co. shall not accept such offer within one calendar month from the date thereof the said Alfred Tennyson shall be at liberty to publish such poem or poems with any publisher that he may think fit.

12. IF under the last preceding Article any poem or poems of the said Alfred Tennyson shall be published in a separate form otherwise than in a magazine or other periodical only and whether by the said C. Kegan Paul & Co. or by any other publisher then and in such case the said C. Kegan Paul & Co. shall be at liberty at the end of one year from the publication thereof in such separate form to include the same in any existing or future general and complete Editions of the works of the said Alfred Tennyson. But in the event of the said C. Kegan Paul & Co. exercising this privilege and being also the publishers of the said Poem or Poems in a separate form they shall always keep in stock a sufficient quantity of the separate Edition thereof to answer the demand which may be made for the same and upon the determination of this Agreement the stereotype plates of the said Poem or Poems as included in the complete works of the said Alfred Tennyson shall become the property of the said Alfred Tennyson without payment Provided Always that nothing contained in this clause or in clause 4 shall prevent the said C. Kegan Paul & Co. from selling separate volumes of any General and complete Edition of the works of the said Alfred Tennyson apart from the other volumes of

such General and complete Edition but so that no such separate volumes shall be sold at a price less than the proportionate price of the volume in the set.

13. C. KEGAN PAUL & Co. shall not advertize any of the existing or future works of the said Alfred Tennyson in any manner which may be distasteful to him and shall immediately withdraw any advertisement to which the said Alfred Tennyson shall signify his objection.

14. THIS Agreement shall continue in force for 5 years — certain from the aforesaid 15th day of January 1879 and thenceforth from year to year unless and until determined by notice as hereinafter provided PROVIDED ALWAYS that 6 months before the 15th day of January 1884 or 6 calendar months before the 15th day of January in any subsequent year notice in writing of his or their intention to determine this agreement on the 15th day of January ensuing the date of such notice then and in such case this agreement shall determine accordingly.

15. IF the said C. Kegan Paul & Co. shall at any time make default in payment of the said annual sum of £2500 or any part thereof for the space of 3 calendar months after the day on which the same ought to be paid as aforesaid the said Alfred Tennyson his executors or administrators shall be at liberty at any time after such default by notice in writing to be given to the said C. Kegan Paul & Co. to determine this agreement at any time not less than one calendar month from the date of the said Notice and this Agreement shall thereupon determine accordingly — PROVIDED ALWAYS that if this agreement shall be determined by notice under this article the said Alfred Tennyson his executors, administrators shall be entitled to receive the whole of the said sum of £2500 which shall become payable on the 15th day of January following the giving of such notice and shall not be bound to allow a proportionate or other part thereof PROVIDED also that any omission by the said Alfred Tennyson his executors or administrators to exercise the right conferred by this Article in respect of any default in any such annual payment as aforesaid shall not prevent him or them from exercising the same in respect of any default of any subsequent annual payment.

16. AFTER the date on which a notice to determine this Agreement under Article 15 shall have been received by the said C. Kegan Paul & Co. the said C. Kegan Paul & Co. shall not without the written consent of the said Alfred Tennyson his executor or administrators print or allow to be printed any more copies of the said works or any of them and after the date on which a notice to determine this

Agreement under Article 14 shall have been received the said C. Kegan Paul & Co. shall not print or allow to be printed more copies of the said works or any of them than there shall be a reasonable prospect of their selling previous to the determination of this Agreement by virtue of such notice and from and after the 15th day of July last preceding the determination of this Agreement by notice or otherwise the said C. Kegan Paul & Co. shall not without the written consent of the said Alfred Tennyson his executors or administrators print or allow to be printed any more copies of the said works or any of them and if at the determination of this Agreement any copies of the said works or any of them shall remain in the hands of the said C. Kegan Paul & Co. unsold the said Alfred Tennyson his executors or administrators shall be at liberty on giving a notice in writing to that effect at any time not later than one calendar month after the determination of this Agreement to purchase the said copies at a sum equal to the cost of production. But if the said Alfred Tennyson his executors or administrators shall not elect to purchase the said copies C. Kegan Paul & Co. shall sell the same in the ordinary course of their business and shall pay the net proceeds of such sale to the said Alfred Tennyson his executors or administrators after deducting the cost of production and a commission of 5 per cent which shall be allowed to the said C. Kegan Paul & Co. on the gross proceeds. The term and cost of production used in this article means a fair and equal proportion of the total cost incurred by the said C. Kegan Paul & Co. in or about the printing or production of the said works such total cost being for this purpose fairly and equally apportioned between the copies which shall have been sold by them under this Agreement and the copies which shall remain unsold at the determination thereof and if the said Alfred Tennyson his executors or administrators shall purchase the stereotype plates under the next article the price paid by him for the same shall be taken into account and allowed for in determining the cost of production and if the parties shall be unable to agree as to the amount to be paid or allowed under this article the same shall be settled by arbitration under the power in that behalf hereinafter contained.

17. UPON the determination of this agreement whether under Article 14 or Article 15 the stereotype plates belonging to the said Alfred Tennyson his executors or administrators shall be delivered to him by the said C. Kegan Paul & Co. and the said Alfred Tennyson his executors or administrators shall be at liberty to purchase the stereotype plates of his works belonging to the said C. Kegan Paul &

Co. at such a price as in case of difference shall be settled by arbitration under the power in that behalf hereinafter contained.

18. ANY notice hereby required or authorized to be given to the said C. Kegan Paul & Co. may be left for them at their office No. 1 Paternoster Square or any substituted place of business of which the said Alfred Tennyson his executors or administrators shall have had notice and any notice hereby required or authorized to be given to the said Alfred Tennyson may be given to him personally or left for him at his usual or last known place of abode in England or Wales.

19. IF any difference shall arise between the parties hereto touching these presents or the construction hereof or any article or thing herein contained or any valuation to be made in pursuance hereof or touching the rights duties or liabilities of either party under these presents the matter in difference shall be referred to two arbitrators or their umpire pursuant to and so as with regard to the mode and consequences of the reference and in all other respects to conform to the provisions in that behalf contained in the Common Law Procedure Act 1854 or any subsisting modification thereof IN WITNESS whereof the said parties to these presents have hereunto set their hands and seals the day and year first above written

THE SCHEDULE ABOVE REFERRED TO FIRST PART
Cabinet Edition
Crown Octavo Edition

SECOND PART
Library Edition
Original Edition
Miniature Edition
Selections
Songs
Tennyson for the Young
Queen Mary

Charles Kegan Paul (Signed)

Alfred Chenevix Trench (Signed)

Notes

Note. Full details of the sources cited in the notes following are given only on first mention and in the Bibliography. Elsewhere sources are identified by author – or editorship, and / or a short title, as necessary. Note, however, the following departures from normal procedure: Sir Charles Tennyson's biography *Alfred Tennyson* is cited simply as *AT*; Hallam Tennyson's *Memoir* of his father as *Memoir*; Christopher Ricks's edition of *The Poems of Tennyson* as *Poems*; and Edgar F. Shannon's *Tennyson and the Reviewers* as "Shannon" (as the other study by Shannon listed is mentioned only in passing in the text).

PREFACE

1. Sir Charles Tennyson, Notebook 8, Tennyson Research Centre, Lincoln, England. (The notebooks are Sir Charles's compilation of quotes and comments for his biography of Tennyson.) Sir Charles no doubt took his figures from Evan J. Cuthbertson, *Tennyson: The Story of His Life* (London and Edinburgh: Chambers, 1898), p. 127.
2. Royal A. Gettmann, *A Victorian Publisher: A Study of the Bentley Papers* (London: Cambridge University Press, 1960), pp. 152–3.
3. J. A. Sutherland, *Victorian Novelists and Publishers* (Chicago: University of Chicago Press, 1976), p. 85.
4. John D. Rosenberg, *The Fall of Camelot: A Study of Tennyson's "Idylls of the King"* (Cambridge, Mass.: Harvard University Press, 1973), p. 5.
5. Tennyson Research Centre, Lincoln, letter of 12 Oct. 1874.

CHAPTER ONE: INTRODUCTION

1. These details are from Gettmann, p. 4. Gettmann's study provides a fascinating overall picture of a publisher of novels in the nineteenth century.
2. See Claude Colleer Abbott, *The Life and Letters of George Darley, Poet and Critic* (London: Oxford University Press, 1928), pp. 8–9; and F. A. Mumby and Ian Norrie, *Publishing and Bookselling*, 5th ed., rev. (London: Cape, 1974), p. 189.
3. John C. Cook and Lionel Stevenson, *English Literature of the Victorian Period* (New York: Appleton–Century–Crofts, 1949), p. 110.
4. Richard D. Altick, *The English Common Reader: A Social History of the Mass Reading Public, 1800–1900* (Chicago: University of Chicago Press, 1957), Appendix B.
5. Gettmann, pp. 7–11.

6. Tim Chilcott, *A Publisher and His Circle: The Life and Work of John Taylor, Keats's Publisher* (London and Boston: Routledge & Kegan Paul, 1972), pp. 184 and 190.

7. Gettmann, p. 10.

8. Thomas Fragnall Dibdin, *Bibliophobia* (London: Henry Bohn, 1832), p. 6.

9. Gettmann, p. 5.

10. Marvin S. Rosen, "Authors and Publishers: 1750–1830," *Science and Society*, 32 (1968), 230–2.

11. Ibid., p. 222.

12. Effingham Wilson, a London publisher, issued *Poems, Chiefly Lyrical* in June 1830.

13. G. C. Moore, "A Critical and Bibliographical Study of the Somersby Library of Dr. George Clayton Tennyson" (MA thesis, Nottingham University, 1966), p. 38.

14. Ibid., p. 39.

15. Hallam Tennyson, *Alfred Tennyson: A Memoir*, 2 vols. (London: Macmillan, 1897), I, p. 17. Sir Charles Tennyson, *Alfred Tennyson* (London: Macmillan, 1949), pp. 33 ff.

16. *Memoir*, II, p. 69.

17. Ibid., I, p. 4.

18. Anne Thackeray Ritchie, *Records of Tennyson, Ruskin and Browning* (London: Macmillan, 1892), p. 10.

19. *AT*, p. 34.

20. *Memoir*, II, p. 93, and I, p. 11.

21. Ibid., I, p. 11.

22. Christopher Ricks, *Tennyson* (New York: Macmillan, 1972), p. 19, quoting Trinity Notebook 34.

23. Ibid., p. 12.

24. Ricks, *Tennyson*, p. 12.

25. *AT*, p. 33.

26. Cook and Stevenson, p. 110.

27. *AT*, p. 50.

28. *Memoir*, I, p. 7.

29. Sir Charles Tennyson and Hope Dyson, *The Tennysons: Background to Genius* (London: Macmillan, 1974), p. 199, suggest that the brothers may have come to the Jacksons as a second choice, after having offered their MS to a Lincoln bookseller and been rejected.

30. See *Memoir*, I, 22; *AT*, p. 49; and Ricks, *Tennyson*, p. 20.

31. Sir Charles Tennyson, unpublished typescript "Tennyson's Dealings with His Publishers" (in the Tennyson Research Centre, Lincoln), p. 2. (Hereafter cited as "Typescript.")

32. Ibid., p. 1.

33. Cuthbertson, p. 22.

34. Joseph Shaylor, *The Fascination of Books* (London: Simpkin, Marshall, Hamilton, Kent, 1912), p. 172.

35. *AT*, p. 49.

36. Ibid.

37. Edgar F. Shannon, Jr, *Tennyson and the Reviewers* (Cambridge, Mass.: Harvard University Press, 1952), p. 1.

38. Ricks, *Tennyson*, p. 20.
39. A bit less than half the book was by Charles; three or four poems were by Frederick; the rest were Alfred's.
40. *Autobiography and Letters of Charles Merivale, Dean of Ely*, ed. Judith Anne Merivale (privately printed, Oxford: Hart, 1898), p. 99.
41. Ibid., p. 171.
42. Ibid., p. 99.
43. T. Wemyss Reid, *The Life, Letters, and Friendships of Richard Monckton Milnes, First Lord Houghton*, 2 vols. (London and New York: Cassell, 1890), I, p. 77.
44. P. F. Jamieson, "Tennyson and His Audience in 1832," *Philological Quarterly*, 31 (1952), 409.
45. Ibid., p. 412.
46. "Former Apostles formed the nuclei of two societies with which [Tennyson] was later connected, the Sterling Club, founded in 1838, and the Metaphysical Society, founded in 1869" (ibid., p. 407).
47. Ricks, *Tennyson*, p. 31.
48. *Memoir*, I, p. 81.
49. Ibid., p. 46.
50. Henry Hallam, in *Tennyson and His Friends*, ed. Hallam Tennyson (London: Macmillan, 1911), p. 447.
51. T. H. Vail Motter, "A 'Lost' Poem by Arthur Hallam," *PMLA*, 50 (1935), 575.
52. Ricks, *Tennyson*, p. 57.
53. Ibid., p. 28.
54. Ibid., p. 32.
55. Ibid. See also *Memoir*, II, p. 355.
56. Christopher Ricks, ed., *The Poems of Tennyson* (London and Harlow: Longmans, Green & Co., 1969), p. 172. Hereafter cited as *Poems*. All quotation of Tennyson's poetry shall be from this standard text.
57. Ibid., p. 170.
58. Ricks, *Tennyson*, p. 37. In *Memoir*, I, p. 47, Hallam Tennyson cuts "morbidness of feeling."
59. *AT*, p. 87.
60. Tennyson Research Centre, Lincoln. Hereafter all primary materials such as letters and accounts which bear no other location note may be assumed to be in this collection. *Memoir*, I, p. 92 has a shortened version of Hallam's letter.
61. Ricks, *Tennyson*, p. 69.
62. Shannon, p. 3.
63. Ibid., p. 5.
64. W. Robertson Nicoll and Thomas J. Wise, *Literary Anecdotes of the Nineteenth Century*, 2 vols. (London: Hodder & Stoughton, 1895), I, pp. 24–5. (Letter of 11 Jan 1831.)
65. *AT*, p. 115.
66. John D. Jump, ed., *Tennyson: The Critical Heritage* (London: Routledge & Kegan Paul, 1967), p. 42, quoting Hallam's unsigned review in the August 1831 *Englishman's Magazine*.
67. *Memoir*, I, p. 81.
68. Ricks, *Tennyson*, p. 69.

CHAPTER TWO: PERSUASIVE FRIENDS

1. Edmund Blunden, *Leigh Hunt: A Biography* (London: Cobden–Sanderson, 1930), p. 289.

2. Edward Moxon left no diary, very few personal letters, no business journal, no memoir or autobiography – in short, very little grist for the biographer's mill. Nonetheless, H. G. Merriam produced in *Edward Moxon: Publisher of Poets* (New York: Columbia University Press, 1939) a detailed study of Moxon's life, based mainly on secondary sources. Much of what follows in this discussion of Moxon's rise in the publishing world is distilled from that now out-of-print volume.

3. Ibid., p. 9.

4. Ibid., p. 8.

5. Ibid., p. 14.

6. William Knight, ed., *Letters of the Wordsworth Family from 1787 to 1855*, 3 vols. (Boston and London: Ginn & Co., 1907), II, pp. 296–7.

7. Merriam, p. 15.

8. Ibid., p. 12.

9. Ibid., pp. 26–7.

10. Ibid., p. 27.

11. Ibid.

12. Ibid., p. 28.

13. Ibid., p. 29.

14. Ibid., p. 31.

15. Walter Graham, *English Literary Periodicals* (New York: Nelson, 1930), p. 292.

16. Merriam, p. 35. Forster, best known now as Dicken's friend and biographer, also became an intimate of the Tennyson family and one of the poet's literary advisors.

17. Ibid., p. 36.

18. Ibid., p. 86.

19. Ibid., pp. 76–7.

20. Ibid., p. 78.

21. Robert Browning to Elizabeth Barrett, 28 Aug. 1846, *Letters of Robert Browning and Elizabeth Barrett* (London: privately printed, 1895), II, p. 485.

22. Blunden, p. 289.

23. *AT*, p. 121. Ricks quotes part of this, giving its source as a letter in the possession of Mr Robert Taylor (*Tennyson*, p. 72).

24. Merriam, p. 100. Quoting British Museum MS. 38110 F67.

25. Ibid., p. 108.

26. Charles and Frances Brookfield, *Mrs. Brookfield and Her Circle*, rev. ed. (London: Pitman, 1906), p. 178.

27. Copy in the hand of Audrey Tennyson (Hallam Tennyson's wife) or Emily Tennyson.

28. Richard Chenevix Trench, *Letters and Memorials*, 2 vols. (London: Kegan Paul, 1888), I, p. 111. (Letter of 20 Mar. 1832.)

29. Copy in an unknown hand, dated 10 Apr. 1832. Also in *Memoir*, I, pp. 84–5.

30. Hugh J. Schonfield, ed., *Letters to Frederick Tennyson* (London: Hogarth Press, 1930), pp. 26–7. (Letter of 20 May 1832.)

31. *AT*, p. 119.

32. Jump, p. 51.
33. Ricks, *Tennyson*, p. 71, quoting Huntington Letter (HM 19464), 3 May 1832 (Hallam to Brookfield).
34. Ricks, *Tennyson*, p. 71, quoting from a Tennyson Research Centre copy in Emily's or Audrey's hand, dated 20 June 1832.
35. *Memoir*, I, p. 93.
36. Catharine B. Johnson, *William Bodham Donne and His Friends* (London and New York: E. P. Dutton, 1905), pp. 10–11, 14.
37. Tennyson Research Centre copies in an unknown hand.
38. Tennyson Research Centre copy in an unknown hand, dated 24 Sep. 1832.
39. *Memoir*, I, pp. 88–9. I date this after 24 Sep. 1832 but before 10 Oct. 1832.
40. Ibid., pp. 89–90.
41. *AT*, p. 121. See note 7.
42. Several copies of "The Lover's Tale" were bound separately before publication of the *Poems* and distributed to friends. George O. Marshall, Jr, *Tennyson Handbook* (New York: Twayne, 1963), p. 184, reports on their history: "All but one of these were recalled, but it eventually got to the Rowfant Library, and in 1868 R. H. Shepherd used this copy for the text of his piracy." It was this pirated edition which forced Tennyson to publish the whole four parts of "The Lover's Tale" in 1879 with publisher Kegan Paul. "Tennyson," Marshall continues, "apologizes for the imperfections in the first two parts, but excuses his publication on the ground that the piracy had kept from dying what he had deemed scarce worthy to live."
43. Although I know of no copy of this letter, I infer that it was written from the following letters.
44. *AT*, p. 129.
45. Hallam Tennyson in *Memoir*, I, pp. 90–1, prints only part of this letter, but he does supply the date, perhaps from a postmarked envelope now missing. Ricks, *Tennyson*, p. 72, quotes part of it, giving the *Memoir* as source.
46. Nicoll and Wise, I, pp. 26–7. (Arthur Hallam to Hunt, 13 Nov. 1832.)
47. To James M. Gaskell on 15 Dec. 1832 Hallam wrote: "One good result of your election is that you will soon come to town. When you do I shall make you buy Alfred Tennyson's book, which may serve by way of recreation after hot stormy debates. I have reviewed it for the 'Edinburgh', but I don't know whether my article will be accepted" – Charles Milnes Gaskell, ed., *An Eton Boy: Letters of James Milnes Gaskell, 1820–1830* (London: Constable, 1939), p. 220.
48. *AT*, p. 137.
49. See Johnson, p. 16.
50. *AT*, p. 137.
51. Merriam, p. 17.
52. Tennyson Research Centre copy in Audrey's hand. Quoted verbatim in *Memoir*, I, p. 91, though undated there. I date it after the April *Quarterly* but before the end of Cambridge's Whitsun term. Sir Charles calls the line about sales "clearly a white lie" (*AT*, p. 141).
53. See *Memoir*, I, pp. 95–6. Tennyson did not print his first version, which would have been even more offensive. "A copy of *1832* (in the possession of Mr W. S. G. Macmillan)," notes Ricks, "shows that Tennyson's original refrain throughout was 'Tipsy Kit'; his [Tennyson's] note reads: 'One of my sisters

when I showed them this version persuaded me that Tipsy Kit was too sharp: so Crusty Xopher took his place'" (*Poems*, p. 461, note). The epigraph as Tennyson published it reads:

> You did late review my lays,
>   Crusty Christopher;
> You did mingle blame and praise,
>   Rusty Christopher.
> When I learnt from whom it came,
> I forgave you all the blame,
>   Musty Christopher;
> I could *not* forgive the praise,
>   Fusty Christopher.

54. *AT*, p. 143.
55. See Ralph Rader, *Tennyson's Maud: The Biographical Genesis* (Berkeley and Los Angeles: University of California Press, 1963), pp. 30–1, and *in toto*.
56. *AT*, p. 144. Sir Charles's source is *Memoir*, 1, p. 103, a letter from Tennant to Septimus Tennyson.
57. *Letters of Edward FitzGerald*, ed. William Aldis Wright, 2 vols. (London: Macmillan, 1901), 1, p. 25.
58. Sir Charles Tennyson, Notebook 3, Frederick Tennyson to George [?], 18 Dec. 1833.
59. *Memoir*, 1, p. 122.
60. Ibid., p. 123.
61. Ibid., p. 12.
62. Ibid., p. 118.
63. The actual changes have been elucidated by J. F. A. Pyre, in *The Formation of Tennyson's Style* (Madison: University of Wisconsin Press, 1921); Edgar F. Shannon, Jr., in *Tennyson and the Reviewers*; and Joyce Green, in "Tennyson's Development During the 'Ten Years' Silence' (1832–1842)," *PMLA*, 66 (1951) pp. 662–97. Of these, Joyce Green gives the most documented, reasonable view. Of real service to the study of these revisions, also, is the Ricks edition of *The Poems of Tennyson*, for Ricks gives all manuscript and published variants in his copious notes, usually without comment. In many cases they speak for themselves.
64. Jerome Buckley, *Tennyson: The Growth of a Poet* (Cambridge, Mass.: Harvard University Press, 1960), p. 70.
65. Mary Joan (Donahue) Ellmann, "Tennyson: Unpublished Letters, 1833–35," *Modern Language Notes*, 65 (Apr. 1950), p. 224.
66. Rader, p. 20.
67. *AT*, p. 149; Buckley, p. 68.
68. Ricks, *Tennyson*, p. 60.
69. *AT*, p. 107.
70. Ricks, *Tennyson*, p. 59.
71. *AT*, pp. 163–4.
72. Ricks, *Tennyson*, p. 71, quoting Merivale, p. 120. (Letter of 14 Aug. 1831.)
73. Ellmann, p. 227, note, from MS in the Harvard College Library. Ellmann surmises that the sonnet was "There are three things which fill my heart with

sighs," published in the *Yorkshire Literary Annual* for 1832.

74. Ellmann, p. 227, gives the complete text of the MS letter in the Huntington Library.

75. Christopher Ricks, in "Tennyson's Methods of Composition," *Proceedings of the British Academy*, 52 (1966), p. 215, explains, "It is not an accident that one reaches for an organic metaphor like 'germ' to describe the relationship of 'O! that 'twere possible' to the completed monodrama. What we find is not any change of context but the providing of a context. As originally published, 'O! that 'twere possible' had no dramatic or psychological setting; itself a cry, it cried out for one. That Tennyson was dissatisfied with it, is clear from his not including it in his volumes of 1842; but by 1855, he had created a context."

76. E. E. Kellett, "The Press," in G. M. Young, *Early Victorian England* (London: Oxford University Press, 1934), p. 91.

77. See Reid, 1, pp. 178–81. The two letters are long and lively and indicative of Tennyson's usual tone with his friends.

78. *Memoir*, 1, p. 145.

79. Cuthbertson, p. 48.

80. This reluctance to write may be attributed in part to "his short sight [which] made the physical task of writing very difficult and distasteful to him," suggests Sir Charles (*AT*, p. 206).

81. *PreRaphaelite Diaries and Letters* (London: Hurst & Blackett, 1900), p. 289.

82. *AT*, pp. 141–2.

83. W. F. Rawnsley, in H. D. Rawnsley, *Memories of the Tennysons* (Glasgow: Maclehose, 1900), pp. 125–6.

84. *Memoir*, 1, p. 124.

85. See Valerie Pitt, *Tennyson Laureate* (London: Barrie & Rockliff, 1962), p. 279, for a description of this volume.

86. *AT*, pp. 240–1.

87. This holds true even though earlier Tennyson published one sonnet in Moxon's *Englishman's Magazine*, for Hallam submitted it, not Tennyson.

88. William Allingham, *Diary*, (1907; repr. Fontwell, Sussex: Centaur, 1967), p. 334.

89. John Pfordresher, *A Variorum Edition of Tennyson's "Idylls of the King"* (New York and London: Columbia University Press, 1973), pp. 11–12.

90. Cuthbertson, p. 61.

91. See my "Tennyson's Revisions to the Last Stanza of 'Audley Court,'" *Costerus*, new ser., 4 (1975), pp. 38–49.

92. Pierpont Morgan Library.

93. *Memoir*, 11, p. 75.

94. *Some New Letters of Edward FitzGerald*, ed. F. R. Barton (London: Williams & Norgate, 1923) p. 13.

95. Thomas R. Lounsbury, *The Life and Times of Tennyson (1809–1850)* (New Haven: Yale University Press, 1915), pp. 357–8.

96. Merriam, p. 57.

97. A. McKinley Terhune, *The Life of Edward FitzGerald* (New Haven: Yale University Press, 1947) pp. 77–8, quoting MS letter to Allen, 31 May 1837.

98. Terhune, p. 79.

99. *Memoir*, 1, p. 155.

100. *AT*, p. 173.

101. Anna O. Allen, *John Allen and His Friends* (London: Hodder & Stoughton, 1922, p. 54.
102. *AT*, p. 173.
103. *Memoir*, I, p. 151.
104. Ibid., p. 150.
105. *AT*, p. 176.
106. Ibid., pp. 176–7.
107. Ibid., p. 177.
108. Ibid., p. 182.

CHAPTER THREE: HEYDAY FOR PUBLISHER AND POET LAUREATE

1. *AT*, p. 121.
2. Ibid., p. 179.
3. John Olin Eidson, "Charles Stearns Wheeler: Emerson's 'Good Grecian,'" *New England Quarterly*, 27 (1954), 475.
4. *Memoir*, I, p. 178.
5. Eidson, in *New England Quarterly*, 27, 476–7.
6. Allingham, p. 168.
7. *AT*, p. 178.
8. Wright, *Letters*, I, p. 93.
9. *Memoir*, I, p. 180.
10. *AT*, p. 191.
11. Sir Charles Tennyson, Notebook 7.
12. Barton, pp. 55–6.
13. Ibid., pp. 57–8. (Letter of 26 Mar. 1842.)
14. *More Letters of Edward FitzGerald*, ed. William Aldis Wright (London: Macmillan, 1901) p. 16.
15. Wright, *Letters*, I, p. 115.
16. Wright, *More Letters*, p. 17.
17. Eidson, in *New England Quarterly*, 27, 477.
18. Caroline Ticknor, *Hawthorne and His Publisher* (Boston and New York: Houghton Mifflin, 1913) p. 5.
19. Marshall, p. 79.
20. *AT*, p. 196.
21. Actually, it was William Moxon, Edward's barrister brother, who used the word, though Edward no doubt shared the feeling. Tennyson wrote to Edmund Lushington on 8 Sep 1842, "I called on Moxon, not at home, gone to the Pyrenees with W. Wordsworth's two sons. 500 of my books are sold: according to Moxon's brother I have made a sensation."
22. Wright, *Letters*, I, p. 119.
23. Johnson, p. 60. (Letter from Donne to Barton, 1 June 1840.)
24. *Robert Browning and Alfred Domett*, ed. F. G. Kenyon (London: Smith, Elder, 1906), p. 42.
25. Merriam, p. 117.
26. Gettmann, p. 23.
27. Kenyon, pp. 40–1.
28. Ibid., p. 97. (Letter of 8 Nov. 1843.)

29. William Jerdan, *Literary Gazette*, 19 Nov. 1842, quoted in Shannon, p. 75.
30. *AT*, p. 196.
31. Ibid., p. 201.
32. Ibid., p. 194.
33. I use "edition" here the way nineteenth-century publishers did; that is, to indicate reissues of a book, with title-page labels of "second," "third," edition, etc., even though unaltered stereoplates were used. In modern bibliographical terminology, these would not be called "editions," because no substantial changes were made in the text.
34. *AT*, p. 198.
35. Ibid., p. 199.
36. Ibid., pp. 203–4.
37. *Memoir*, I, p. 219.
38. *AT*, p. 522.
39. Terhune, p. 125. For more on Tennyson's water-cures, see Elizabeth Jenkins, *Tennyson and Dr. Gully*, Tennyson Society Occasional Paper No. 3 (Lincoln: The Tennyson Society, 1974).
40. Ricks, *Tennyson*, p. 186.
41. *AT*, p. 210. Both of Tennyson's poems, later retitled "Literary Squabbles," were published under the name "Alcibiades."
42. Allen, p. 81.
43. Wilfrid Ward, *Aubrey de Vere: A Memoir* (London: Longmans, Green & Co., 1904), pp. 71–4.
44. Ibid., p. 87.
45. Alethea Hayter, *A Sultry Month: Scenes of London Literary Life in 1846* (London: Faber & Faber, 1965), pp. 64–5. Tennyson and Moxon did visit Dickens in Lausanne. Hayter's description of this visit includes this: "He gave them Liebfraumilch and crisp unsweetened biscuits and a great many cigars. Moxon was wearing a deplorable straw hat, and talked in bursts with 'you know' at the end of every sentence, and altogether seemed to Dickens . . . 'an odd companion for a man of genius'" (pp. 191–2).
46. Wright, *Letters*, I, p. 207.
47. Brookfield, p. 199.
48. *AT*, p. 212.
49. *Memoir*, I, pp. 230–1. The entries from the journal go on to p. 233, and should be read *in toto* by anyone interested in Tennyson's responses to Alpine scenery.
50. Hayter, p. 191.
51. *Memoir*, I, pp. 233–4.
52. Ricks, *Tennyson*, p. 184.
53. Allingham, p. 150.
54. Hugh L'Anson Fausset, *Tennyson: A Modern Portrait* (New York: Appleton, 1923), p. 254.
55. *Letters of Robert Browning to Elizabeth Barrett*, I, 427.
56. Shannon, p. 92.
57. John Killham, *Tennyson and "The Princess": Reflections of an Age* (London: University of London, Athlone Press, 1958), p. 3.
58. *Westminster Review*, Jan. 1831, quoted in Shannon, p. 93.
59. *AT*, p. 164.
60. Ibid., p. 177.

61. See Catherine Barnes Stevenson, "Emily Tennyson in Her Own Right" (forthcoming), for more on Emily's influence.
62. Ricks, *Tennyson*, p. 218.
63. Killham, p. 4.
64. Catherine Barnes Stevenson, "Narrative Form and Point of View in *The Princess, Maud,* and *Idylls of the King*" (PhD dissertation, New York University, 1973), p. 66.
65. Ibid.
66. Killham, p. 14.
67. *AT*, p. 221.
68. *Memoir*, I, pp. 240–1.
69. Killham, p. 13.
70. Shannon, p. 97.
71. Killham, pp. 5–6.
72. Shannon, p. 118.
73. *Memoir*, I, p. 254.
74. *AT*, p. 223.
75. *Memoir*, II, pp. 70–1.
76. See Isobel Armstrong, ed., *The Major Victorian Poets: Reconsiderations* (Lincoln: University of Nebraska Press; London: Routledge & Kegan Paul, 1969).
77. Shannon, p. 114.
78. Wright, *More Letters*, p. 22.
79. Ward, p. 154.
80. *Memoir*, I, pp. 304–5.
81. Allingham, p. 55.
82. The major biographical sources seem to be in error about the terms for *In Memoriam*'s publication. Sir Charles (*AT*, p. 248) suggests that Tennyson stood to "benefit more by the success of the book" under this new agreement. This conclusion is predicated on Sir Charles's assumption that for previous publications Moxon and Tennyson had split the profits equally. The accounts show that this was not the case. Both Hallam Tennyson (*Memoir*, I, 328) and Ricks (*Tennyson*, p. 207), moreover, refer to "a small yearly royalty" from *In Memoriam* and the other poems which Moxon paid Tennyson. Since this royalty does not appear in any accounts, I believe it was not part of any agreement and thus never paid.
83. *AT*, p. 241.
84. In the letters accompanying the yearly accounts, Moxon refers to these as "editions," though he specified in the accounts themselves that they were "reprinted from standing type." Ricks has chosen to use this nineteenth-century terminology also, writing, "The 2nd edition appeared in the latter half of July; the 3rd, end of August; the 4th, Jan. 1851" (*Poems*, p. 857). Most sources, furthermore, say that 5000 were published in June 1850 and 60,000 copies sold in a few months, but the accounts list 8000 printed the first year and 16,000 sold during the first six years – still a sizeable sale, but nowhere near 60,000.
85. *Poems*, p. 857.
86. Shannon, pp. 141–2.
87. Marshall, p. 122.
88. *AT*, p. 252.

89. *Memoir*, I, p. 333.
90. James O. Hoge, ed., *The Letters of Emily Lady Tennyson* (University Park, Pa, and London: Pennsylvania State University Press, 1974), p. 19.
91. Ibid., p. 20.
92. Ricks, *Tennyson*, p. 232.
93. Ibid. Charles Knight once referred to Tennyson's "chief aversion, the 'digito monstrari'" – *Passages of a Working Life During Half a Century*, 3 vols. (London: Bradbury & Evans, 1864), III, p. 40.
94. Pierpont Morgan Library. (Tennyson to Moxon, 7 May [1851].)
95. Pierpont Morgan Library.
96. *Memoir*, I, p. 362.
97. Marshall, p. 133.
98. Ricks, *Tennyson*, p. 239; and *AT*, p. 272. Ricks observes of the line "The last great Englishman is low," "This is better than anybody was able to do on the death of Churchill – indeed, found itself quoted on that occasion" (*Tennyson*, p. 239). I might note here that the deaths of national leaders seem inherently difficult to effectively capture in poetry. Whitman did well by Lincoln in "When lilacs last in the dooryard bloom'd," but who has caught Great Britain's mourning for Churchill or America's for Franklin Roosevelt or John Kennedy? Tennyson achieved remarkable success in portraying the nation's farewell to the Duke of Wellington when we acknowledge the difficulty of such occasional poetry.
99. *AT*, p. 279.
100. *Memoir*, I, p. 378.
101. See *AT*, pp. 276–9, for a description of the house and grounds; also, Sir Charles's pamphlet, *Farringford* (Lincoln: The Tennyson Society, 1976).
102. Sir Charles summarizes Tennyson's receipts from Moxon's during these years: "1851 and 1852 . . . under £800 a year. In 1853, with the publication at the end of 1852 of the Ode on the Death of the Duke of Wellington . . . and of a new Edition of the 'Poems' of 1842, the receipts jumped up to over £1,600" (Typescript, pp. 6–7).
103. Ibid., p. 7.
104. *Memoir*, I, p. 365. Emily had written to Mr Seymour, the owner of Farringford, informing him that Tennyson would become the tenant for one, two, or three years at £104 yearly rent with the option of purchasing – the rentals to be then deducted from the purchase price.
105. Ibid., I, p. 381. Ricks (*Poems*, p. 1034) notes that the editorial writer on 14 Nov. in *The Times* had spoken of "some hideous blunder."
106. *Memoir*, I, p. 411.
107. *Poems*, p. 1035, note.
108. *AT*, p. 288.
109. *Memoir*, I, p. 507.
110. Ricks, *Tennyson*, p. 245.
111. *Memoir*, I, p. 377.
112. Ibid., p. 379.
113. Hallam Tennyson, *Materials for a Life of A.T.*, 4 vols. (privately printed, 1895), II, p. 108.
114. *Memoir*, I, p. 282.
115. Ibid., p. 409.

116. Ibid., p. 385.
117. Tennyson's lawyer for this transaction, Charles W. Estcourt, had estimated the whole at £6500; the check Tennyson sent to settle the purchase was for £6051 9s. 5d. (the previous years' rents had been deducted); the total price, however, was more likely £6750 plus £150 for the orchard opposite (Sir Charles's figures in Notebook 8); yet in late June "Franklin Lushington [spoke] of A. T. having £7,000 to pay and the house to patch up" (Sir Charles Tennyson, Notebook 6).
118. *Memoir*, I, p. 415.
119. *AT*, p. 301.
120. Ibid., p. 286.
121. Ibid., p. 289.
122. *Memoir*, I, p. 468.
123. Allingham, p. 117.
124. *AT*, p. 287.
125. Stevenson, "Narrative Form," p. 171.
126. Ibid., p. 185.
127. *Memoir*, I, p. 402.
128. *Memoir*, I, p. 396; Gordon N. Ray, "Tennyson Reads *Maud*," *Sedgewick Memorial Lecture* (Vancouver, BC: University of British Columbia Press, 1968), p. 20; *Memoir*, I, p. 401.
129. Merriam, p. 190.
130. Ibid., pp. 191–2.
131. Ibid., p. 193.

CHAPTER FOUR: TROUBLED YEARS WITH MOXON & CO.

1. This period poses unusual problems for the researcher because important primary material is missing. The firm of Ward Lock, who bought Moxon & Co. in 1871, reported to me that much correspondence and all accounts with Moxon & Co. after Edward's death, that is from 1858 to 1868, were lost in the fires of World War II. Other sources, however, can partially fill this gap. The Tennyson Research Centre, for example, does have letters between Tennyson and his intermediaries, Emily's Journal, a list of income in her hand, and bank books.
2. Merriam, p. 181.
3. 11 Jan. 1854. The bottom third of this letter in the Tennyson Research Centre is ripped off diagonally at this point.
4. Sir Charles Tennyson, Typescript, pp. 7–8.
5. See George Somes Layard, *Tennyson and His Pre-Raphaelite Illustrators* (London: Elliot Stock, 1894), pp. 6–7.
6. *Memoir*, I, p. 371.
7. *AT*, p. 305.
8. *Memoir*, I, p. 421.
9. *AT*, p. 341.
10. Dante Gabriel Rossetti, *Letters to William Allingham, 1854–1870*, ed. G. B. Hill (London: T. Fisher Unwin, 1897), p. 111.
11. *AT*, p. 293.
12. D. G. Rossetti, p. 104.

13. Ibid., p. 104.
14. Ibid., p. 97.
15. Sir Charles Tennyson, Notebook 6.
16. Letter of 10 Nov. 1870.
17. Merriam, p. 183.
18. This difficulty was remedied in 1872, when "a method discovered a few years previously was for the first time put systematically into practice, by which a drawing on paper could be photographed on to the block" (Layard, pp. 23–4).
19. D. G. Rossetti, p. 191.
20. Merriam, pp. 183–4.
21. Marcia Allentuck, "New Light on Rossetti and the Moxon Tennyson," *Apollo*, 97 (Feb. 1973), 176, quoting William Michael Rossetti, *Dante Gabriel Rossetti as Designer and Writer* (London: Cassell, 1889), pp. 29–30.
22. Merriam, p. 185.
23. Ibid., p. 184, quoting Hunt, *Pre-Raphaelitism and the Pre-Raphaelite Brotherhood* (London: Macmillan, 1905), II, p. 103.
24. Routledge, Kegan Paul Publication Books, Vol. 3. Routledge & Kegan Paul Ltd have made available microfilms of the firm's accounts and publication books for the Tennyson years via the firm of Chadwyck-Healey Ltd, Bishops Stortford, Herts. Also, see Weld's 27 Oct. 1858 letter below. "The exclusive sale of this edition," Moxon wrote to Tennyson, " . . . I have promised to Messrs. Appleton and Co. of New York, who are in a position to do more with it than any other house in America."
25. Sir Charles Tennyson, Typescript, p. 9.
26. Tennyson's help to Mrs Moxon continued many years after his leaving the firm, though he was forced to reduce the sum to £100 a year. She discovered that he was the donor in 1874. In 1878, when the sales of his books fell off somewhat and he entered into a contract with Kegan Paul for half of what he had been getting from Strahan, Tennyson reluctantly informed Mrs Moxon that his aid to her would end.
27. Hoge, p. 120.
28. Routledge, Kegan Paul Publication Books, Vol. 3. Routledge also remaindered 3000 of *The Princess* in its illustrated form, but the royalties to Tennyson on this do not appear in the Routledge records.
29. Sir Charles Tennyson, Typescript, p. 10.
30. Rosenberg, p. 143. Because my study of Tennyson and his publishers does not have room for extensive commentary on Tennyson's longest poem, I point here to several worthwhile studies. I recommend Rosenberg's, *The Fall of Camelot*, as being the finest critical study of the *Idylls of the King* to date. Professor Rosenberg manages to combine great insight with clarity of presentation, and, as good criticism should, his book drives the reader back to the poem in question instead of trying to be in itself a replacement for that poem. Anyone wishing to follow the sequence of the composition and publication of the *Idylls* should consult John Pfordresher's introduction to his Variorum Edition and the headnote and footnotes to the poem in Ricks's edition of Tennyson's *Poems*. Ricks's complaints about the poem have been answered by Rosenberg (pp. 13–33) and by Stevenson ("Narrative Form," pp. 264–9), who draws upon Nancy Engbretsen, "The Thematic Evolution of the *Idylls of the King*," *Victorian Newsletter*, no. 26 (1964), 1–5; and Kathleen Tillotson, "Tennyson's Serial

Poem," in *Mid-Victorian Studies* (London: University of London, Athlone Press, 1965), pp. 80–109. F. E. L. Priestley, in "The Creation of New Genres," *Language and Structure in Tennyson's Poetry* (London: Deutsch, 1973), pp. 125–36, offers thoughts on the *Idylls* as "a dramatic parable of enormous variety, richness, and complexity [which retains] the strong and relatively simple shape of tragedy" (p. 136); Priestley's article "Tennyson's *Idylls*," in *Critical Essays on the Poetry of Tennyson*, ed. John Killham (New York: Barnes & Noble, 1960), pp. 239–55, is worth reading also. "The City Built to Music," Jerome H. Buckley's *Idylls* chapter in *Tennyson: The Growth of the Poet* (Cambridge, Mass.: Harvard University Press, 1960), serves as good introduction to the whole poem.

31. Rosenberg, pp. 10–11.
32. Ibid., p. 33.
33. Ibid., pp. 5–6.
34. In Jump, pp. 230, 264.
35. P. G. Scott, *Tennyson's "Enoch Arden": A Victorian Best-Seller*, Tennyson Society Monograph No. 2 (Lincoln: The Tennyson Society, 1970), p. 18. Scott's study is one of the more balanced ones.
36. Scott, p. 2.
37. Ibid., p. 17.
38. Sir Charles Tennyson, Notebook 7; and Scott, p. 35, note 94.
39. Shaylor, *Fascination*, p. 53.
40. Allingham, p. 168.
41. Merriam, p. 194.
42. *AT*, p. 354.
43. Ibid.
44. Merriam, p. 186.
45. Sir Charles Tennyson, Typescript, p. 13.
46. See Chapter 6 for more on "Lucretius."
47. Hoge, p. 227. "Property," actually entitled "Northern Farmer, New Style," first appeared in *The Holy Grail and Other Poems* (1869).
48. Leonard M. Findlay, "Swinburne and Tennyson," *Victorian Poetry*, 9 (Spring–Summer 1971), 227.
49. Ibid.
50. *Memoir*, II, p. 63.
51. *AT*, p. 376.
52. Merriam, p. 194.

CHAPTER FIVE: SUCCESSORS

1. Merriam, p. 181, quoting Joseph Shaylor, *Sixty Years a Bookman* (London: Selwyn & Blount, 1923), p. 88.
2. Ibid. See my Chapter 4 for details on the terms of the contract.
3. Sir Charles Tennyson, Notebook 8.
4. Fausset, pp. 247–8.
5. Emily Tennyson's Journal, 11 Nov. 1871, cited in Hoge, p. 233, and Brown, p. 19.
6. *Memoir*, II, p. 59, based on Tennyson's letter-book entry of 23 Nov.
7. A. W. Brown, *The Metaphysical Society: Victorian Minds in Crisis*, 1869–80 (New York: Columbia University Press, 1947), pp. 180–3.

8. Prefatory Sonnet to the *Nineteenth Century, Poems*, p. 1239.

9. Alexander Strahan, "Our Very Cheap Literature," *Contemporary Review*, 14 (1870), 439–60.

10. Sutherland, pp. 74–5.

11. Mumby and Norrie, p. 228.

12. Ibid.

13. F. A. Mumby, *The House of Routledge, 1834–1934* (London: Routledge, 1934), p. 187.

14. Sir Charles Tennyson, Typescript, pp. 10–11.

15. See Pfordresher, pp. 36–45, for a full discussion of the composition and various proof stages of the *Idylls* written from 1868 to 1873.

16. *AT*, pp. 278–9; and *Memoir*, II, pp. 61–2.

17. Hoge, p. 246. Sir Charles (*AT*, p. 383) records that 40,000 copies of *The Holy Grail* volume were ordered before publication.

18. *AT*, p. 383.

19. Jump, p. 313.

20. *Memoir*, II, pp. 126–7.

21. Ibid., p. 127.

22. Rosenberg, p. 22.

23. Pfordresher, p. 50.

24. Ibid., p. 55.

25. Sir Charles Tennyson, Notebook 8.

26. Arthur Waugh, *Alfred Lord Tennyson* (New York: Macmillan, 1896) p. 169.

27. *Memoir*, II, p. 113.

28. Ibid., p. 116.

29. Hoge, p. 290.

30. *AT*, p. 403, gives 1873 receipts from Strahan of around £7000.

31. Pfordresher, pp. 50–1.

32. Ricks, *Poems*, pp. 1196–7, gives more on this publication, including a letter from Grove to Tennyson in which the musicologist expands on his idea of a song-cycle like those of Schumann and Beethoven and a letter from Tennyson to Strahan in which the poet outlines his provisions for publication.

33. Sir Charles Tennyson, Notebook 8.

34. Hoge, p. 242, note, and p. 243.

35. *Memoir*, II, pp. 53–4.

36. Ibid., p. 54.

37. Sir Charles Tennyson, Notebook 8.

38. The piracy problem was to persist throughout Tennyson's career. As far back as 1842 he had had to publish a new volume of *Poems* before an American publisher reissued the old 1832 *Poems* without permission; in 1879 he was forced to publish – again, because of piracy – "The Lover's Tale," a poem he had been trying to suppress since 1833; and in 1882 he complained about a pirated copy of the Royal Edition. For a summary of "The Lover's Tale" difficulty, see Hoge, p. 319, note. The Royal Edition complaint appears in Hoge, pp. 324–5. For more on Tennyson and his American publishing, see John Olin Eidson, *Tennyson in America* (Athens: University of Georgia, 1943), and the continuation of that work which Professor Eidson is now preparing; W. S. Tryon and W. Charvat, *The Cost Books of Ticknor and Fields* (New York: Bibliographical Society of America, 1949); and Ticknor.

39. Charles Kegan Paul, *Memories*, new ed. (London: Routledge & Kegan Paul, 1971), p. 274. (First ed. 1899.)
40. Mumby, p. 180.
41. Kegan Paul, *Memories*, p. 275.
42. Ibid., pp. 279–80.
43. Ibid., p. 276.
44. Tennyson Research Centre, letters and copies of letters: James Virtue to Arnold White, 3 Apr. 1873; King to Tennyson, 29 Mar. 1873; Knowles to Emily Tennyson, 2 Apr. 1873; Tennyson to White and Tennyson to King, 16 Apr. 1873.
45. *Memoir*, II, p. 153.
46. Hoge, p. 307.
47. *Memoir*, II, p. 383.
48. Sir Charles Tennyson, Typescript, pp. 19–20.
49. Terry Otten, *The Deserted Stage: The Search for Dramatic Form in Nineteenth-Century England* (Athens: Ohio University Press, 1972), pp. 91–2.
50. Jump, p. 48.
51. Ricks, *Tennyson*, pp. 292–3.
52. See Sir Charles Tennyson, *Tennyson Collection: Usher Gallery, Lincoln* (Lincoln: City of Lincoln Libraries, Museum and Art Gallery Committee, 1963), pp. 12–14; Otten, pp. 76–107; Paull F. Baum, *Tennyson Sixty Years After* (Chapel Hill, University of North Carolina Press, 1948), pp. 214–20; C. G. H. Japikse, *The Dramas of Alfred Lord Tennyson* (New York: Macmillan, 1926); and *AT*.
53. Sir Charles Tennyson, Typescript, p. 20.
54. Marshall, pp. 180–2.
55. Brian Hill, *Julia Margaret Cameron: A Victorian Family Portrait* (London: Peter Owen, 1973), p. 119.
56. Ibid., p. 122.
57. *Tennyson in Lincoln*, compiled by Nancie Campbell, II (Lincoln: The Tennyson Society, 1973), lists this as a "reissue" of Strahan's 1872 edition, but Kegan Paul's letter of 13 Jan. 1877 to Hallam Tennyson, which states, "I am glad you are pleased with the book. It is far more correct than the old Edn. which was not in typography quite what you fancied it was," suggests that either there was substantial correction of the old plates or the whole of the type was reset, making this a new edition, not simply a reissue.
58. *AT*, p. 356.
59. Kegan Paul, *Memories*, p. 220.
60. B. E. Maidment, in his introduction to the microfilms of the Routledge, Kegan Paul, Trench, and Trübner archives (which include Henry S. King), refers to the firms as being among those

> smaller specialist publishing firms whose list was built almost entirely round one or two subjects. Thus Trench & Co. published mainly theological works, Kegan Paul were particularly interested in scientific works of a cheap, popularizing nature, and Trübner's list was centered on oriental subjects. In all these firms can be seen the drive towards fulfilling the need of a newly defined and newly educated serious popular readership which dominated so much of late Victorian publishing. With these firms this drive is held in check by the

erudite nature of many of these books, yet still the sense of newly opened markets, and the accepted need to fulfill popular needs at low prices adds a new dimension to very specialized projects. The archives say almost as much about late Victorian seriousness and the interest in the age in education, in self-help and in gaining knowledge on a wide range of subjects, as about publishing history. On either subject the range of information is remarkably complete. No letter books of any of the firms survive, but all the details of printing, costs, and distribution remain, as well as many of the Kegan Paul contracts.

Maidment errs a bit here, for the details of some first editions, such as *Queen Mary, Harold, The Lover's Tale,* and *Ballads and Other Poems,* are not on the films. Good records of the Crown, Cabinet and Shilling Editions, however, are. Of particular interest for this study of Tennyson is the inclusion of the publisher's total yearly receipts and expenses for each particular edition, for with the other publishers we have had to estimate such figures, basing them on Tennyson's receipts.

61. Kegan Paul, *Memories,* p. 277.
62. Mumby, p. 189.
63. Ibid., p. 196.
64. Kegan Paul, *Memories,* p. 290.
65. Charles Kegan Paul, "The Production and Life of Books," *Faith and Unfaith and Other Essays* (London: Kegan Paul, Trench, Trübner, 1891), p. 208.
66. Kegan Paul, *Memories,* p. 294.
67. Ibid., pp. 333−4.
68. Ibid., p. 339.
69. See John Churton Collins's articles in *The Cornhill,* 1880 and 1881.
70. Kegan Paul, *Memories,* pp. 278−9.
71. Sir Charles Tennyson, Typescript, p. 23.
72. Kegan Paul microfilms, Account Book, Vol. 2, p. 81 (Reel 5).
73. Tennyson used this edition as his standard for pricing. In the new agreement with Kegan Paul, for example, he specified that no edition of the complete works was to be sold for less than six shillings, the bottom price of the Crown Edition. See Kegan Paul microfilms, Account Book, Vol. 2, p. 207 (Reel 5), for profits records on the Crown Edition.
74. *Memoir,* II, p. 225.
75. The term "stereotype plate" refers to the end product of a process in which the type was set and corrected in the usual way, locked in a forme, and then made permanent by means of a metal cast taken from a plaster of paris cast of that forme. As Marjorie Plant explains in *The English Book Trade: An Economic History of the Making and Sale of Books,* 2nd ed. (London: George Allen & Unwin, 1965), p. 303, "The saving where a new impression was called for was no slight one: the casting of plates was far less expensive than the founding and composition of individual types; there was, moreover, a total abolition of proof-correcting for the second impression, with all that it involved in time and money."
76. John[?] King to Arnold White, 17 Jan. 1880.
77. Marshall, p. 200.
78. Ibid., p. 224.

79. Ricks (*Poems*, pp. 299–301) adds information on Tennyson's original decision to withdraw "The Lover's Tale."
80. *AT*, p. 455.
81. Sir Charles has this remark in Notebook 8: "Sidney [Colvin?] told John Bailey that he heard AT read the Revenge . . . in his deep chaunt, a sort of intoning with little variation of expression & he ended 'to be lost evermore in the main!' adding immediately in exactly the same voice & attitude without any pause, 'And the scoundrels only gave me £300 for that; it was worth £500.'"
82. Ricks, *Tennyson*, p. 292.

CHAPTER SIX: FINAL CHOICE

1. Copy, Macmillan & Co. to White, 27 Sep. 1883.
2. British Museum, 1 Nov. 1883. All material noted "BM" is from the British Museum, Macmillan Archives, Add. MSS. 54888, 54980–1, 55438–9 and 55986.
3. Charles Morgan, *The House of Macmillan (1843–1943)* (London: Macmillan, 1943), p. 174.
4. *AT*, p. 230.
5. A. Aingier, "Alexander Macmillan: A Personal Reminiscence," *Macmillan's Magazine*, 73 (Mar. 1896), 398.
6. Charles L. Graves, *Life and Letters of Alexander Macmillan* (London: Macmillan, 1910), p. 399.
7. Ibid., p. 369.
8. Aingier, p. 399.
9. *AT*, p. 230.
10. The old quarterlies cost five shillings and the magazines 2s. 6d.
11. *Letters of Alexander Macmillan*, ed. George A. Macmillan (Glasgow: privately printed, 1908), p. 21. (Letter of 6 Oct. 1859.)
12. Ibid., p. 24. Macmillan seems to use "manly" in the sense of "not vacuous," for in a letter to Franklin Lushington he stated: "I cannot tell you how anxious I am that everything that we put into our *Magazine* should be manly and elevating. I don't in the least believe that the aimless and frivolous is as interesting in the long run as that which means something" (ibid., p. 25).
13. Ibid., p. 24.
14. Brookfield, p. 481. Letter from Stephen Spring-Rice to Mrs. Brookfield, 1859.
15. Along the way Macmillan also mentioned that *The Princess* is epic, an observation which Tennyson himself could not certify. Macmillan apologized in a letter to Lady Tennyson: "If Mr. Tennyson does not know whether the *Princess* is Epic or not, it was surely presumptuous in me to lay down the law on the subject. It is quite clear, however, that it is a story told in a narrative form of some kind, which is all we meant to maintain. It is very strange to find how hard it is to get people impressed with the simple distinction that was sought to be enforced in that short paper" (Macmillan, p. 31). (Letter of 6 Dec. 1859.)
16. Graves, p. 82.
17. Ibid., p. 86.
18. Aingier, p. 400.
19. Macmillan, pp. 117–18. (Letter of 21 June 1862.)

20. Ibid., pp. 236–7. (Letter of 6 Jan. 1868.)
21. *Poems*, p. 1214, note. See William E. Buckler, "Tennyson's 'Lucretius' Bowdlerized?" *English Studies*, new ser., 5 (1954), 269–71, for the view that Tennyson's critical judgment was at play here, too, when he allowed the aborted version. No other Tennyson poem first printed in *Macmillan's Magazine* – "Sea-Dreams" (1859), "Wages" (1868), "The Charge of the Heavy Brigade" (1882), "Vastness" (1885), and "Carmen Seculare" (1887) – required bowdlerization.
22. Graves, pp. 359–60.
23. William E. Buckler, *Matthew Arnold's Books: Towards a Publishing Diary* (Geneva: Librarie Droz, 1958), p. 169, note.
24. Morgan, p. 107.
25. Ibid., p. 69.
26. Ibid., p. 140.
27. *AT*, p. 522.
28. Ibid., p. 527.
29. Ibid., p. 532.
30. Ibid., p. 535. Punctuation is exactly as given in *AT*.
31. See *AT*, p. 535, note, for details on Irving's admiration for *Becket*.
32. *AT*, p. 524.
33. Sir Charles Tennyson, Notebook 9.
34. *Memoir*, I, p. 345, note 1.
35. *AT*, p. 483.
36. Marshall, p. 204.
37. *AT*, p. 467.
38. Pierpont Morgan Library, MA 808. Copy of a note in Pollock's hand, enclosed in a letter presumably from Pollock to the Rev. George Crabbe, 17 June 1883, and quoted in part in Terhune, p. 344. The poem referred to is the prologue to "Tiresias"; before publication, Tennyson added an epilogue which referred to his friend Fitz's death.
39. Marshall, pp. 222–3.
40. *Memoir*, II, pp. 329–30.
41. *AT*, p. 523.
42. Marshall, p. 225.
43. See *AT*, p. 515.
44. Ibid., p. 518.
45. Marshall, p. 241.
46. *AT*, pp. 524–5.
47. BM, Hallam Tennyson to Macmillan, 18 Mar. 1892. The telegram is quoted in this letter.
48. *AT*, p. 531.
49. Ibid., p. 533.
50. Ibid., p. 536.
51. Shortly after Tennyson's death, Macmillan quickly reprinted 40,000 copies of the 7s. 6d. *Complete Works* and sold about 29,000 before 1892 was over. Because of these extremely high sales, the account for 1892 registered £117 19s. 3d. from commission books, £9897 2s. 4d. from English royalties, and £612 4s. 3d. from American royalties – a grand total of £10,627 5s. 10d. When he enclosed the account, Craik advised Hallam on 13 Jan. 1893, "We can't expect a

result like this again, but I hope for a good if less result next year." Macmillan had going two additional Tennyson projects: a volume with illustrations by William Morris and a facsimile edition of *Poems by Two Brothers* (1827). The 1893 payment from Macmillan decreased to £7214, with 1894 bringing in £8129, and a bit more than £4000 in both 1895 and 1896. Although the ten-year contract made between Tennyson and Alexander Macmillan had run out in 1893, Hallam Tennyson stayed with the firm for publication of his two-volume *Alfred Lord Tennyson: A Memoir* in 1897. This boosted the family's yearly income from Macmillan to over £10,000. In 1898 the figure went to £6448, in 1899 to £7310, and then remained stable at close to £3000 for several years. Macmillan in 1907–8 published the Eversley Edition of Tennyson's poems, with notes by the poet and Hallam, and Hallam's *Tennyson and His Friends* in 1911. Sir Charles Tennyson kept up the connection between Macmillans and the Tennyson family by publishing with the firm both his biography of the poet (1949) and the family biography, *The Tennysons: Background to Genius* (1974), which he co-authored with Hope Dyson.

Bibliography

Extensive bibliographies of the book trade may be found in Frank A. Mumby and Ian Norrie, *Publishing and Bookselling*, 5th ed., rev. (London: Cape, 1974), pp. 586–649, and in Robin Myers, *The British Book Trade: From Caxton to the Present Day* (London: Deutsch, 1973). Guinevere L. Griest gives in *Mudie's Circulating Library and The Victorian Novel* (Bloomington and London: Indiana University Press, 1970), pp. 226–31, a useful brief bibliography on publishing practices in nineteenth-century England.

Abbott, Claude Colleer. *The Life and Letters of George Darley, Poet and Critic*. London: Oxford University Press, 1928.

Aingier, A. "Alexander Macmillan: A Personal Reminiscence." *Macmillan's Magazine*, 73 (Mar. 1896), 397–400.

Allen, Anna O. *John Allen and His Friends*. London: Hodder & Stoughton, 1922.

Allentuck, Marcia. "New Light on Rossetti and the Moxon Tennyson." *Apollo*, 97 (Feb. 1973), 176.

Allingham, William. *Diary*. 1907; repr. Fontwell, Sussex: Centaur, 1967.

Altick, Richard D. *The English Common Reader: A Social History of the Mass Reading Public, 1800–1900*. Chicago: University of Chicago Press, 1957.

Armstrong, Isobel, ed. *The Major Victorian Poets: Reconsiderations*. Lincoln: University of Nebraska Press; London: Routledge & Kegan Paul, 1969.

Baum, Paull F. *Tennyson Sixty Years After*. Chapel Hill: University of North Carolina Press, 1948.

Blunden, Edmund. *Leigh Hunt: A Biography*. London: Cobden–Sanderson, 1930.

British Museum Add. MSS. 54888, 54980–1, 55438–9, 55986, Macmillan Archives.

Brookfield, Charles and Frances. *Mrs. Brookfield and Her Circle*. Rev. ed. London: Pitman, 1906.

Brown, A. W. *The Metaphysical Society: Victorian Minds in Crisis, 1869–80.* New York: Columbia University Press, 1947.

Browning, Robert. *Letters of Robert Browning and Elizabeth Barrett.* 2 vols. London: privately printed, 1895.

——. *Robert Browning and Alfred Domett.* Ed. F. G. Kenyon. London: Smith, Elder, 1906.

Buckler, William E. *Matthew Arnold's Books: Towards a Publishing Diary.* Geneva: Librarie Droz, 1958.

——. "Tennyson's 'Lucretius' Bowdlerized?" *English Studies,* new ser., 5 (1954), 269–71.

Buckley, Jerome. *Tennyson: The Growth of a Poet.* Cambridge, Mass.: Harvard University Press, 1960.

Chilcott, Tim. *A Publisher and His Circle: The Life and Work of John Taylor, Keats's Publisher.* London and Boston: Routledge & Kegan Paul, 1972.

Cook, John C. and Stevenson, Lionel. *English Literature of the Victorian Period.* New York: Appleton–Century–Crofts, 1949.

Cuthbertson, Evan J. *Tennyson: The Story of His Life.* London and Edinburgh: Chambers, 1898.

Dibdin, Thomas Fragnall. *Bibliophobia.* London: Henry Bohn, 1832.

Eidson, John Olin. "Charles Stearns Wheeler: Emerson's 'Good Grecian.'" *New England Quarterly,* 27 (1954), 472–83.

——. *Tennyson in America.* Athens: University of Georgia, 1943.

Ellmann, Mary Joan (Donahue). "Tennyson: Unpublished Letters, 1833–35." *Modern Language Notes,* 65 (Apr. 1950), 223–8.

Engbretsen, Nancy. "The Thematic Evolution of the *Idylls of the King.*" *Victorian Newsletter,* no. 26 (1964), 1–5.

Fausset, Hugh L'Anson. *Tennyson: A Modern Portrait.* New York: Appleton, 1923.

Findlay, Leonard M. "Swinburne and Tennyson." *Victorian Poetry,* 9 (Spring–Summer 1971), 217–36.

FitzGerald, Edward. *Letters of Edward FitzGerald.* Ed. William Aldis Wright. 2 vols. London: Macmillan, 1901.

——. *More Letters of Edward FitzGerald.* Ed. William Aldis Wright. London: Macmillan, 1901.

——. *Some New Letters of Edward FitzGerald.* Ed. F. R. Barton. London: Williams and Norgate, 1923.

Gaskell, Charles Milnes, ed. *An Eton Boy: Letters of James Milnes Gaskell, 1820–1830.* London: privately printed, 1883; Constable, 1939.

Gettmann, Royal A. *A Victorian Publisher: A Study of the Bentley*

Papers. London: Cambridge University Press, 1960.

Graham, Walter. *English Literary Periodicals*. New York: Nelson, 1930.

Graves, Charles L. *Life and Letters of Alexander Macmillan*. London: Macmillan, 1910.

Green, Joyce. "Tennyson's Development During the 'Ten Years' Silence' (1832–1842)." *PMLA*, 66 (1951), 662–97.

Hagen, June Steffensen. "Tennyson's Revisions to the Last Stanza of 'Audley Court,'" *Costerus*, new ser., 4 (1975), 38–49.

Hallam, Arthur Henry. "On Some of the Characteristics of Modern Poetry and on the Lyrical Poems of Alfred Tennyson." *Englishman's Magazine*, 1 (Aug. 1831), 616–28. In Jump, pp. 34–49.

Hayter, Alethea. *A Sultry Month: Scenes of London Literary Life in 1846*. London: Faber & Faber, 1965.

Hill, Brian. *Julia Margaret Cameron: A Victorian Family Portrait*. London: Peter Owen, 1973.

Hoge, James O., ed. *The Letters of Emily Lady Tennyson*. University Park, Pa., and London: Pennsylvania State University Press, 1974.

Hunt, W. Holman. *Pre-Raphaelitism and the Pre-Raphaelite Brotherhood*. 2 vols. London: Macmillan, 1905.

Jamieson, P. F. "Tennyson and His Audience in 1832." *Philological Quarterly*, 31 (1952), 407–13.

Japikse, C. G. H. *The Dramas of Alfred Lord Tennyson*. New York: Macmillan, 1926.

Jenkins, Elizabeth. *Tennyson and Dr. Gully*. Tennyson Society Occasional Paper No. 3. Lincoln: The Tennyson Society, 1974.

Johnson, Catharine' B., ed. *William Bodham Donne and His Friends*. London and New York: E. P. Dutton, 1905.

Jump, John D., ed. *Tennyson: The Critical Heritage*. London: Routledge & Kegan Paul, 1967.

Kegan Paul, Charles. *Memories*. London: Routledge & Kegan Paul, 1971. 1st ed. 1899.

———. "The Production and Life of Books." *Faith and Unfaith and Other Essays*. London: Kegan Paul, Trench, Trübner, 1891.

Kellett, E. E. "The Press." In G. M. Young, *Early Victorian England*. London: Oxford University Press, 1934.

Killham, John. *Tennyson and "The Princess": Reflections of an Age*. London: University of London, Athlone Press, 1958.

Knight, Charles. *Passages of a Working Life During Half a Century*. 3 vols. London: Bradbury & Evans, 1864.

Knight, William, ed. *Letters of the Wordsworth Family from 1787 to 1855.* 3 vols. Boston and London: Ginn & Co., 1907.

Layard, George Somes. *Tennyson and His Pre-Raphaelite Illustrators.* London: Elliot Stock, 1894.

Lounsbury, Thomas R. *The Life and Times of Tennyson (1809–1850).* New Haven: Yale University Press, 1915.

Macmillan, Alexander. *Letters of Alexander Macmillan.* Ed. George A. Macmillan. Glasgow: privately printed, 1908.

Maidment, B. E. Introduction to Routledge, Kegan Paul, Trench, Trübner Archives Microfilms. Chadwyck – Healey Ltd.

Marshall, George O., Jr. *Tennyson Handbook.* New York: Twayne, 1963.

Merivale, Charles. *Autobiography and Letters of Charles Merivale, Dean of Ely.* Ed. Judith Anne Merivale. Privately printed, Oxford: Hart, 1898.

Merriam, H. G. *Edward Moxon: Publisher of Poets.* New York: Columbia University Press, 1939.

Moore, G. C. "A Critical and Bibliographical Study of the Somersby Library of Dr. George Clayton Tennyson." MA thesis, Nottingham University, 1966.

Morgan, Charles. *The House of Macmillan (1843–1943).* London: Macmillan, 1943.

Motter, T. H. Vail. "A 'Lost' Poem by Arthur Hallam." *PMLA,* 50 (1935), 568–75.

Mumby, Frank A. *The House of Routledge, 1834–1934.* London: Routledge, 1934.

—— and Norrie, Ian. *Publishing and Bookselling.* 5th ed., rev. London: Cape, 1974.

Nicoll, W. Robertson and Wise, Thomas J. *Literary Anecdotes of the Nineteenth Century.* 2 vols. London: Hodder & Stoughton, 1895.

Otten, Terry. *The Deserted Stage: The Search for Dramatic Form in Nineteenth Century England.* Athens: Ohio University Press, 1972.

Pfordresher, John. *A Variorum Edition of Tennyson's "Idylls of the King."* New York and London: Columbia University Press, 1973.

Pierpont Morgan Library, New York. Letters.

Pitt, Valerie. *Tennyson Laureate.* London: Barrie & Rockliff, 1962.

Plant, Marjorie. *The English Book Trade: An Economic History of the Making and Sale of Books.* 2nd ed. London: George Allen & Unwin, 1965.

Priestley, F. E. L. *Language and Structure in Tennyson's Poetry.* London: Deutsch, 1973.

Priestley, F. E. L. "Tennyson's *Idylls*." *Critical Essays on the Poetry of Tennyson.* Ed. John Killham. New York: Barnes & Noble, 1960, pp. 239–55.

Pyre, J. F. A. *The Formation of Tennyson's Style.* Madison: University of Wisconsin Press, 1921.

Rader, Ralph. *Tennyson's Maud: The Biographical Genesis.* Berkeley and Los Angeles: University of California Press, 1963.

Rawnsley, H. D. *Memories of the Tennysons.* Glasgow: Maclehose, 1900.

Ray, Gordon N. "Tennyson Reads *Maud*." *Sedgewick Memorial Lecture.* Vancouver, BC: University of British Columbia Press, 1968.

Reid, T. Wemyss. *The Life, Letters, and Friendships of Richard Monckton Milnes, First Lord Houghton.* 2 vols. London and New York: Cassell, 1890.

Ricks, Christopher. *Tennyson.* London and New York: Macmillan, 1972.

——. "Tennyson's Methods of Composition." *Proceedings of the British Academy,* 52 (1966), 209–30.

Ritchie, Anne Thackeray. *Records of Tennyson, Ruskin and Browning.* London: Macmillan, 1892.

Rosen, Marvin S. "Authors and Publishers: 1750–1830." *Science and Society,* 32 (1968), 218–32.

Rosenberg, John D. *The Fall of Camelot: A Study of Tennyson's "Idylls of the King."* Cambridge, Mass.: Harvard University Press, 1973.

Rossetti, Dante Gabriel. *Letters to William Allingham, 1854–1870.* Ed. G. B. Hill. London: T. Fisher Unwin, 1897.

Rossetti, William Michael. *Dante Gabriel Rossetti as Designer and Writer.* London: Cassell, 1889.

——. *PreRaphaelite Diaries and Letters.* London: Hurst & Blackett, 1900.

Routledge Kegan Paul Publication Books. Microfilms. Bishop's Stortford, Herts.: Chadwyck–Healey.

Schonfield, Hugh J., ed. *Letters to Frederick Tennyson.* London: Hogarth Press, 1930.

Scott, P. G. *Tennyson's "Enoch Arden": A Victorian Best-Seller.* Tennyson Society Monograph No. 2. Lincoln: The Tennyson Society, 1970.

Shannon, Edgar F., Jr. "The Coachman's Part in the Publication of *Poems by Two Brothers.*" *Modern Language Notes,* 64 (1949), 107–10.

Shannon, Edgar F., Jr. *Tennyson and the Reviewers.* Cambridge, Mass.: Harvard University Press, 1952.

Shaylor, Joseph. *The Fascination of Books.* London: Simpkin, Marshall, Hamilton, Kent, 1912.

——. *Sixty Years a Bookman.* London: Selwyn and Blount, 1923.

Stevenson, Catherine Barnes. "Emily Tennyson in Her Own Right." Forthcoming.

——. "Narrative Form and Point of View in *The Princess, Maud,* and *Idylls of the King.*" PhD dissertation, New York University, 1973.

Strahan, Alexander. "Our Very Cheap Literature." *Contemporary Review,* 14 (1870), 439–60.

Sutherland, J. A. *Victorian Novelists and Publishers.* Chicago: University of Chicago Press, 1976.

Tennyson, Alfred. *The Poems of Tennyson.* Ed. Christopher Ricks. London: Longmans, 1969.

Tennyson, Charles. *Alfred Tennyson.* London: Macmillan, 1950.

——. *Farringford.* Lincoln: The Tennyson Society, 1976.

——. Notebooks. Tennyson Research Centre, Lincoln.

——. *Tennyson Collection: Usher Gallery, Lincoln.* Lincoln: City of Lincoln Libraries, Museum and Art Gallery Committee, 1963.

——. Unpublished typescript "Tennyson's Dealings with His Publishers." Tennyson Research Centre.

Tennyson, Charles and Dyson, Hope. *The Tennysons: Background to Genius.* London: Macmillan, 1974.

Tennyson, Emily. Journal. Tennyson Research Centre.

Tennyson, Frederick. *See under* Schonfield.

Tennyson, Hallam. *Alfred Lord Tennyson: A Memoir.* 2 vols. London: Macmillan, 1897.

——. *Materials for a Life of A.T.* 4 vols. Privately printed, 1895.

——. *Tennyson and His Friends.* London: Macmillan, 1911.

Tennyson in Lincoln. Compiled Nancie Campbell. 2 vols. Lincoln: The Tennyson Society, 1971 and 1973.

Tennyson Research Centre. Lincoln, England. Personal and business letters and accounts.

Terhune, A. McKinley. *The Life of Edward FitzGerald.* New Haven: Yale University Press, 1947.

Ticknor, Caroline. *Hawthorne and His Publisher.* Boston and New York: Houghton Mifflin, 1913.

Tillotson, Kathleen. "Tennyson's Serial Poem." *Mid-Victorian Studies.* London: University of London, Athlone Press, 1965, pp. 80–109.

Trench, Richard Chenevix. *Letters and Memorials.* Ed. M. Trench. 2 vols. London: Kegan Paul, 1888.

Tryon, W. S. and Charvat, W. *The Cost Books of Ticknor and Fields and Their Predecessors, 1832–1858.* New York: Bibliographical Society of America, 1949.

Ward, Wilfrid. *Aubrey de Vere: A Memoir.* London: Longmans, Green & Co., 1904.

Waugh, Alfred. *Alfred Lord Tennyson.* New York: Macmillan, 1896.

Wordsworth. *See under* Knight, William.

Index

Tennyson's works are indexed under the name of the poem or play, and also under the names of collections and editions. The works of other writers are indexed under their authors' names.